THE WICKED + THE DIVINE
VOL. 6, IMPERIAL PHASE PART 2

GILLEN

MᶜKELVIE

WILSON

COWLES

KIERON GILLEN
WRITER

JAMIE McKELVIE
ARTIST

MATTHEW WILSON
COLOURIST

CLAYTON COWLES
LETTERER

SERGIO SERRANO
DESIGNER

CHRISSY WILLIAMS
EDITOR

DEE CUNNIFFE
FLATTER

THE WICKED + THE DIVINE, VOL. 6, IMPERIAL PHASE PART 2
First printing. January 2018.
ISBN: 978-1-5343-0473-4
Published by Image Comics Inc.
Office of publication: 2701 NW Vaughn St., Suite 780, Portland, OR 97210.

This book was designed by Sergio Serrano, based on a design by Hannah
Donovan and Jamie McKelvie, and set into type by Sergio Serrano in Edmonton,
Canada. The text face is Gotham, designed and issued by Hoefler & Co. in 2000.
The paper is Liberty 60 matte.

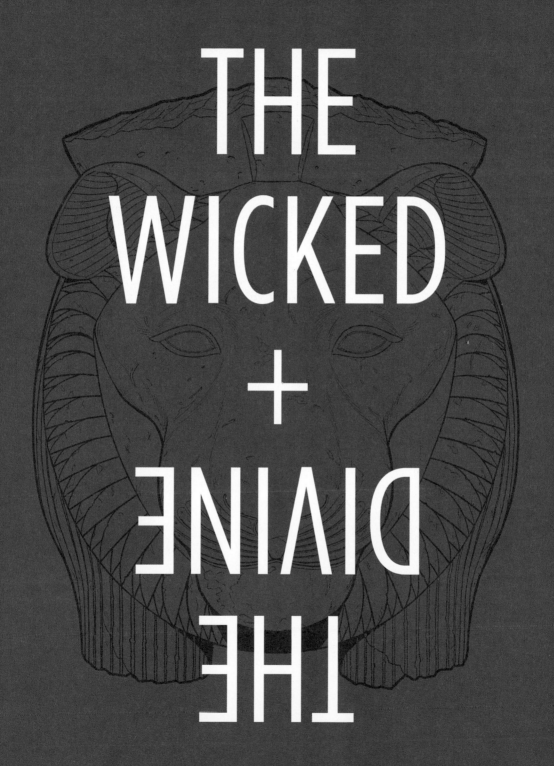

GILLEN MᶜKELVIE WILSON COWLES

THE
WICKED
+
DIVINE
THE

VOL. 6, IMPERIAL PHASE PART 2

PREVIOUSLY...

Every ninety years twelve gods return as young people. They are loved. They are hated. In two years, they are all dead. It's happening now. It's happening again.

Her secrets uncovered, Ananke claimed to have been killing gods to avert "The Great Darkness" for thousands of years, before being murdered by Persephone to avenge her family. The gods covered it up. Enter stage right, The Great Darkness. The gods voted on what to do next and are now split into three separate factions: fight, study and anarchy. Everyone's gone off the rails. Sakhmet murders a bunch of people in a moment of pique. Life goes on.

Persephone. Is in hell. Ascended fangirl Laura. Current lover of Sakhmet. The Destroyer.

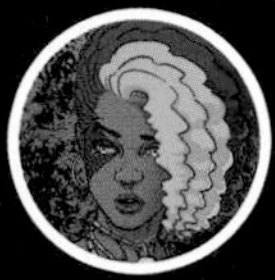

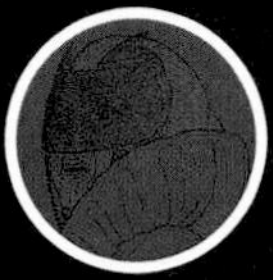

Ananke. Murderous manipulative ~~immortal~~ god of destiny. A bad 'un.

THE PANTHEON

Lucifer. Underworld god. Framed for murder. Killed by Ananke.

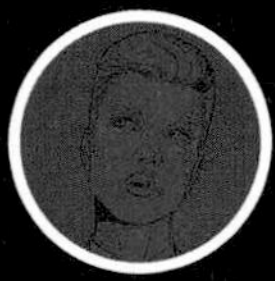

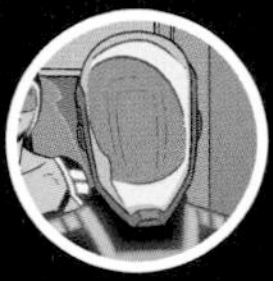

Woden. Shithead god. Secretly collaborated with Ananke due to some mysterious hold over him.

Baphomet. Punderworld god. The Morrigan's lover. Cheated with Persephone. Beaten by Morrigan.

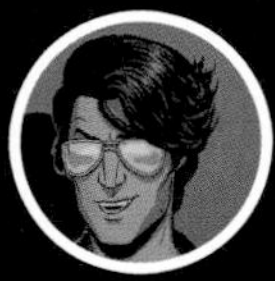

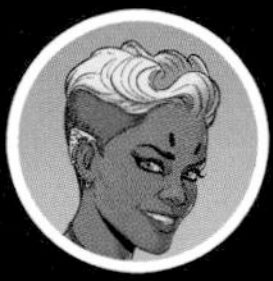

Sakhmet. Feline war god. Ate her dad. Went on rampage when she realised the Pantheon lied to her.

The Morrigan. Triple-formed underworld god ruling in increasingly disturbing isolation.

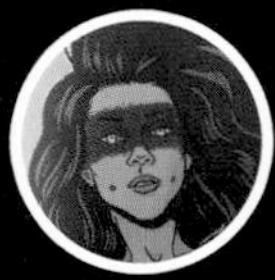

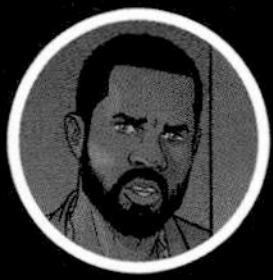

Baal. Storm god. Ex-lover of Inanna and Persephone. The Great Darkness killed his dad.

Dionysus. Hivemind dancefloor god. Doesn't sleep. Working tirelessly on Cassandra's projects.

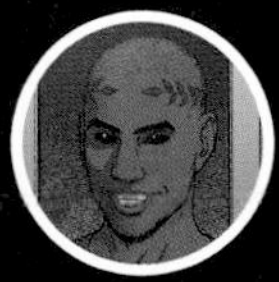

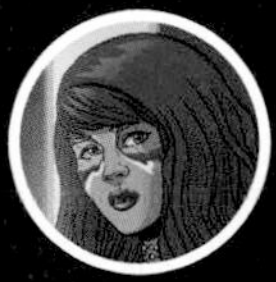

Amaterasu. Sun god. Started her own cult, ShinTwo™. Accidentally revealed truth to Sakhmet.

The Norns. Cynical journo Cassandra and crew obsessively researching Ananke's Machine.

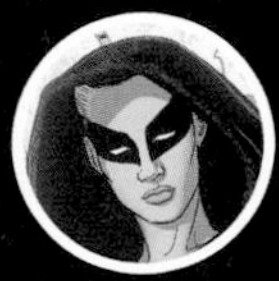

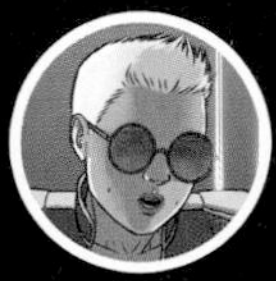

Minerva. Wisdom god. Parents murdered. Baal is legal guardian. Tortured by Ananke on Machine.

Inanna. Queen of heaven. Ex-lover of Baal. Murdered by Ananke.

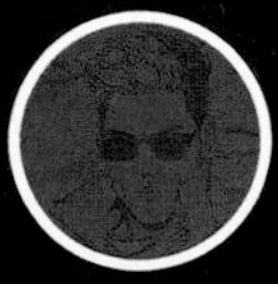

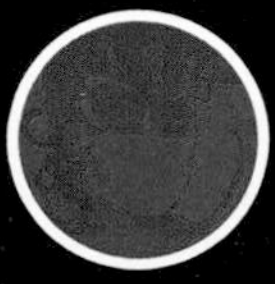

Tara. Secretly killed by Ananke in assisted suicide to frame Baphomet. No one buys it now.

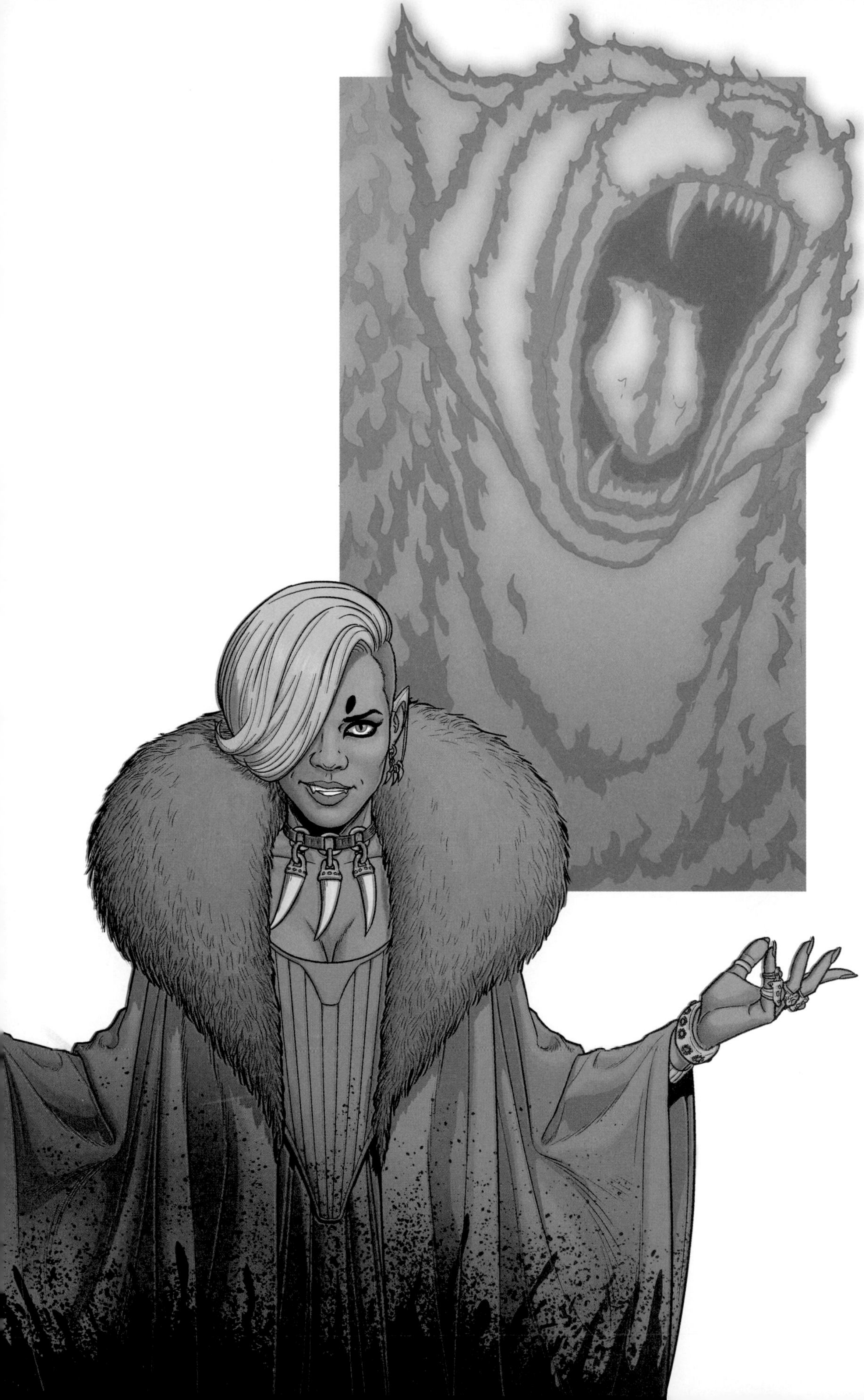

THE WICKED + THE DIVINE

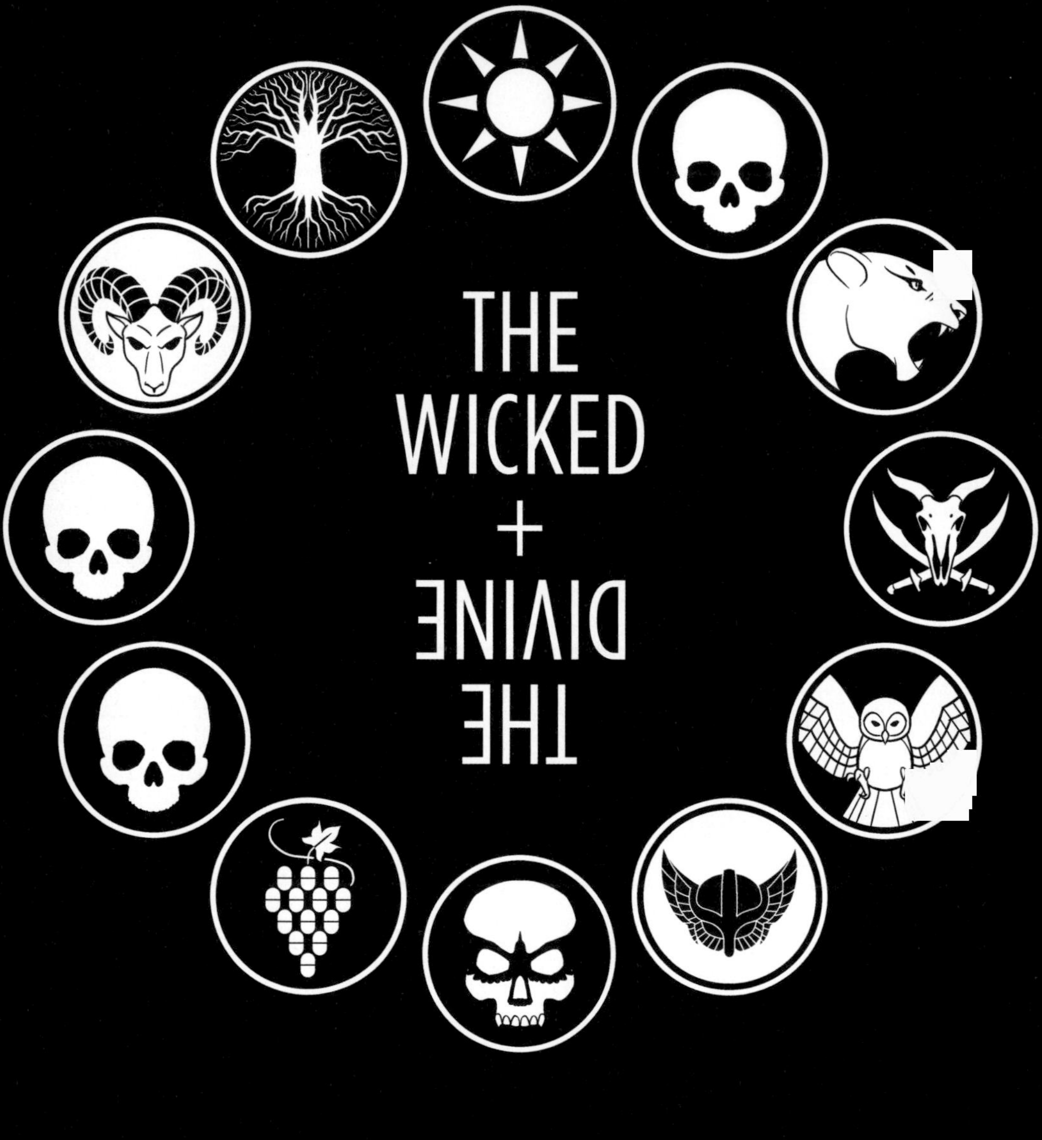

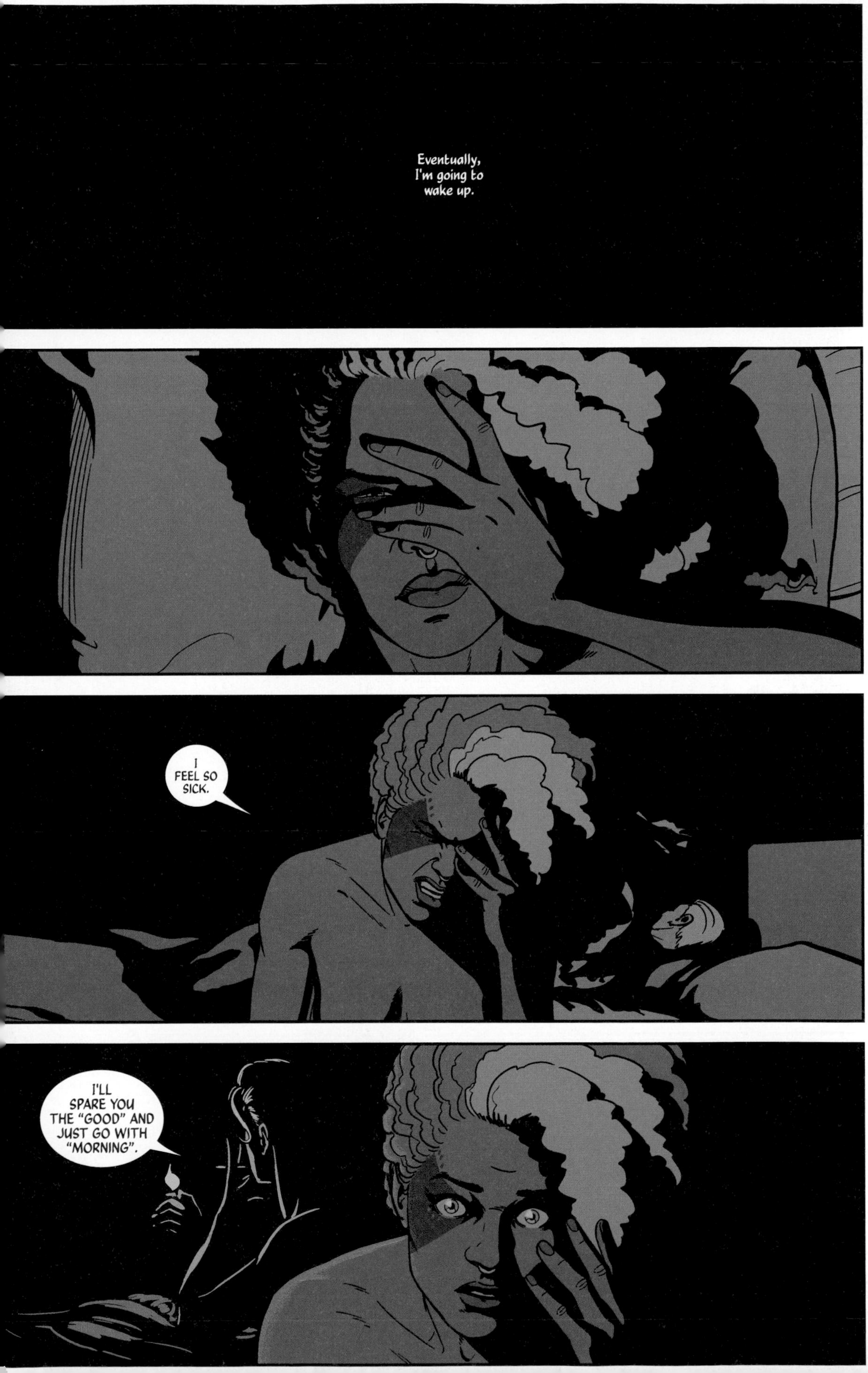
Eventually, I'm going to wake up.
I FEEL SO SICK.
I'LL SPARE YOU THE "GOOD" AND JUST GO WITH "MORNING".

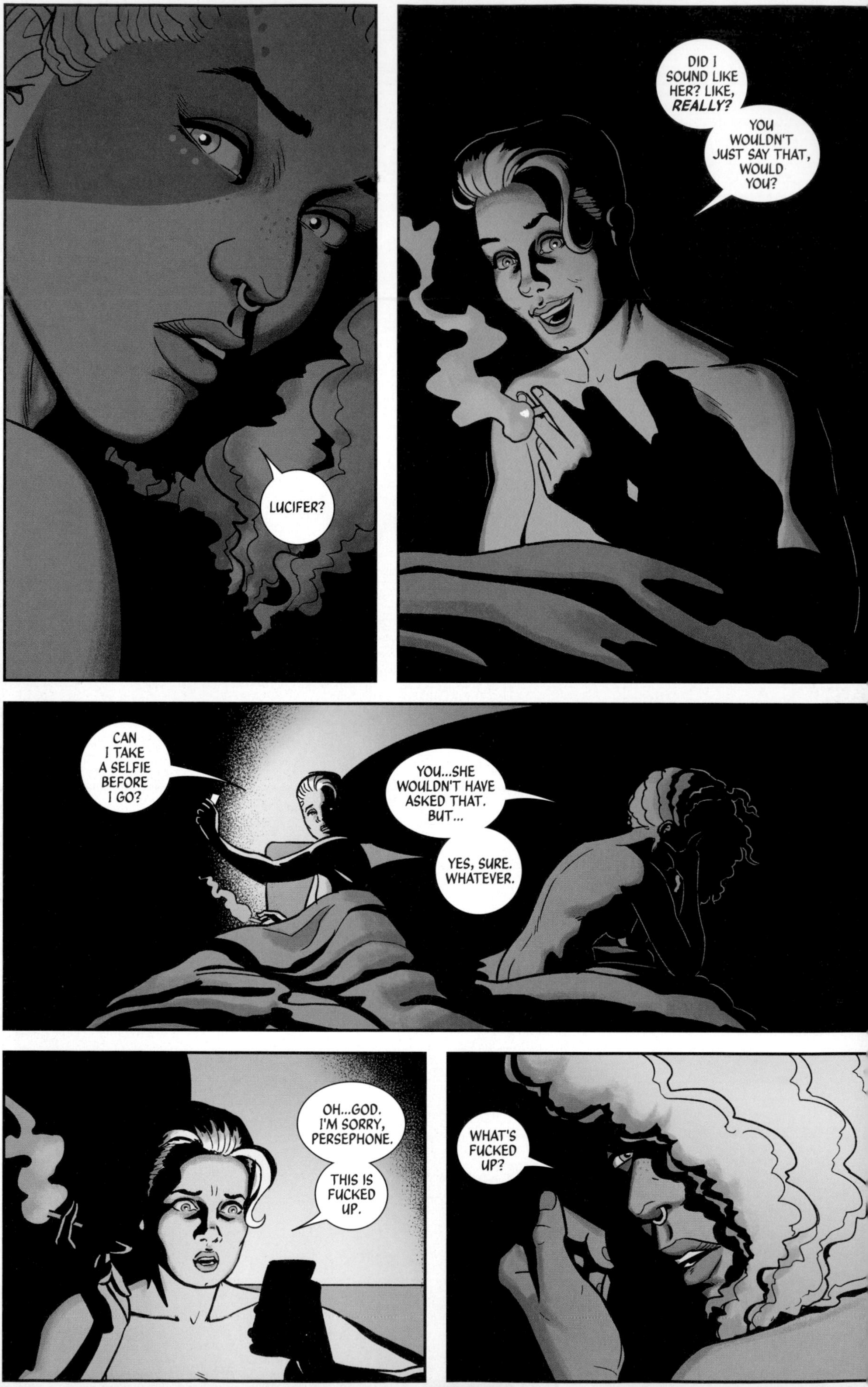
LUCIFER?
DID I SOUND LIKE HER? LIKE, ***REALLY?***
YOU WOULDN'T JUST SAY THAT, WOULD YOU?
CAN I TAKE A SELFIE BEFORE I GO?
YOU...SHE WOULDN'T HAVE ASKED THAT. BUT...
YES, SURE. WHATEVER.
OH...GOD. I'M SORRY, PERSEPHONE.
THIS IS FUCKED UP.
WHAT'S FUCKED UP?

THE FIRST DEGREE

6 MARCH 2015

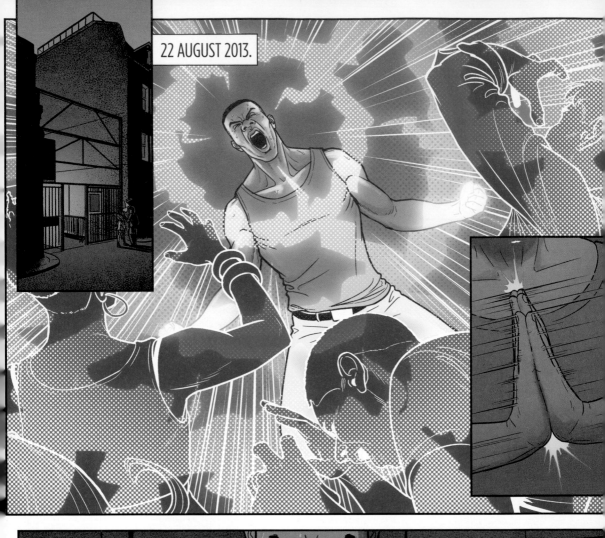

22 AUGUST 2013.

HEH.

THAT'S MY HELLO.

MY FIRST TIME AND YOURS...

WELCOME TO THE RECURRENCE. AND GUESS WHAT?

I'M DONE, BUT THE SHOW'S NOT OVER. I'VE BROUGHT COMPANY...

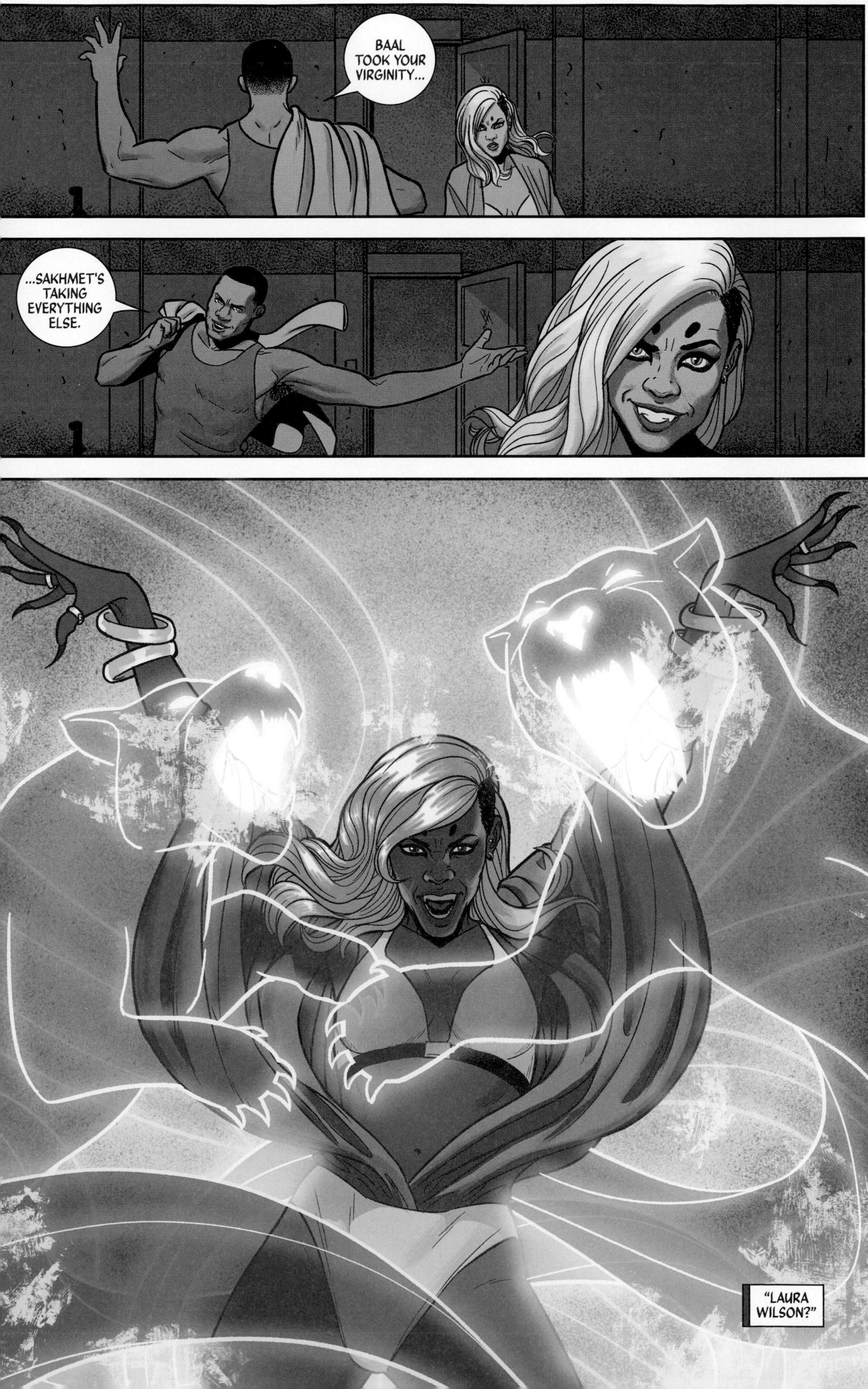
BAAL TOOK YOUR VIRGINITY...
...SAKHMET'S TAKING EVERYTHING ELSE.
"LAURA WILSON?"

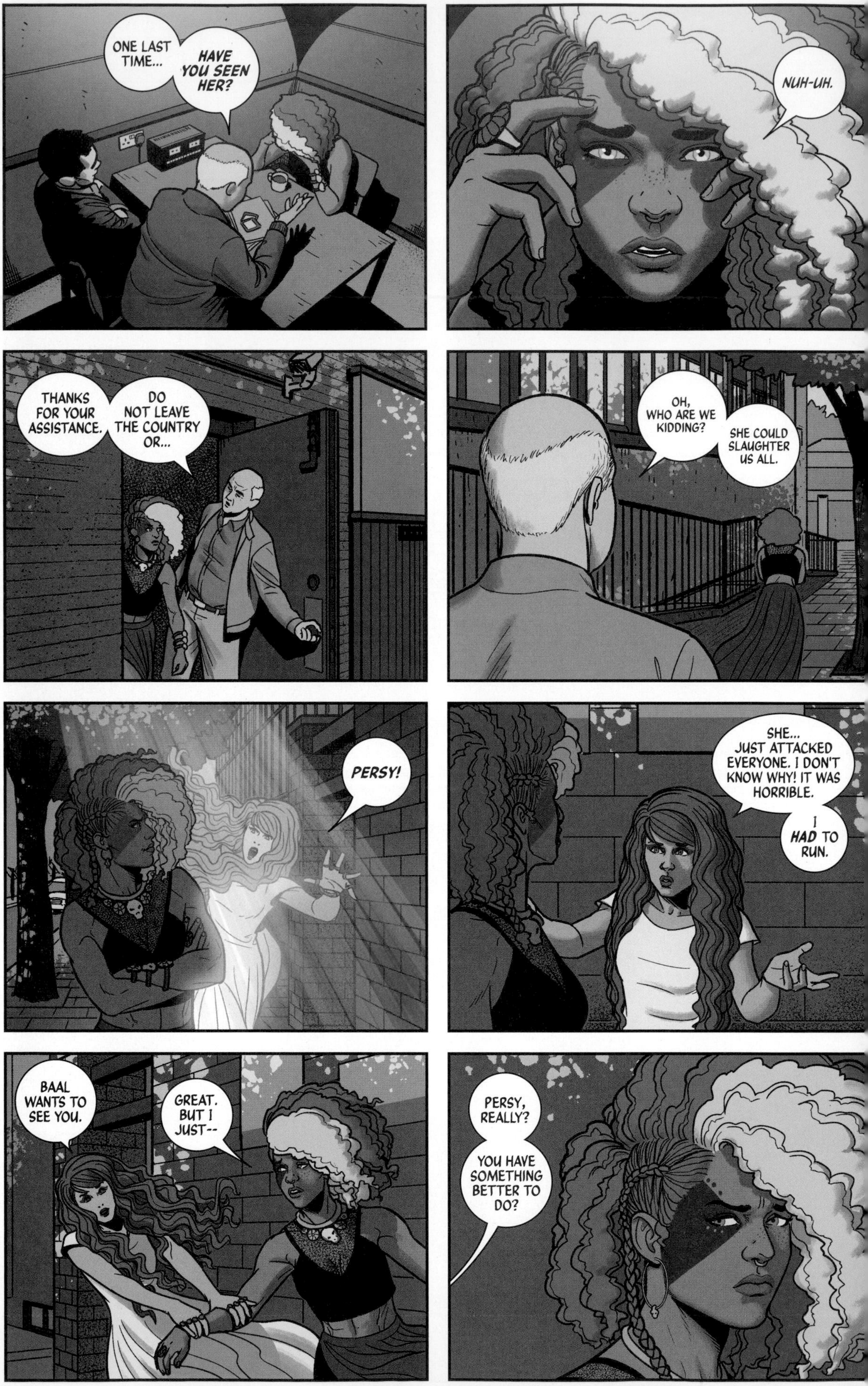
ONE LAST TIME...
HAVE YOU SEEN HER?
NUH-UH.
THANKS FOR YOUR ASSISTANCE.
DO NOT LEAVE THE COUNTRY OR...
OH, WHO ARE WE KIDDING?
SHE COULD SLAUGHTER US ALL.
PERSY!
SHE... JUST ATTACKED EVERYONE. I DON'T KNOW WHY! IT WAS HORRIBLE.
I HAD TO RUN.
BAAL WANTS TO SEE YOU.
GREAT. BUT I JUST--
PERSY, REALLY?
YOU HAVE SOMETHING BETTER TO DO?

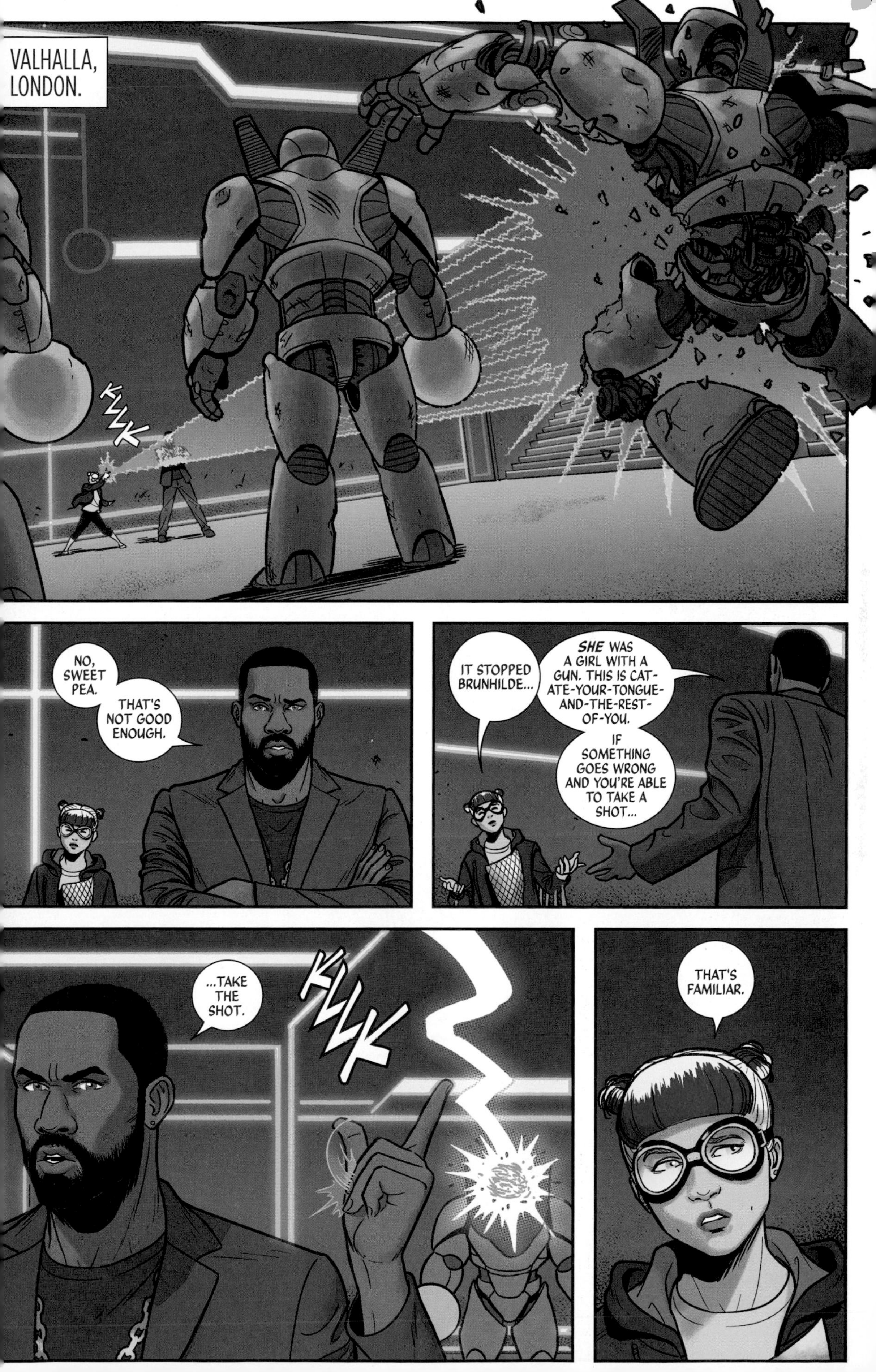
VALHALLA, LONDON.
KLLK
NO, SWEET PEA.
THAT'S NOT GOOD ENOUGH.
IT STOPPED BRUNHILDE...
SHE WAS A GIRL WITH A GUN. THIS IS CAT-ATE-YOUR-TONGUE-AND-THE-REST-OF-YOU.
IF SOMETHING GOES WRONG AND YOU'RE ABLE TO TAKE A SHOT...
...TAKE THE SHOT.
KLLK
THAT'S FAMILIAR.

ARE YOU JUST GOING TO COPY ANANKE?

ANANKE WAS A KILLER. SHE KILLED MORE PEOPLE THAN ANYONE.

SHE HAD PRACTICE AND WAS DAMNED GOOD AT IT.

IN THIS PARTICULAR AREA, WE *HAVE* TO BE LIKE ANANKE.

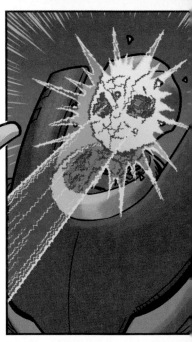

FOCUS.

YAY!

HEY! I GOT US A PERSY!

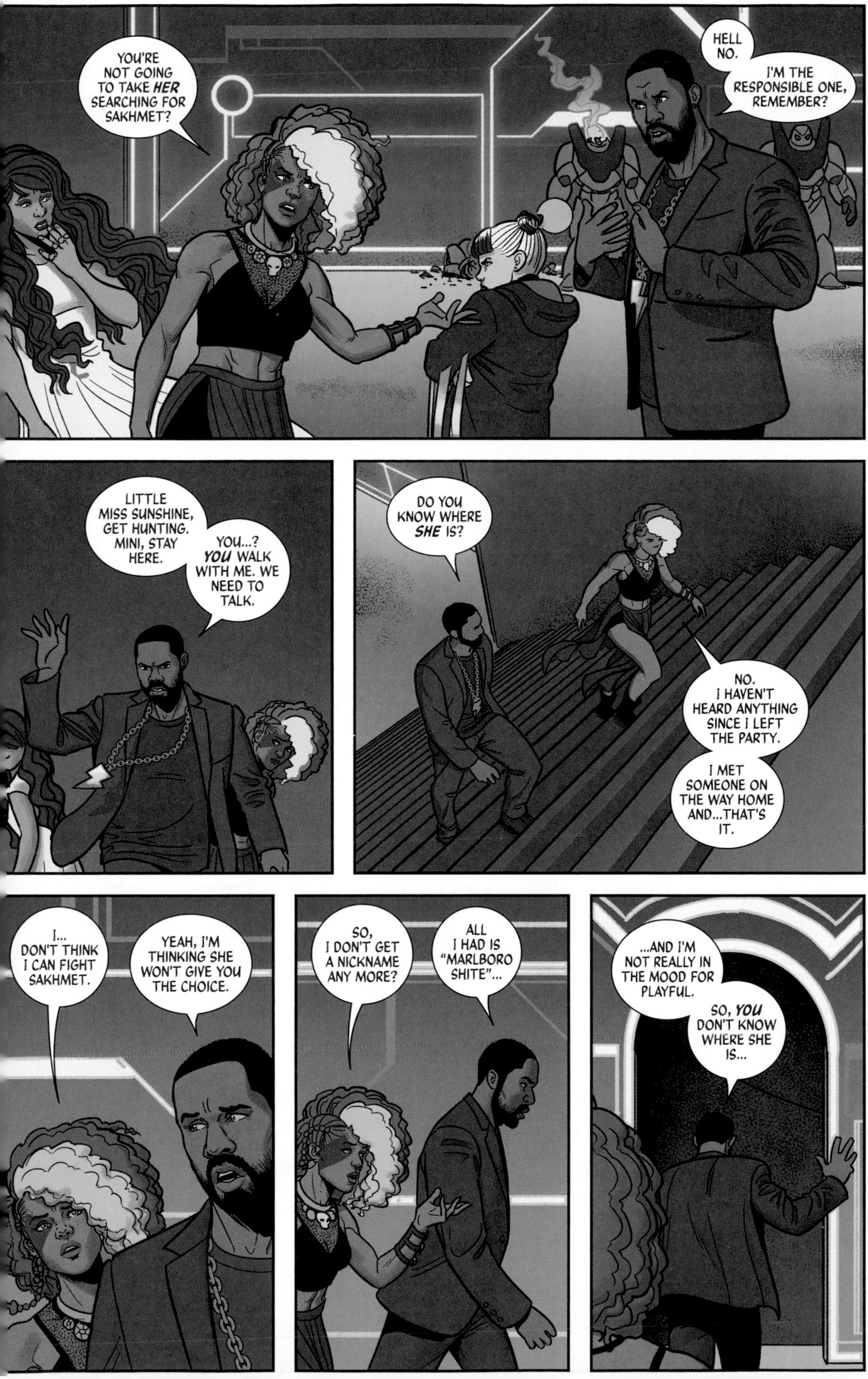
YOU'RE NOT GOING TO TAKE *HER* SEARCHING FOR SAKHMET?
HELL NO.
I'M THE RESPONSIBLE ONE, REMEMBER?
LITTLE MISS SUNSHINE, GET HUNTING. MINI, STAY HERE.
YOU...? *YOU* WALK WITH ME. WE NEED TO TALK.
DO YOU KNOW WHERE *SHE* IS?
NO. I HAVEN'T HEARD ANYTHING SINCE I LEFT THE PARTY.
I MET SOMEONE ON THE WAY HOME AND...THAT'S IT.
I... DON'T THINK I CAN FIGHT SAKHMET.
YEAH, I'M THINKING SHE WON'T GIVE YOU THE CHOICE.
SO, I DON'T GET A NICKNAME ANY MORE?
ALL I HAD IS "MARLBORO SHITE"...
...AND I'M NOT REALLY IN THE MOOD FOR PLAYFUL.
SO, *YOU* DON'T KNOW WHERE SHE IS...

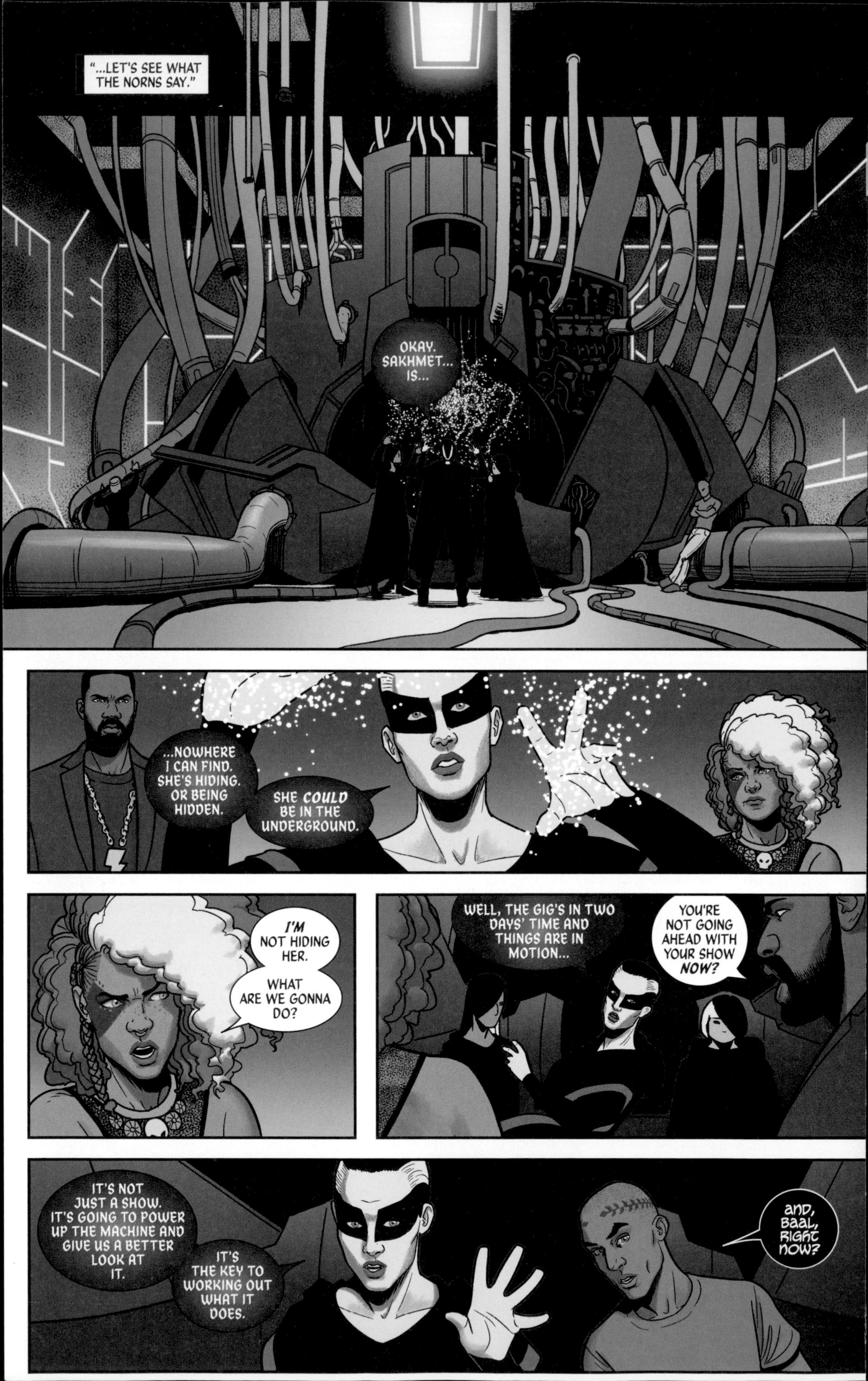
"...LET'S SEE WHAT THE NORNS SAY."
OKAY. SAKHMET... IS...
...NOWHERE I CAN FIND. SHE'S HIDING. OR BEING HIDDEN.
SHE COULD BE IN THE UNDERGROUND.
I'M NOT HIDING HER.
WHAT ARE WE GONNA DO?
WELL, THE GIG'S IN TWO DAYS' TIME AND THINGS ARE IN MOTION...
YOU'RE NOT GOING AHEAD WITH YOUR SHOW NOW?
IT'S NOT JUST A SHOW. IT'S GOING TO POWER UP THE MACHINE AND GIVE US A BETTER LOOK AT IT.
IT'S THE KEY TO WORKING OUT WHAT IT DOES.
AND, BAAL, RIGHT NOW?

WE NEED A REASON FOR PEOPLE NOT TO BE AFRAID OF US.

HMPH.

I GUESS MR. MISOGYNIST, FREE HUGS, AND SARCASM-IN-TRIPLICATE REALLY *AREN'T* FIGHTERS.

CAN YOU DO *ANYTHING* USEFUL?

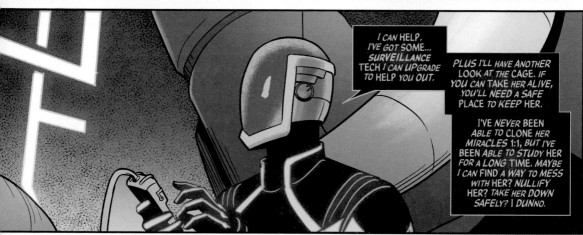

I CAN HELP. I'VE GOT SOME... *SURVEILLANCE* TECH I CAN *UPGRADE* TO HELP YOU OUT.

PLUS I'LL HAVE ANOTHER LOOK AT THE CAGE. IF YOU CAN TAKE *HER* ALIVE, YOU'LL NEED A *SAFE* PLACE TO KEEP HER.

I'VE *NEVER* BEEN ABLE TO CLONE HER MIRACLES 1:1, BUT I'VE BEEN ABLE TO STUDY HER FOR A *LONG* TIME. MAYBE I CAN FIND A WAY TO MESS WITH HER? NULLIFY HER? TAKE HER DOWN SAFELY? I DUNNO.

OKAY, DO THAT. BUT WE NEED ANYONE WHO *CAN* FIGHT ON SPEED DIAL.

TALK TO THE GOTHS.

FINE. IT'S NOT AS IF WE DIDN'T HAVE TO SPEAK TO MORRIGAN ANYWAY!

TO THE UNDERGROUND, UNDERGROUND GODS!

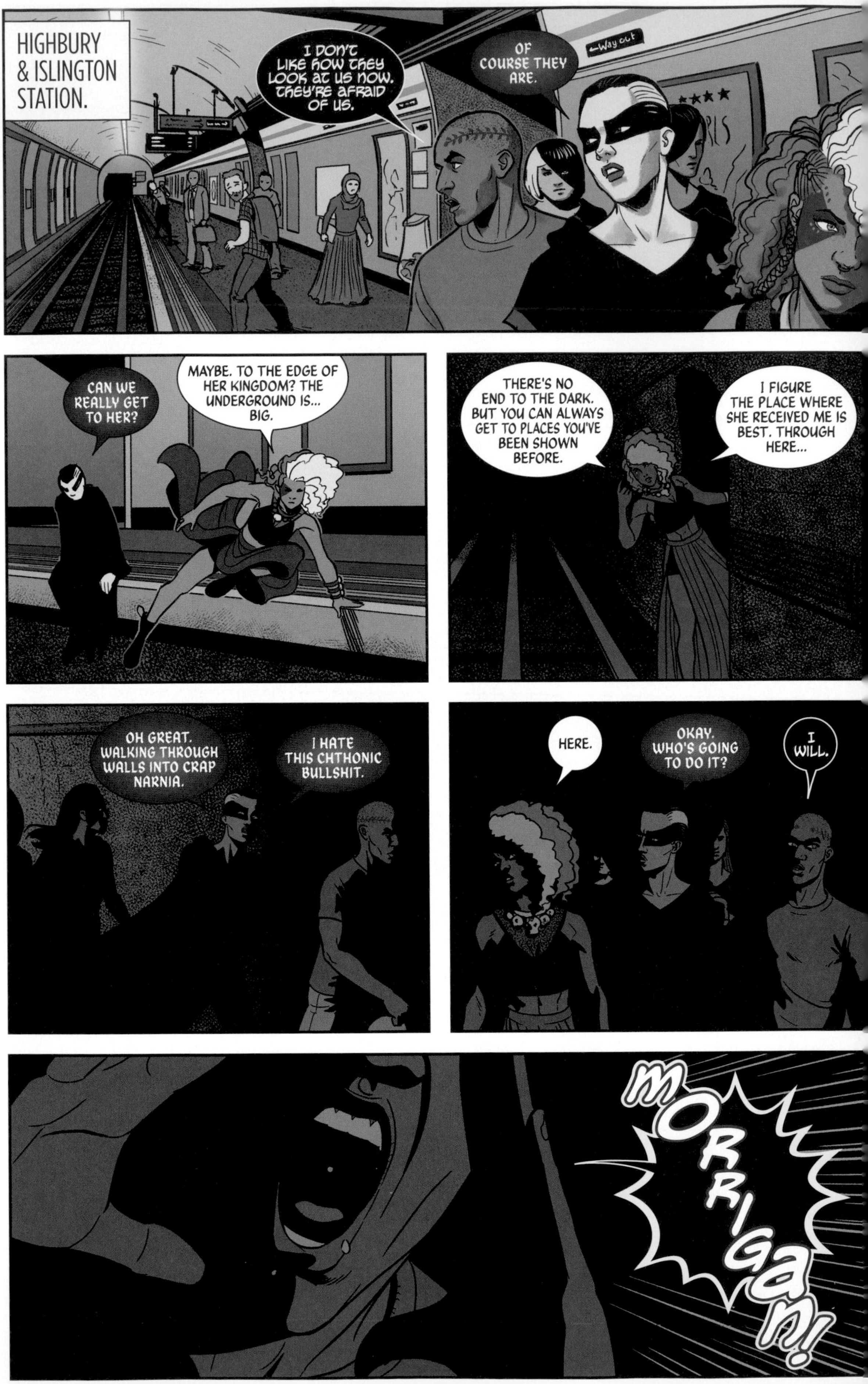
HIGHBURY & ISLINGTON STATION.
I DON'T LIKE HOW THEY LOOK AT US NOW. THEY'RE AFRAID OF US.
OF COURSE THEY ARE.
←Way out
CAN WE REALLY GET TO HER?
MAYBE. TO THE EDGE OF HER KINGDOM? THE UNDERGROUND IS... BIG.
THERE'S NO END TO THE DARK. BUT YOU CAN ALWAYS GET TO PLACES YOU'VE BEEN SHOWN BEFORE.
I FIGURE THE PLACE WHERE SHE RECEIVED ME IS BEST. THROUGH HERE...
OH GREAT. WALKING THROUGH WALLS INTO CRAP NARNIA.
I HATE THIS CHTHONIC BULLSHIT.
HERE.
OKAY. WHO'S GOING TO DO IT?
I WILL.
MORRIGAN!

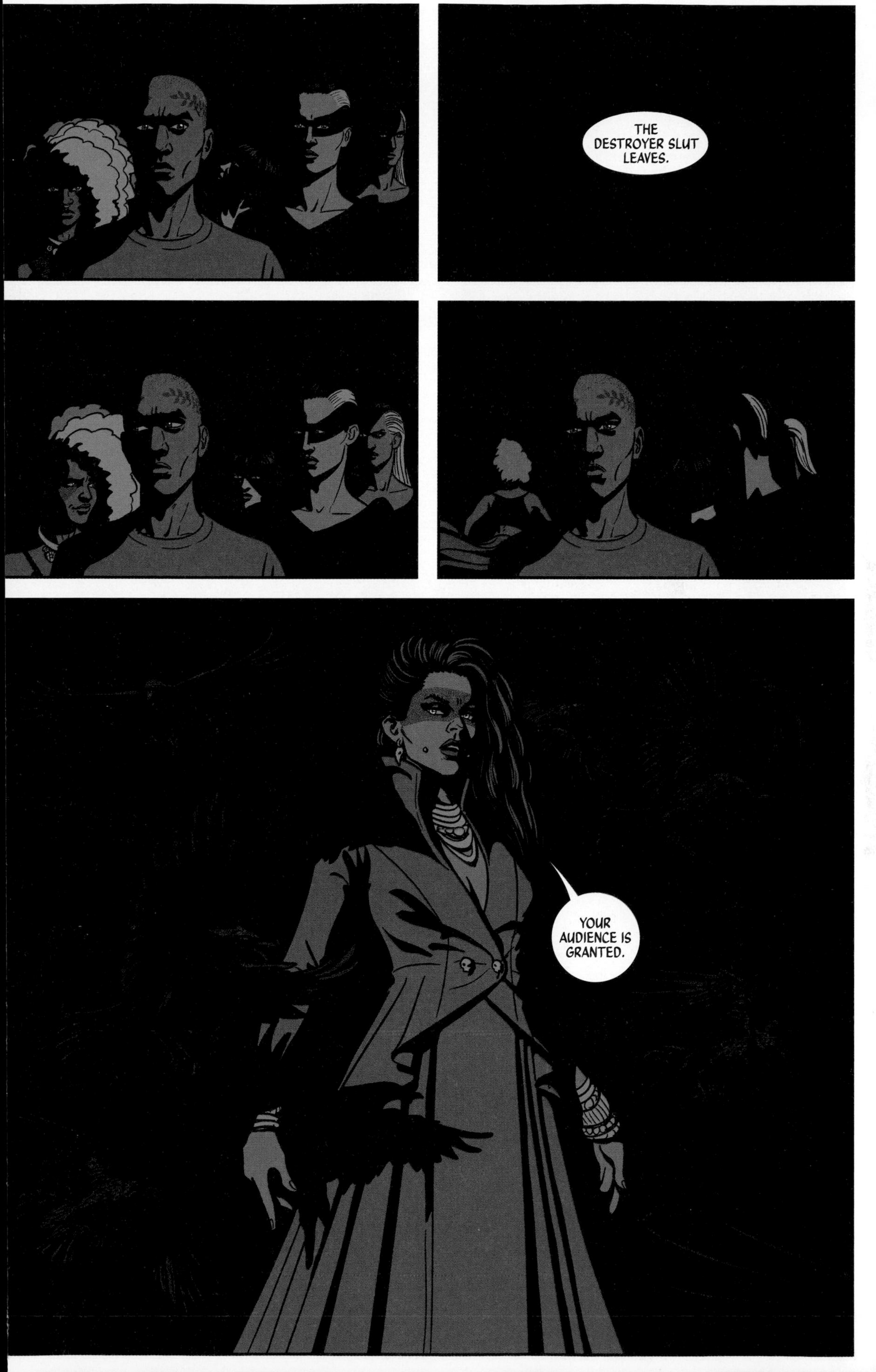
THE DESTROYER SLUT LEAVES.
YOUR AUDIENCE IS GRANTED.

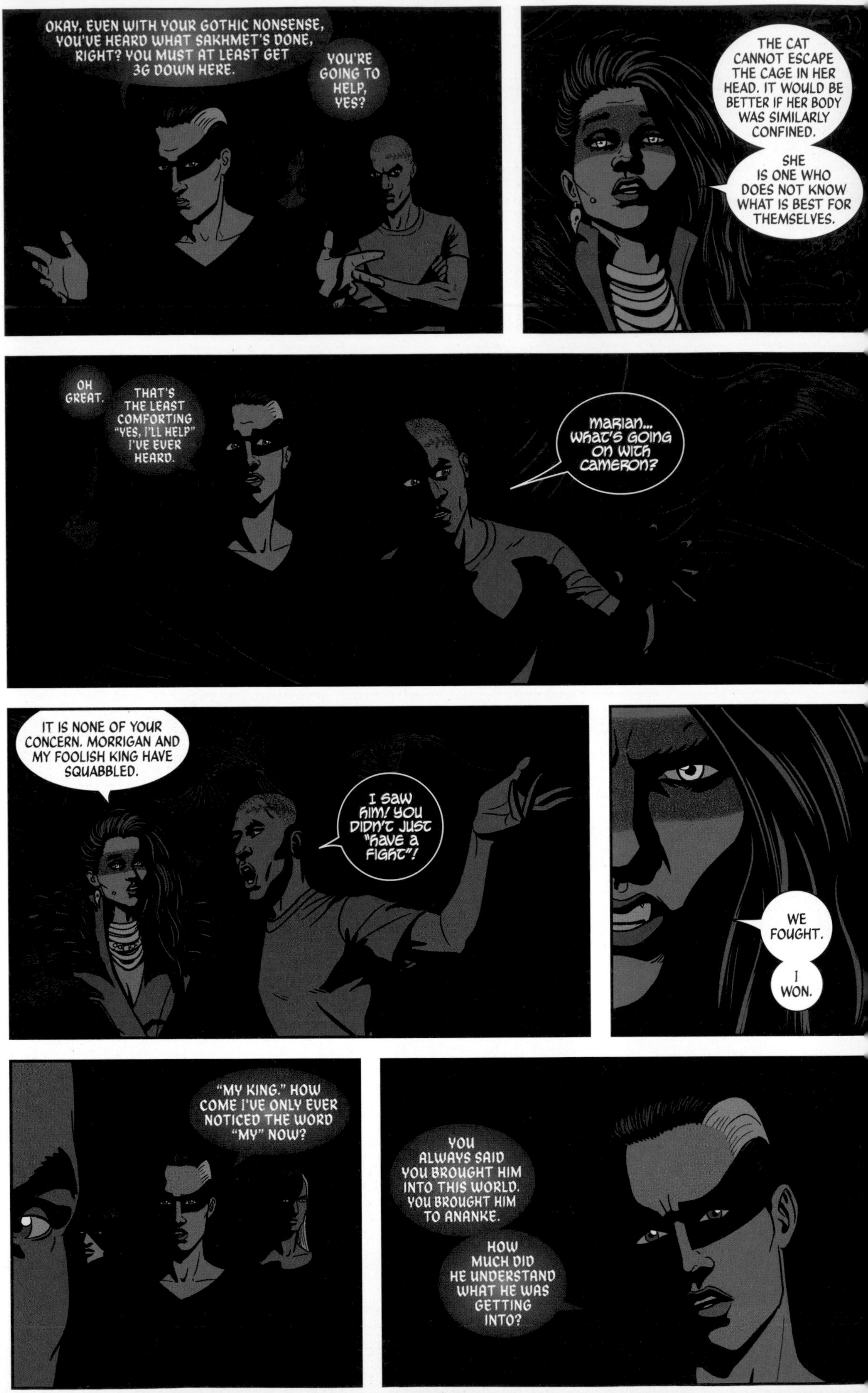
OKAY, EVEN WITH YOUR GOTHIC NONSENSE, YOU'VE HEARD WHAT SAKHMET'S DONE, RIGHT? YOU MUST AT LEAST GET 3G DOWN HERE.
YOU'RE GOING TO HELP, YES?
THE CAT CANNOT ESCAPE THE CAGE IN HER HEAD. IT WOULD BE BETTER IF HER BODY WAS SIMILARLY CONFINED.
SHE IS ONE WHO DOES NOT KNOW WHAT IS BEST FOR THEMSELVES.
OH GREAT.
THAT'S THE LEAST COMFORTING "YES, I'LL HELP" I'VE EVER HEARD.
MARIAN... WHAT'S GOING ON WITH CAMERON?
IT IS NONE OF YOUR CONCERN. MORRIGAN AND MY FOOLISH KING HAVE SQUABBLED.
I SAW HIM! YOU DIDN'T JUST "HAVE A FIGHT"!
WE FOUGHT.
I WON.
"MY KING." HOW COME I'VE ONLY EVER NOTICED THE WORD "MY" NOW?
YOU ALWAYS SAID YOU BROUGHT HIM INTO THIS WORLD. YOU BROUGHT HIM TO ANANKE.
HOW MUCH DID HE UNDERSTAND WHAT HE WAS GETTING INTO?

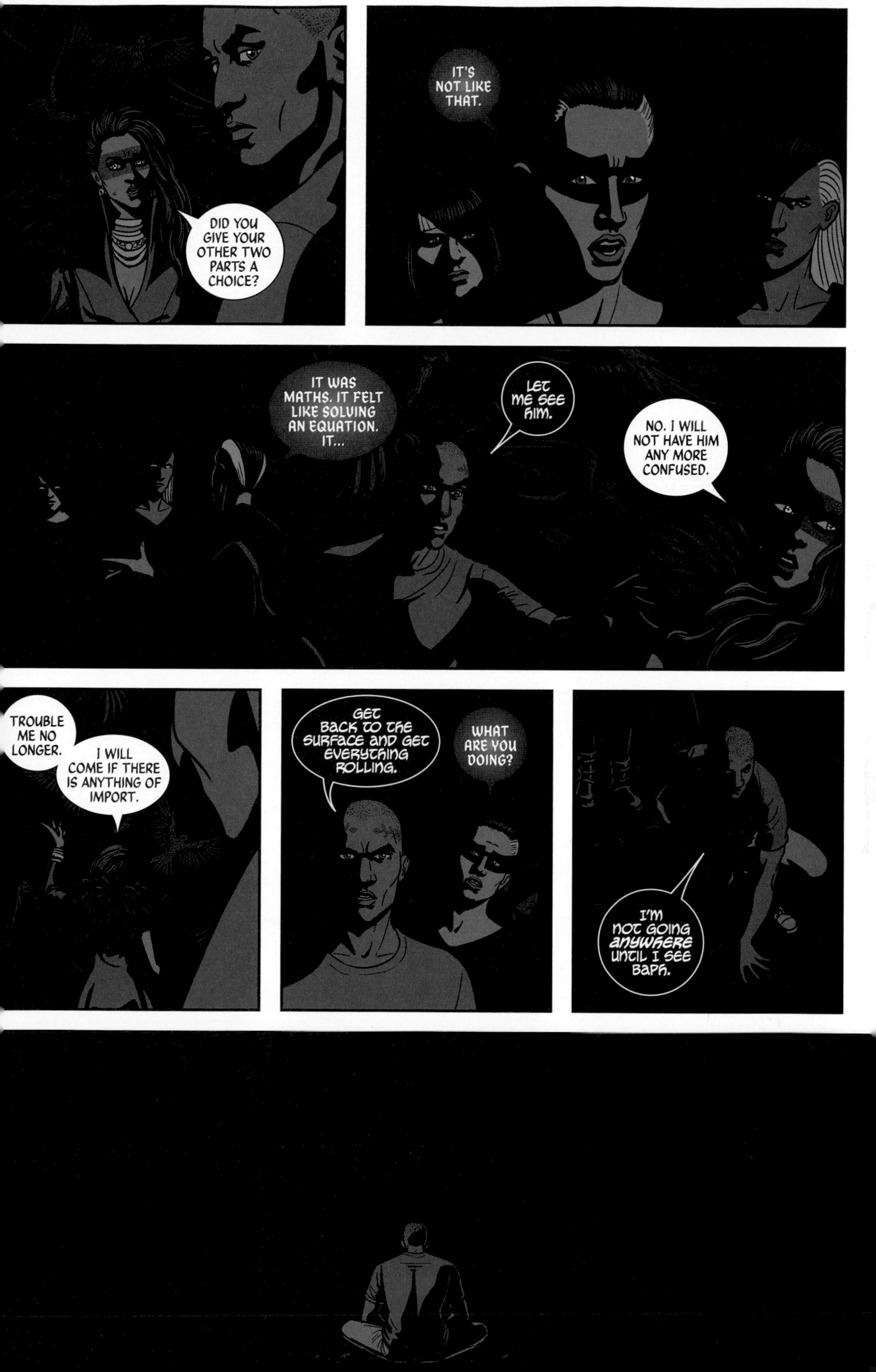
DID YOU GIVE YOUR OTHER TWO PARTS A CHOICE?
IT'S NOT LIKE THAT.
IT WAS MATHS. IT FELT LIKE SOLVING AN EQUATION. IT...
LET ME SEE HIM.
NO. I WILL NOT HAVE HIM ANY MORE CONFUSED.
TROUBLE ME NO LONGER.
I WILL COME IF THERE IS ANYTHING OF IMPORT.
GET BACK TO THE SURFACE AND GET EVERYTHING ROLLING.
WHAT ARE YOU DOING?
I'M NOT GOING ANYWHERE UNTIL I SEE BAPH.

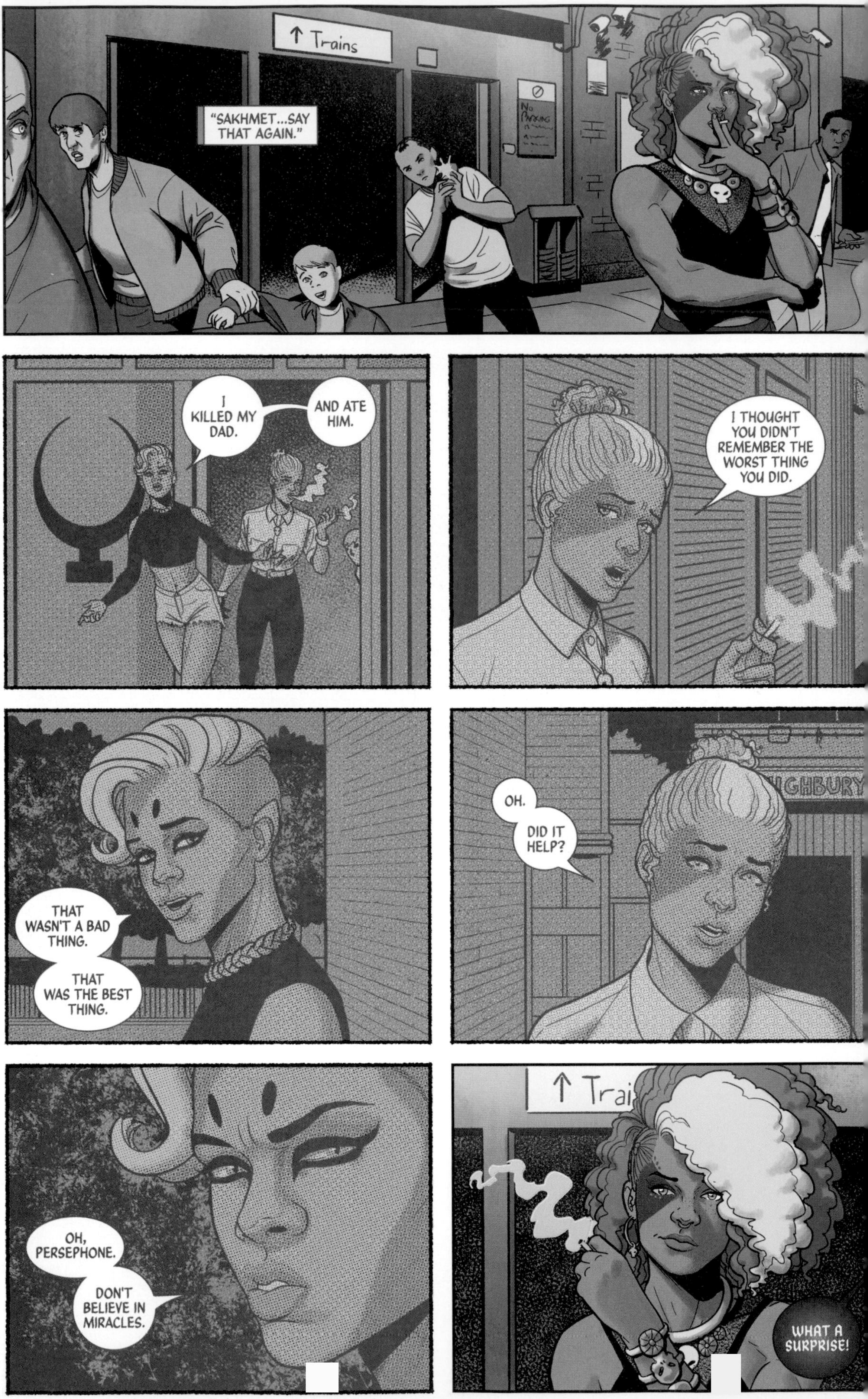
"SAKHMET...SAY THAT AGAIN."
↑ Trains
I KILLED MY DAD.
AND ATE HIM.
I THOUGHT YOU DIDN'T REMEMBER THE WORST THING YOU DID.
THAT WASN'T A BAD THING.
THAT WAS THE BEST THING.
OH.
DID IT HELP?
OH, PERSEPHONE.
DON'T BELIEVE IN MIRACLES.
WHAT A SURPRISE!

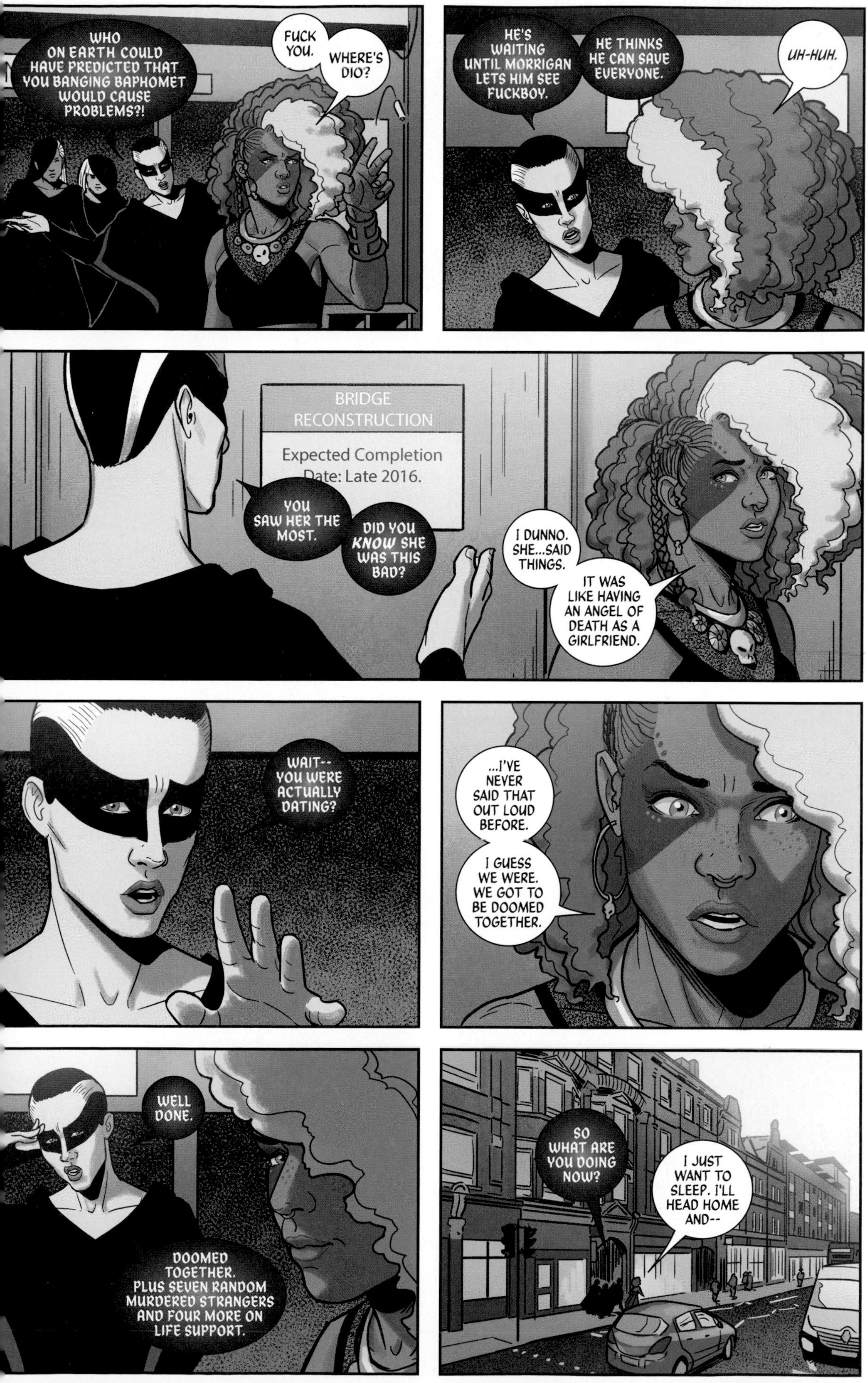

WHO ON EARTH COULD HAVE PREDICTED THAT YOU BANGING BAPHOMET WOULD CAUSE PROBLEMS?!
FUCK YOU.
WHERE'S DIO?
HE'S WAITING UNTIL MORRIGAN LETS HIM SEE FUCKBOY.
HE THINKS HE CAN SAVE EVERYONE.
UH-HUH.
BRIDGE RECONSTRUCTION
Expected Completion Date: Late 2016.
YOU SAW HER THE MOST.
DID YOU KNOW SHE WAS THIS BAD?
I DUNNO. SHE...SAID THINGS.
IT WAS LIKE HAVING AN ANGEL OF DEATH AS A GIRLFRIEND.
WAIT-- YOU WERE ACTUALLY DATING?
...I'VE NEVER SAID THAT OUT LOUD BEFORE.
I GUESS WE WERE. WE GOT TO BE DOOMED TOGETHER.
WELL DONE.
DOOMED TOGETHER. PLUS SEVEN RANDOM MURDERED STRANGERS AND FOUR MORE ON LIFE SUPPORT.
SO WHAT ARE YOU DOING NOW?
I JUST WANT TO SLEEP. I'LL HEAD HOME AND--

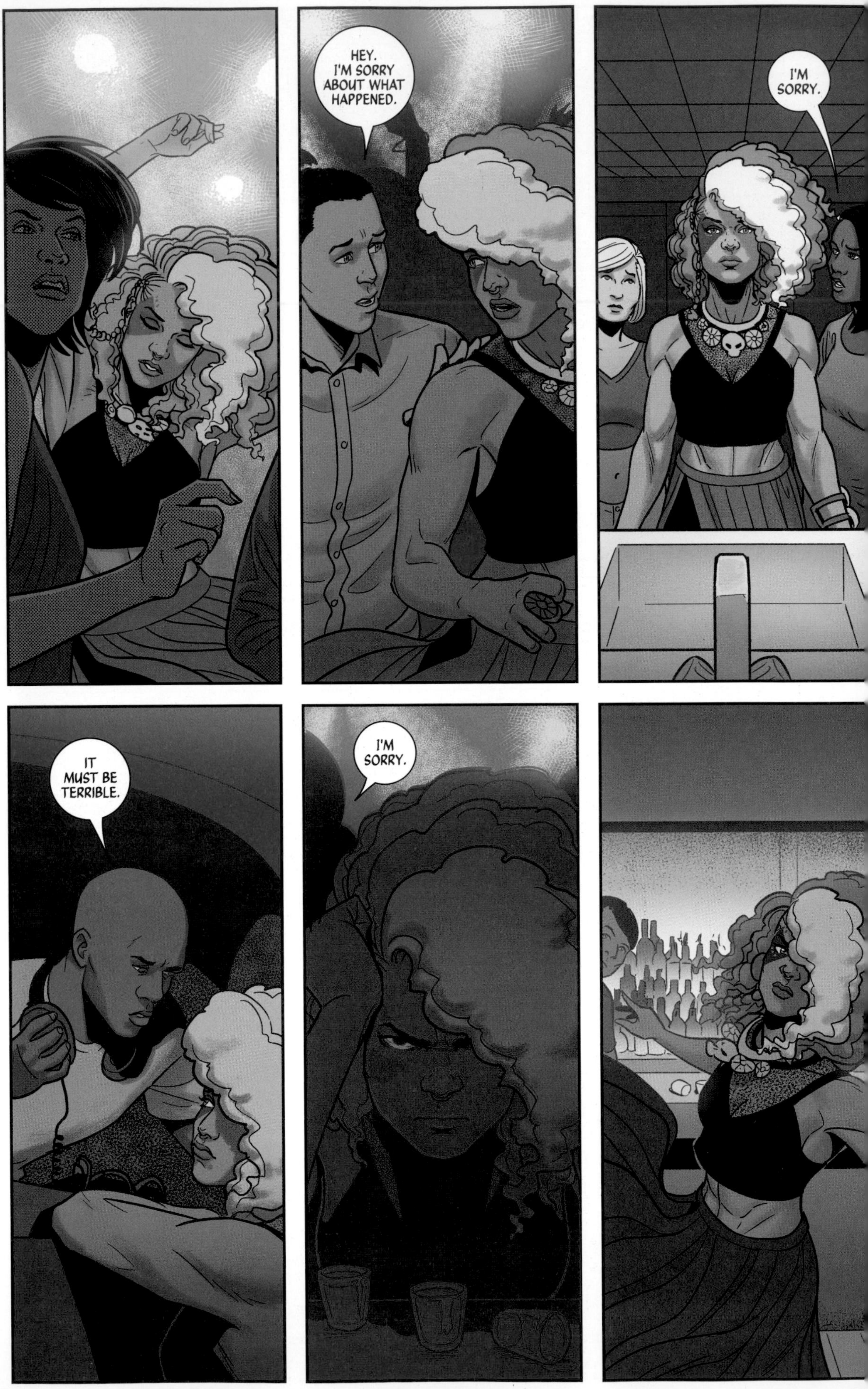
HEY. I'M SORRY ABOUT WHAT HAPPENED.
I'M SORRY.
IT MUST BE TERRIBLE.
I'M SORRY.

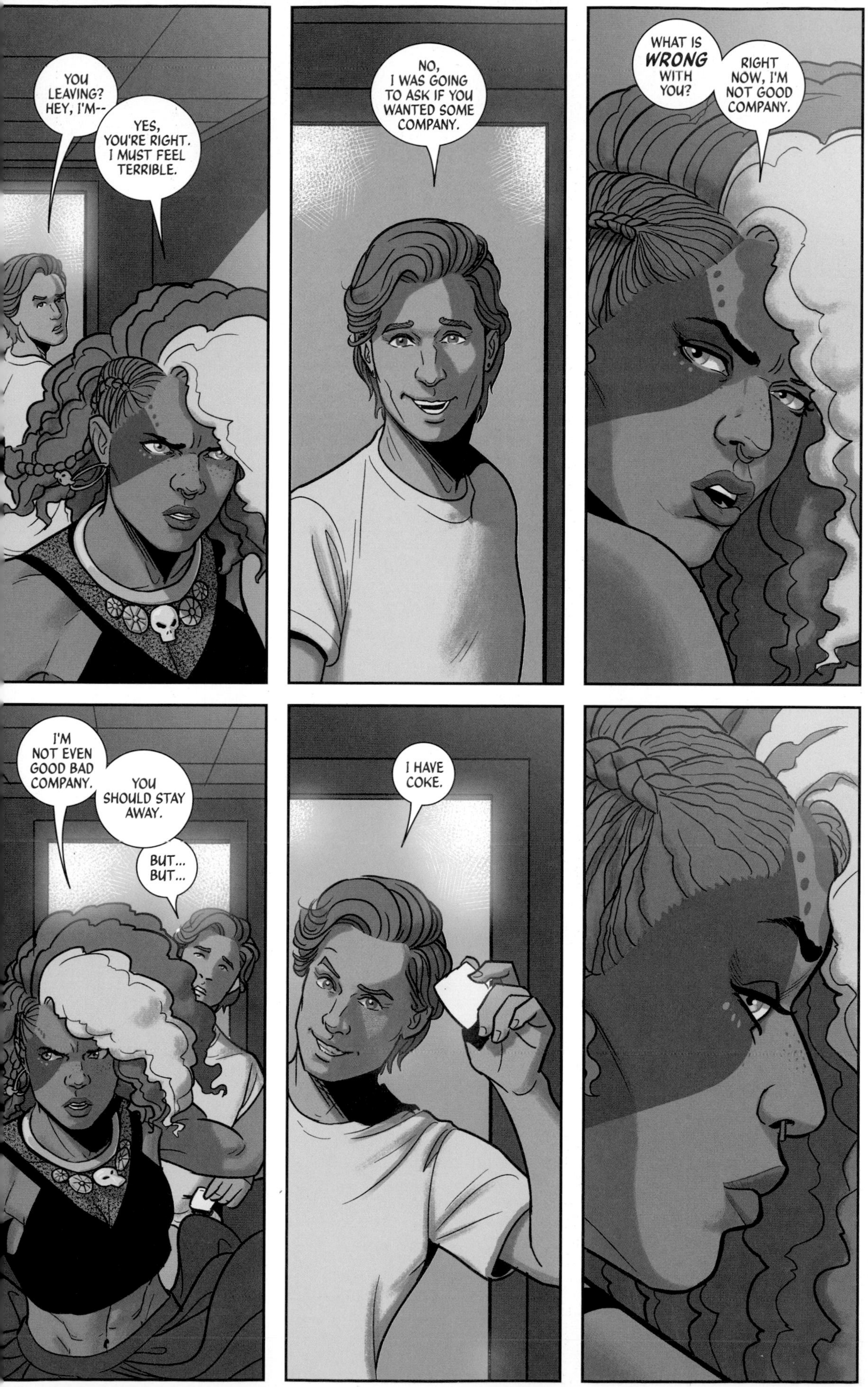
YOU LEAVING? HEY, I'M--
YES, YOU'RE RIGHT. I MUST FEEL TERRIBLE.
NO, I WAS GOING TO ASK IF YOU WANTED SOME COMPANY.
WHAT IS WRONG WITH YOU?
RIGHT NOW, I'M NOT GOOD COMPANY.
I'M NOT EVEN GOOD BAD COMPANY.
YOU SHOULD STAY AWAY.
BUT... BUT...
I HAVE COKE.

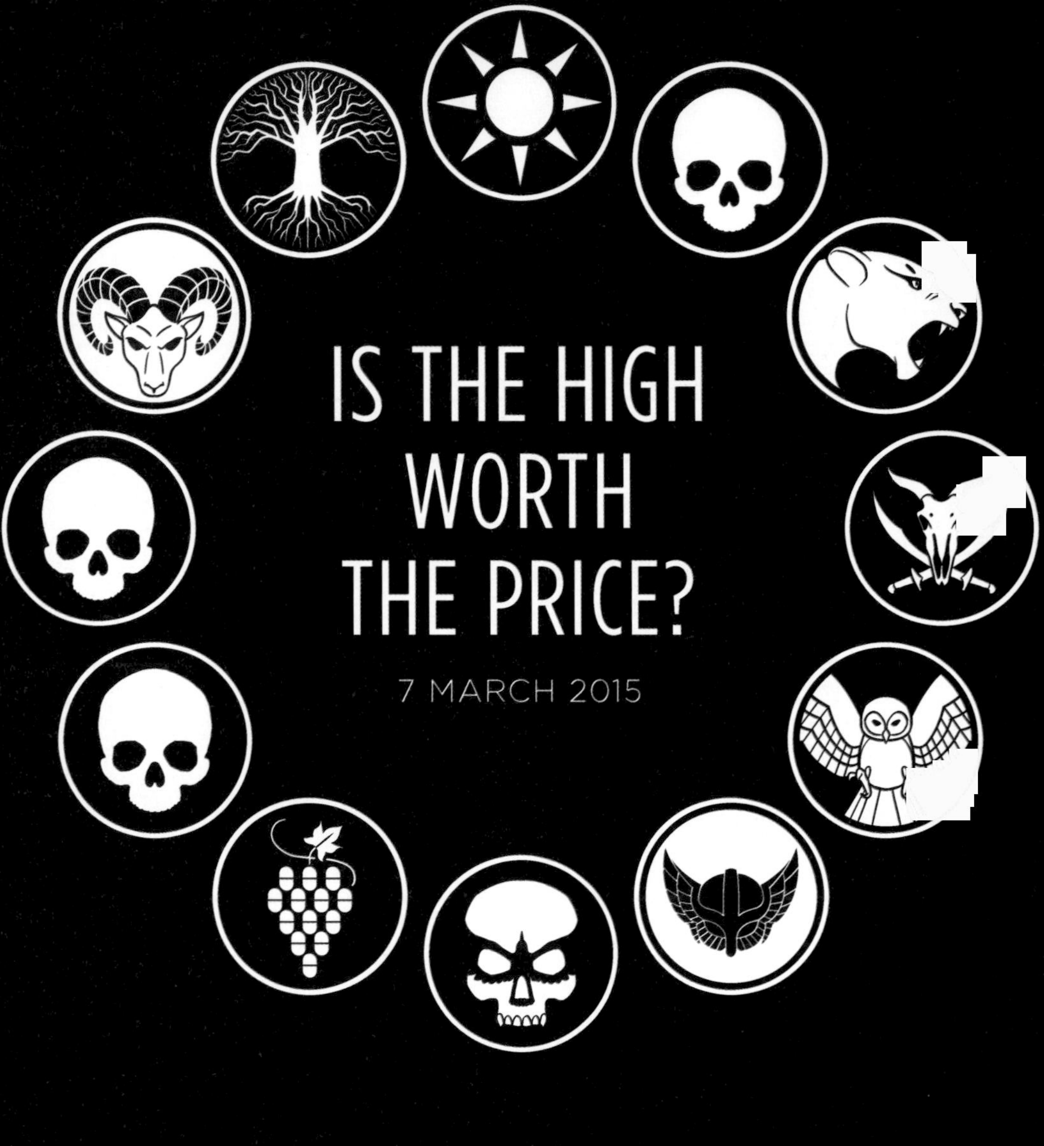
IS THE HIGH
WORTH
THE PRICE?
7 MARCH 2015

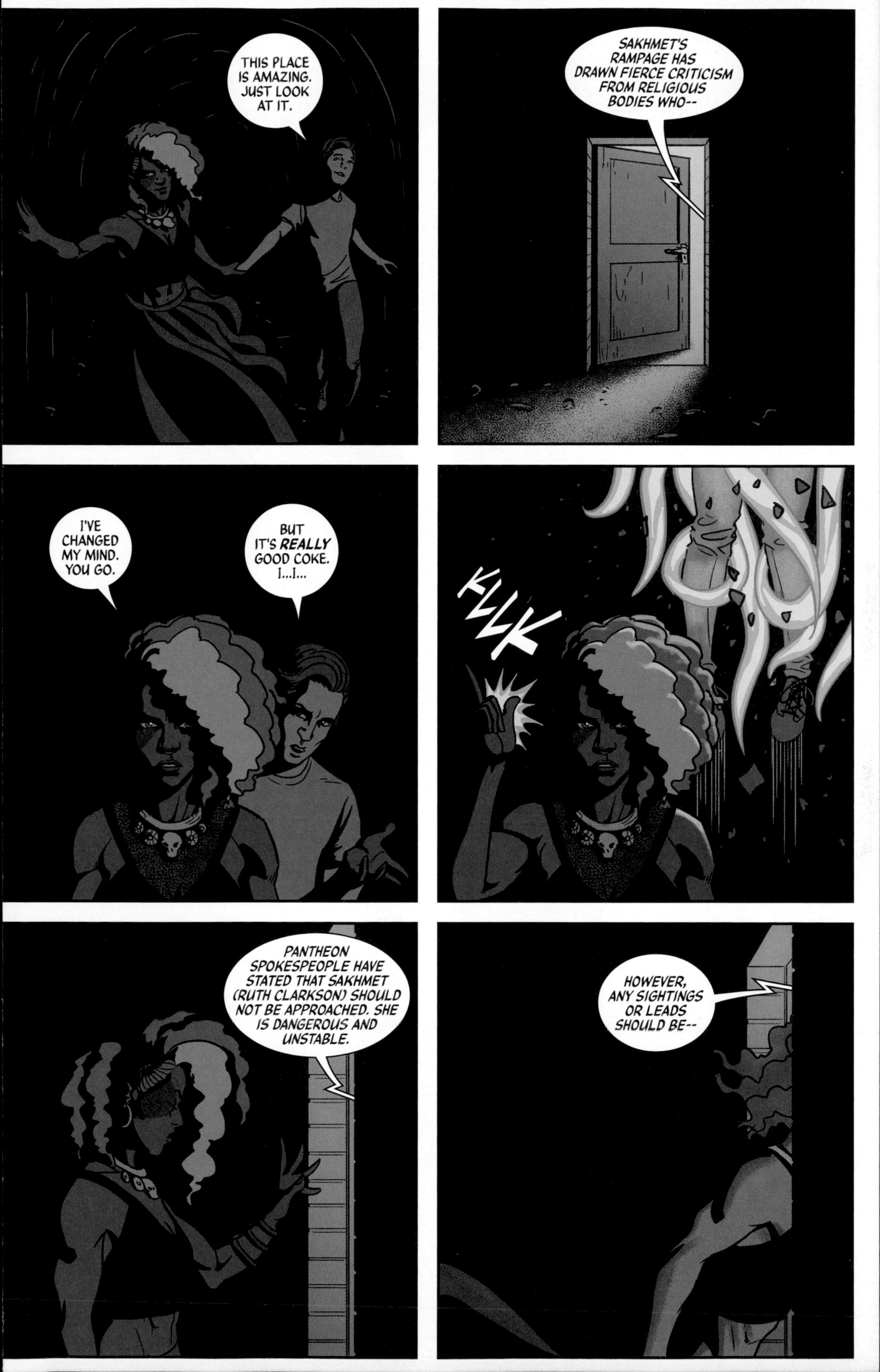
THIS PLACE IS AMAZING. JUST LOOK AT IT.
SAKHMET'S RAMPAGE HAS DRAWN FIERCE CRITICISM FROM RELIGIOUS BODIES WHO--
I'VE CHANGED MY MIND. YOU GO.
BUT IT'S *REALLY* GOOD COKE. I...I...
KLLK
PANTHEON SPOKESPEOPLE HAVE STATED THAT SAKHMET (RUTH CLARKSON) SHOULD NOT BE APPROACHED. SHE IS DANGEROUS AND UNSTABLE.
HOWEVER, ANY SIGHTINGS OR LEADS SHOULD BE--

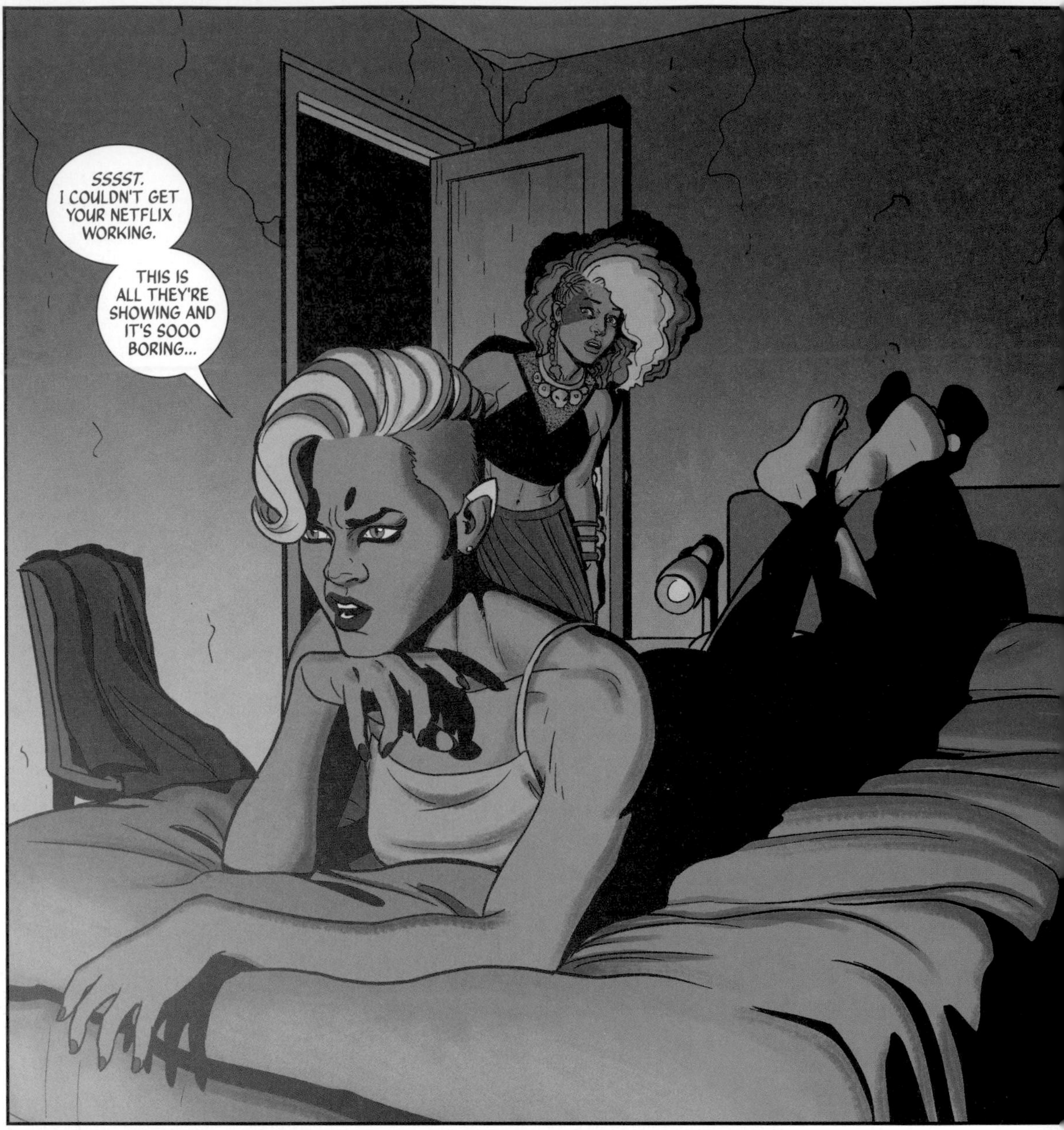
SSSST. I COULDN'T GET YOUR NETFLIX WORKING.
THIS IS ALL THEY'RE SHOWING AND IT'S SOOO BORING...

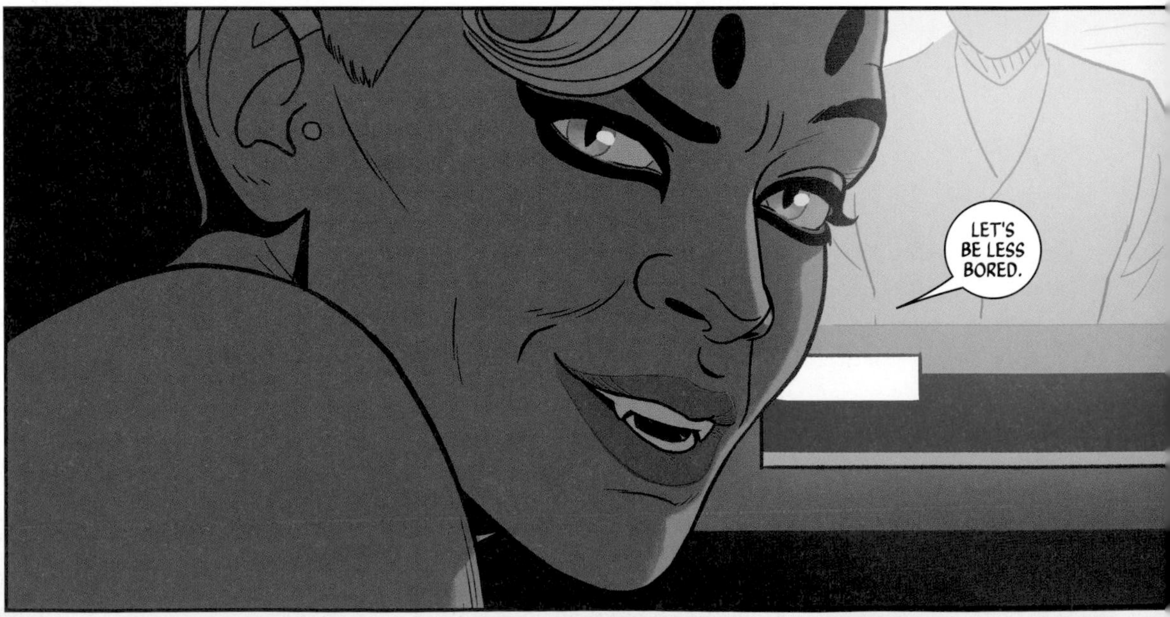
LET'S BE LESS BORED.

NETFLIX
AND KILL

7 MARCH 2015

30

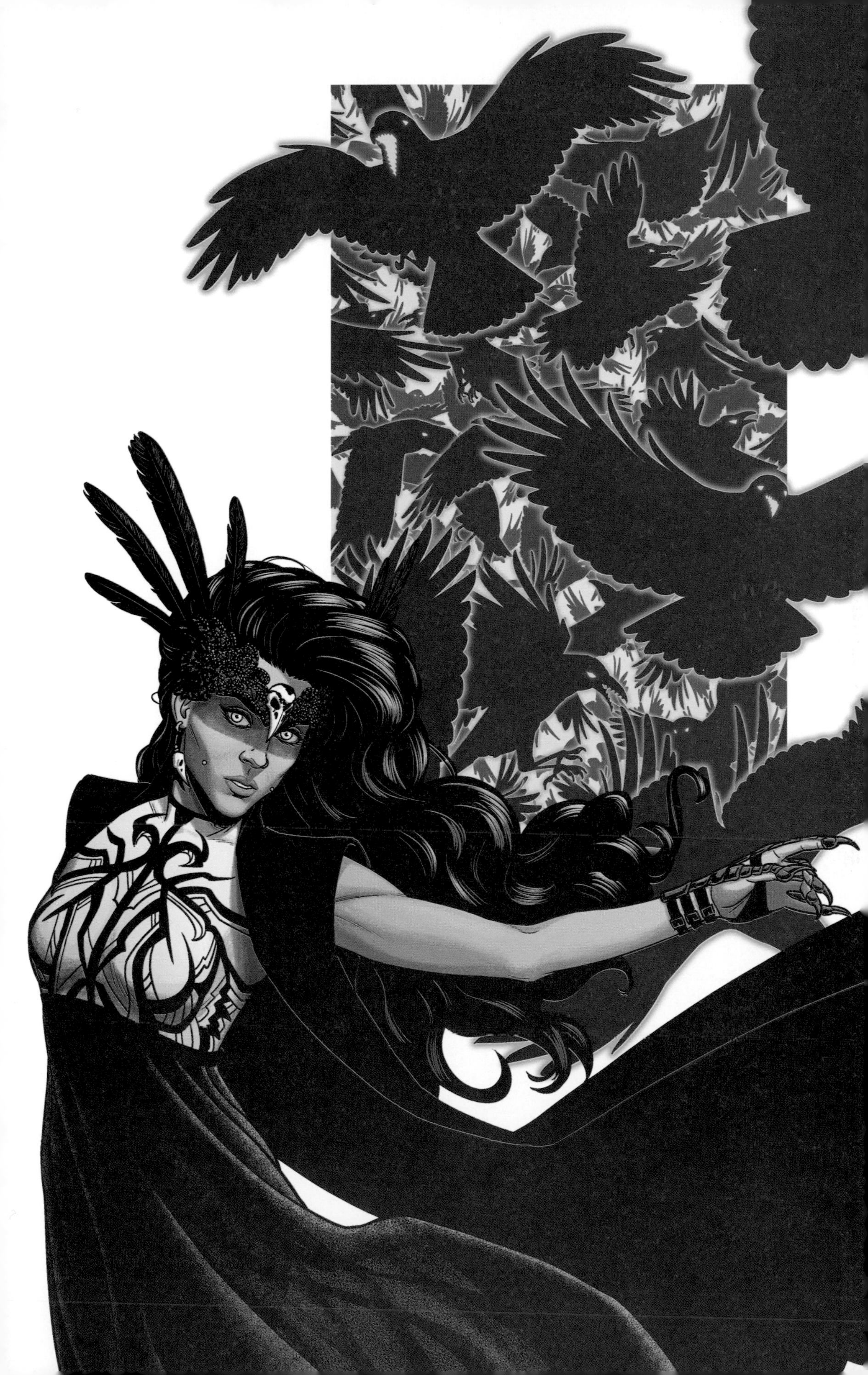

THE
WICKED
+
ƎNIΛIꓷ
ƎHꓕ

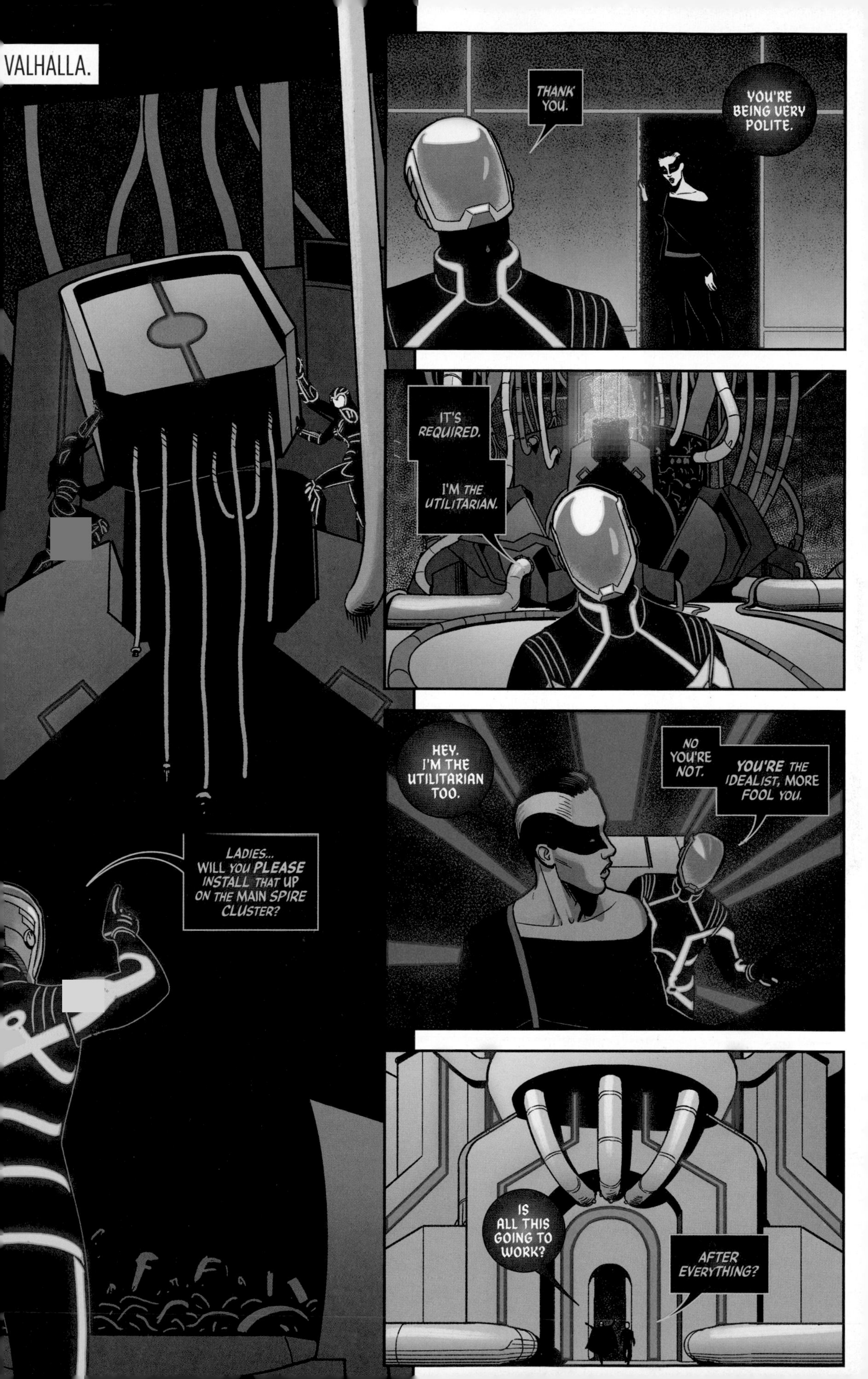
VALHALLA.
LADIES... WILL YOU PLEASE INSTALL THAT UP ON THE MAIN SPIRE CLUSTER?
THANK YOU.
YOU'RE BEING VERY POLITE.
IT'S REQUIRED.
I'M THE UTILITARIAN.
HEY. I'M THE UTILITARIAN TOO.
NO YOU'RE NOT.
YOU'RE THE IDEALIST, MORE FOOL YOU.
IS ALL THIS GOING TO WORK?
AFTER EVERYTHING?

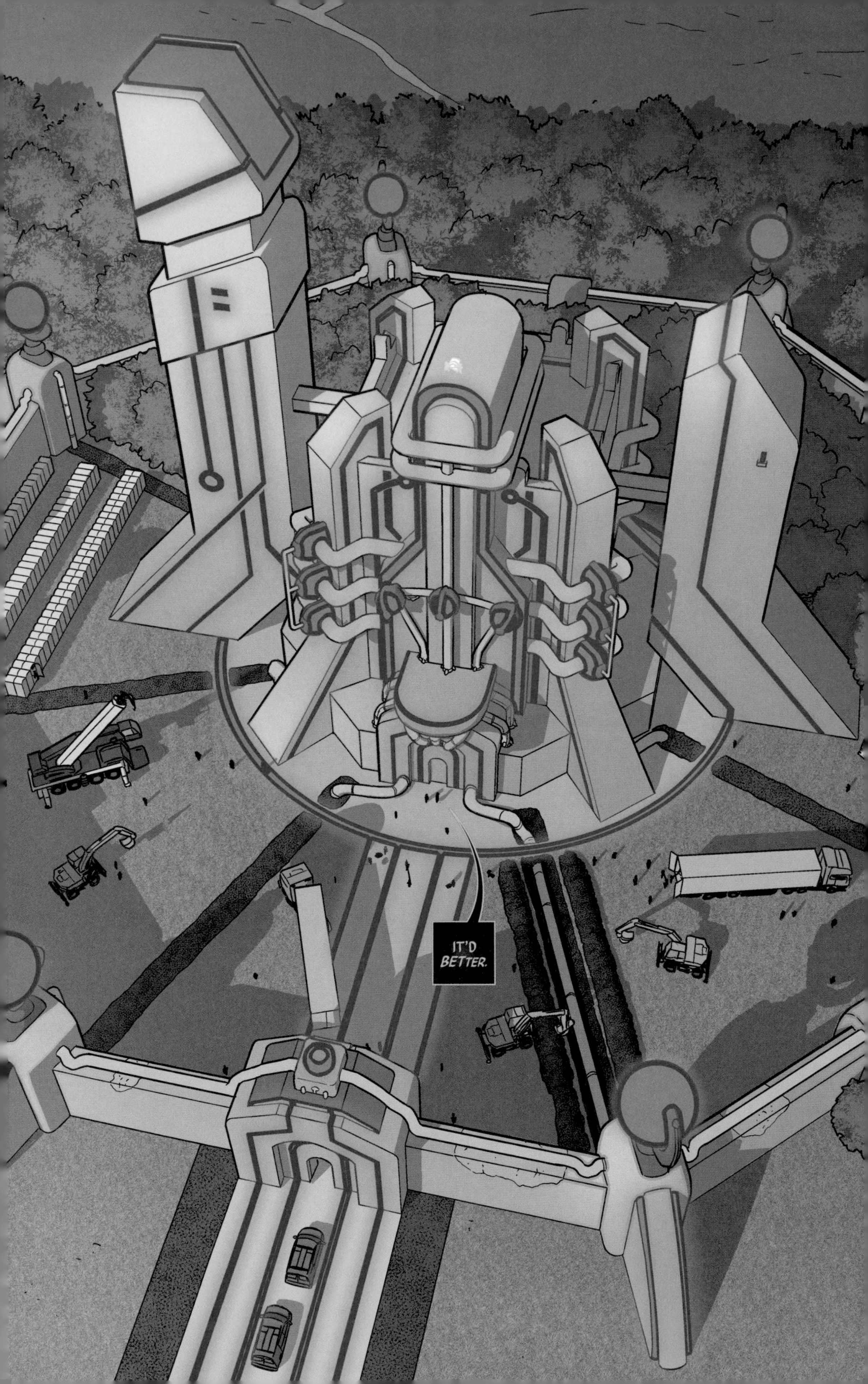
IT'D BETTER.

TOMORROW NIGHT, THERE'LL BE 44,444 PEOPLE IN THE GROUNDS. DIO PULLS A HIVEMIND. IT POWERS UP THE MACHINE AND THEN... WHAT?

IF THE MACHINE GOES FIZZ, IT'S GOING TO BE A SHITSTORM.

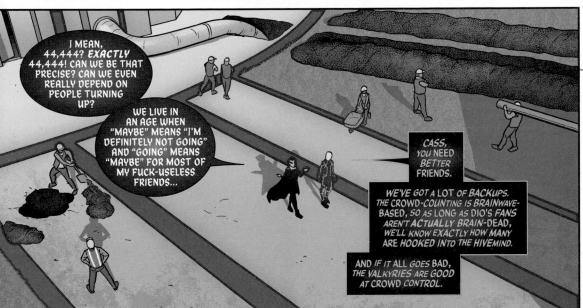

I MEAN, 44,444? *EXACTLY* 44,444! CAN WE BE THAT PRECISE? CAN WE EVEN REALLY DEPEND ON PEOPLE TURNING UP?

WE LIVE IN AN AGE WHEN "MAYBE" MEANS "I'M DEFINITELY NOT GOING" AND "GOING" MEANS "MAYBE" FOR MOST OF MY FUCK-USELESS FRIENDS...

CASS, YOU NEED BETTER FRIENDS.

WE'VE GOT A LOT OF BACKUPS. THE CROWD-COUNTING IS BRAINWAVE-BASED, SO AS LONG AS DIO'S FANS AREN'T *ACTUALLY* BRAIN-DEAD, WE'LL KNOW EXACTLY HOW MANY ARE HOOKED INTO THE HIVEMIND.

AND IF IT ALL GOES BAD, THE *VALKYRIES* ARE GOOD AT CROWD CONTROL.

WHAT'S THE ACTUAL DEAL WITH THEM?

THEY *GET* TO DO THE WARM-UP SETS. UPGRADES ON MY NEW WAVE OF PERFORMANCE TECH. PLUS MONEY!

THEY *STILL NEED* ME. THEY *JUST GET* TO PRETEND THEY DON'T.

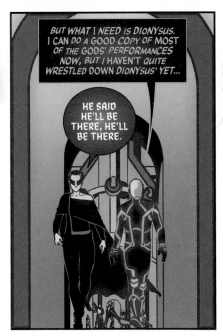

BUT WHAT I NEED IS DIONYSUS. I CAN DO A GOOD *COPY* OF MOST OF THE GODS' PERFORMANCES NOW, BUT I HAVEN'T QUITE WRESTLED DOWN *DIONYSUS'* YET...

HE SAID HE'LL BE THERE, HE'LL BE THERE.

SO...IS THAT A PIECE OF *GENUINE PROPHECY* OR UNCHARACTERISTIC OPTIMISM?

NO REST FOR
THE DIVINE TOO

7 MARCH 2015

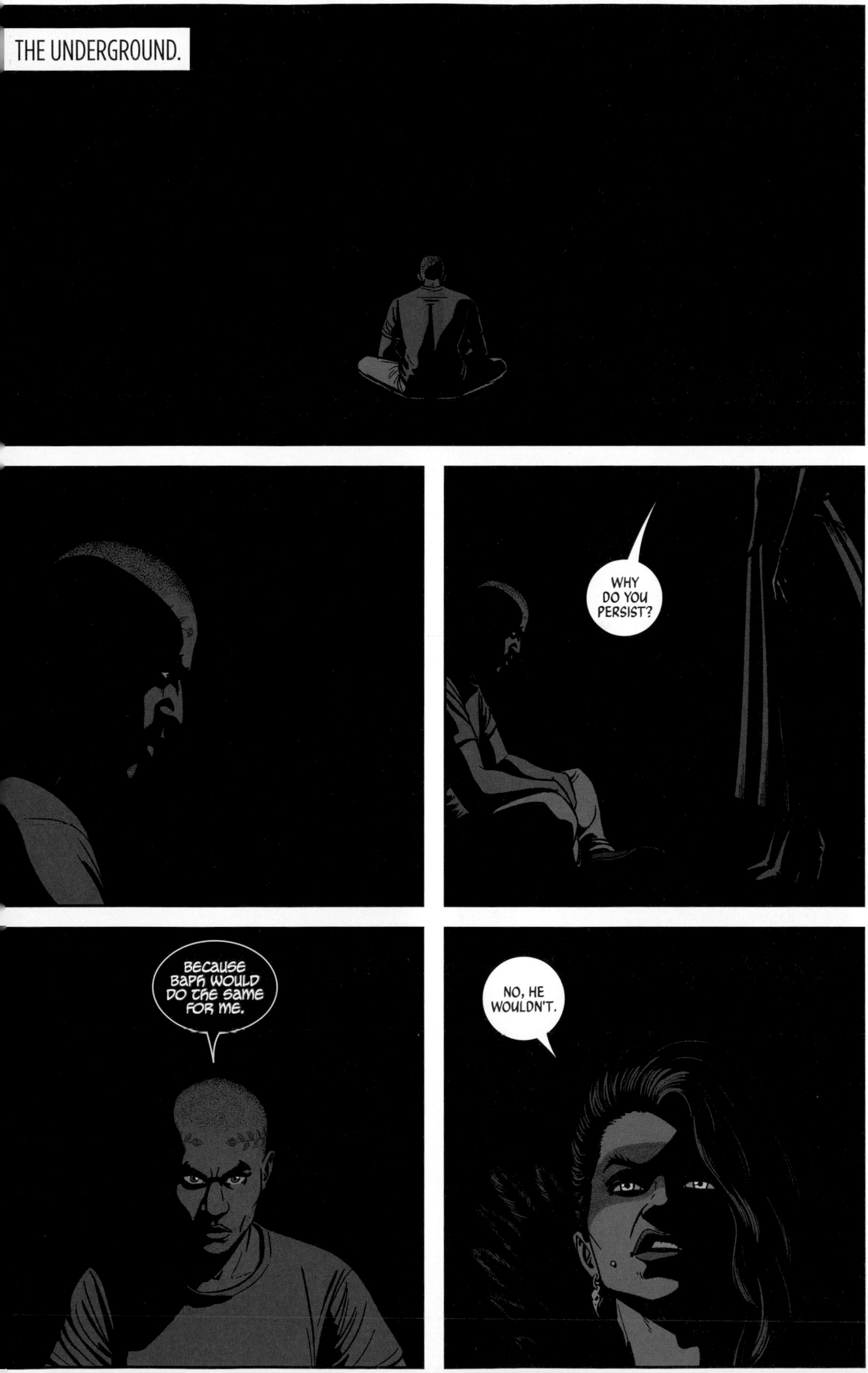
THE UNDERGROUND.
WHY DO YOU PERSIST?
BECAUSE BAPH WOULD DO THE SAME FOR ME.
NO, HE WOULDN'T.

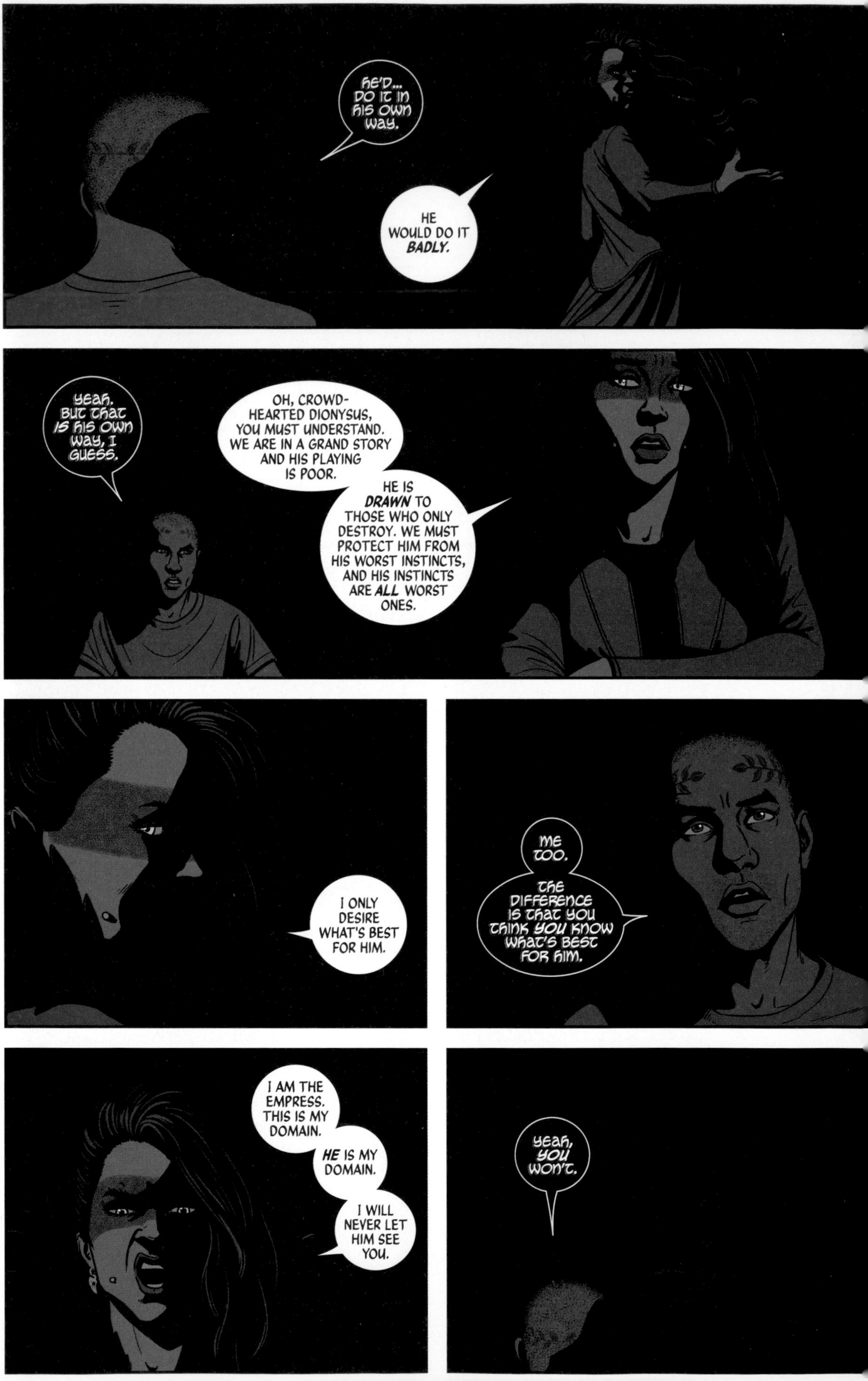

HE'D... DO IT IN HIS OWN WAY.
HE WOULD DO IT *BADLY.*
YEAH. BUT THAT *IS* HIS OWN WAY, I GUESS.
OH, CROWD-HEARTED DIONYSUS, YOU MUST UNDERSTAND. WE ARE IN A GRAND STORY AND HIS PLAYING IS POOR.
HE IS *DRAWN* TO THOSE WHO ONLY DESTROY. WE MUST PROTECT HIM FROM HIS WORST INSTINCTS, AND HIS INSTINCTS ARE *ALL* WORST ONES.
I ONLY DESIRE WHAT'S BEST FOR HIM.
ME TOO.
THE DIFFERENCE IS THAT YOU THINK *YOU* KNOW WHAT'S BEST FOR HIM.
I AM THE EMPRESS. THIS IS MY DOMAIN.
HE IS MY DOMAIN.
I WILL NEVER LET HIM SEE YOU.
YEAH, *YOU* WON'T.

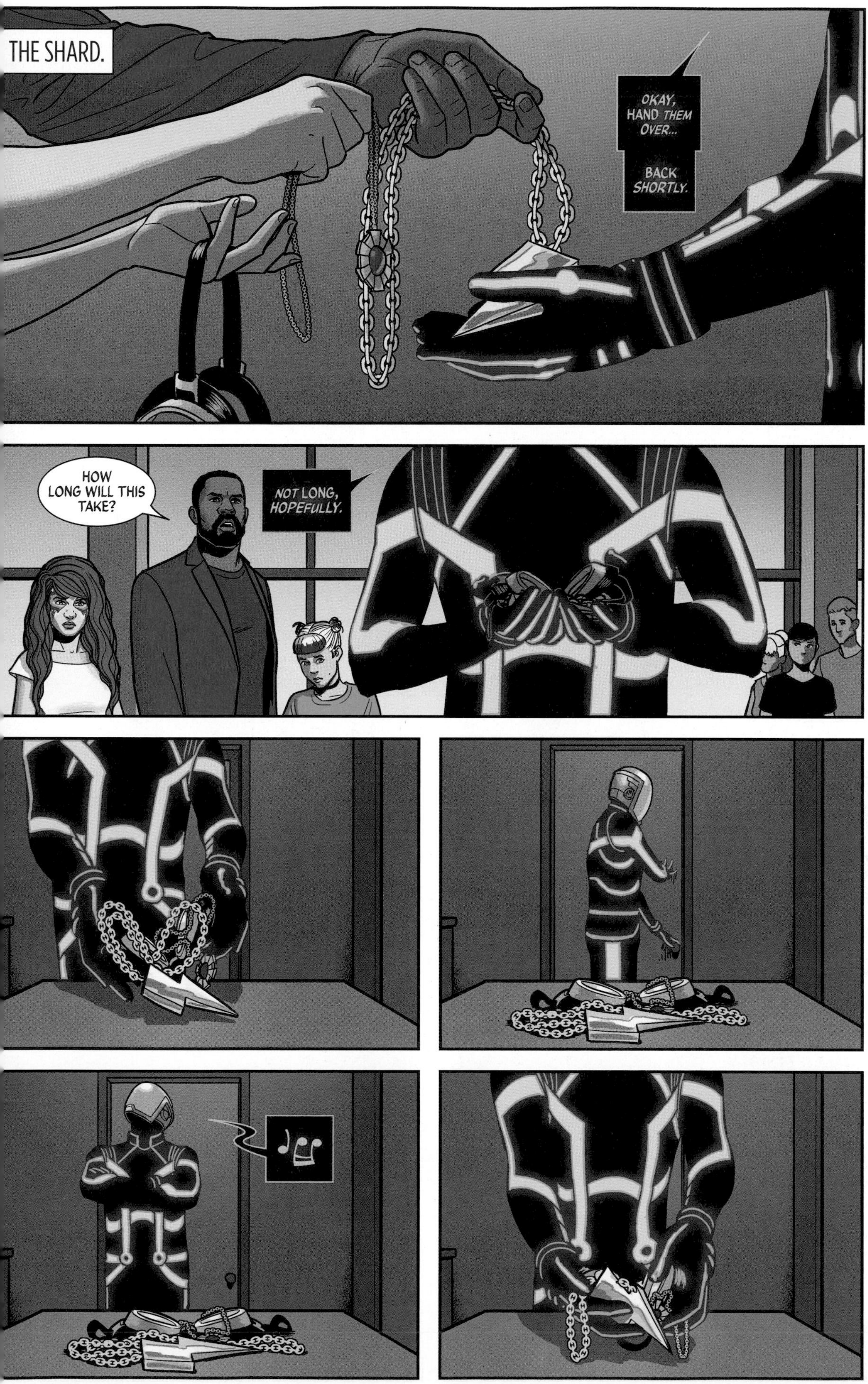
THE SHARD.
OKAY, HAND THEM OVER...
BACK SHORTLY.
HOW LONG WILL THIS TAKE?
NOT LONG, HOPEFULLY.

OKAY, I'VE, ER, ADDED THE TRACKING AND RECORDING FUNCTIONALITY.

WE'LL KNOW *WHERE* YOU ARE, WILL *BROADCAST FOOTAGE* SO YOU CAN COORDINATE.

CLK

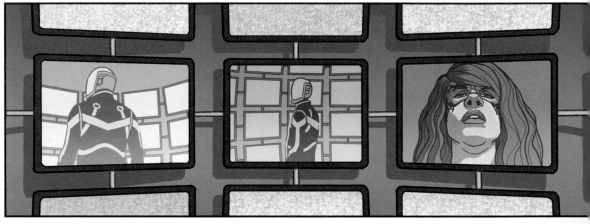

WHAT ABOUT PERSY?

I'D *HAVE* TO MAKE ONE *FROM SCRATCH* FOR HER. SAME AS *DIONYSUS, MORRIGAN* AND *BAPHOMET* IF THEY EVER WANT TO JOIN *THIS* PARTY...

WAIT...WHAT IF WE DON'T *WANT* SOMETHING RECORDED?

YOU TAKE IT OFF, DUH.

ER...CAN WE HAVE ACCESS TO THIS FOOTAGE FOR THE DOCUMENTARY?

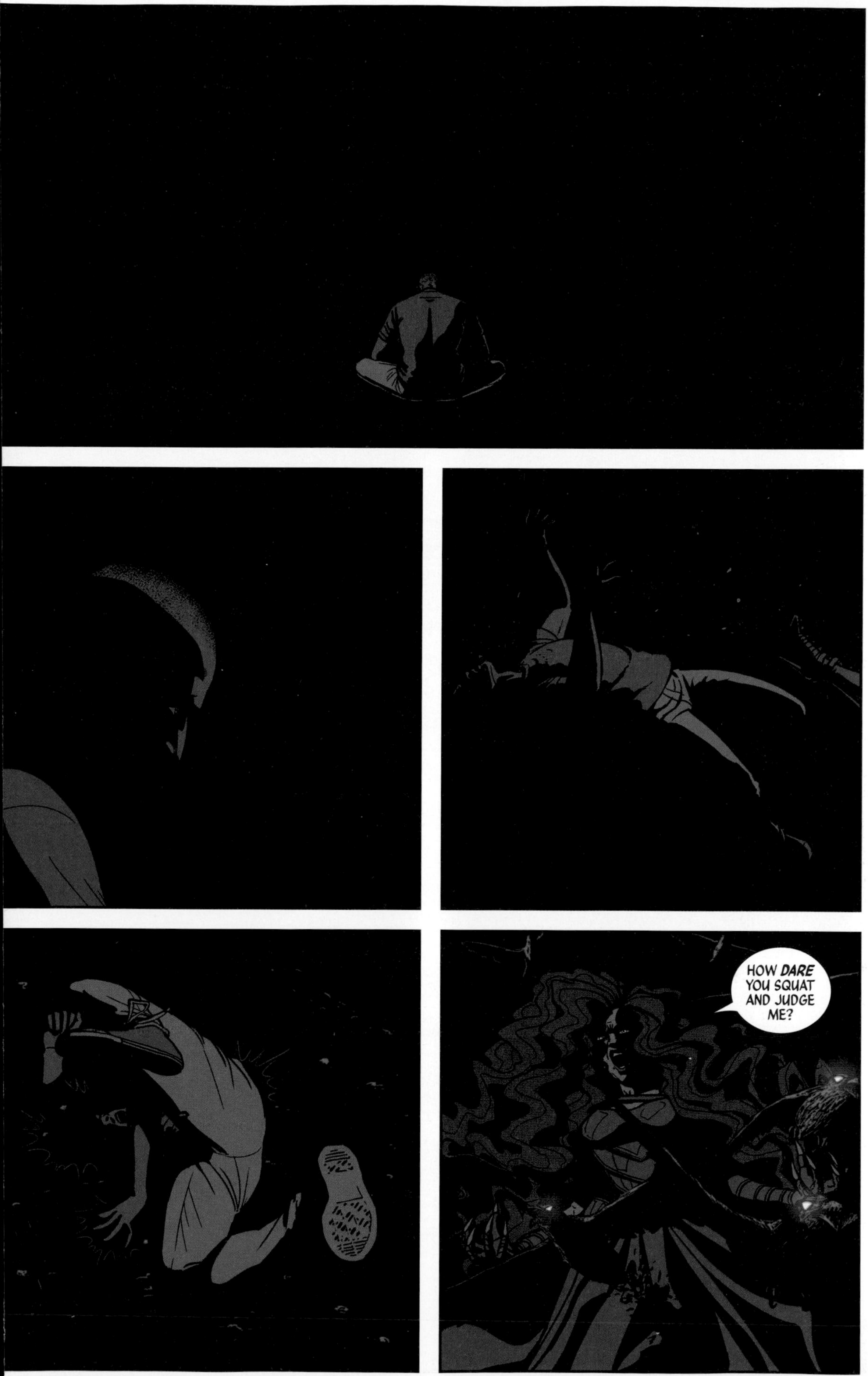
HOW DARE YOU SQUAT AND JUDGE ME?

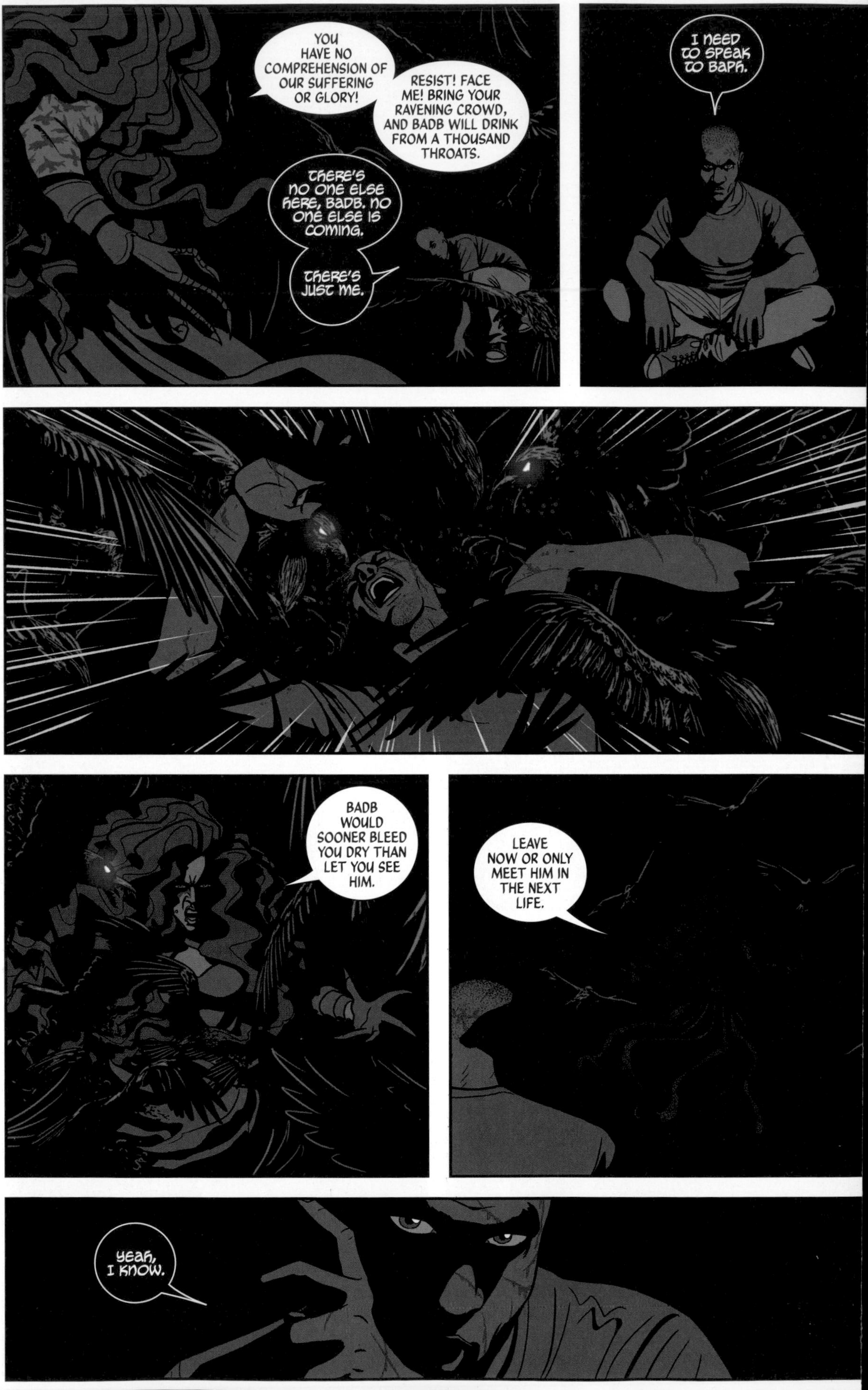
YOU HAVE NO COMPREHENSION OF OUR SUFFERING OR GLORY!
RESIST! FACE ME! BRING YOUR RAVENING CROWD, AND BADB WILL DRINK FROM A THOUSAND THROATS.
THERE'S NO ONE ELSE HERE, BADB. NO ONE ELSE IS COMING.
THERE'S JUST ME.
I NEED TO SPEAK TO BAPH.
BADB WOULD SOONER BLEED YOU DRY THAN LET YOU SEE HIM.
LEAVE NOW OR ONLY MEET HIM IN THE NEXT LIFE.
YEAH, I KNOW.

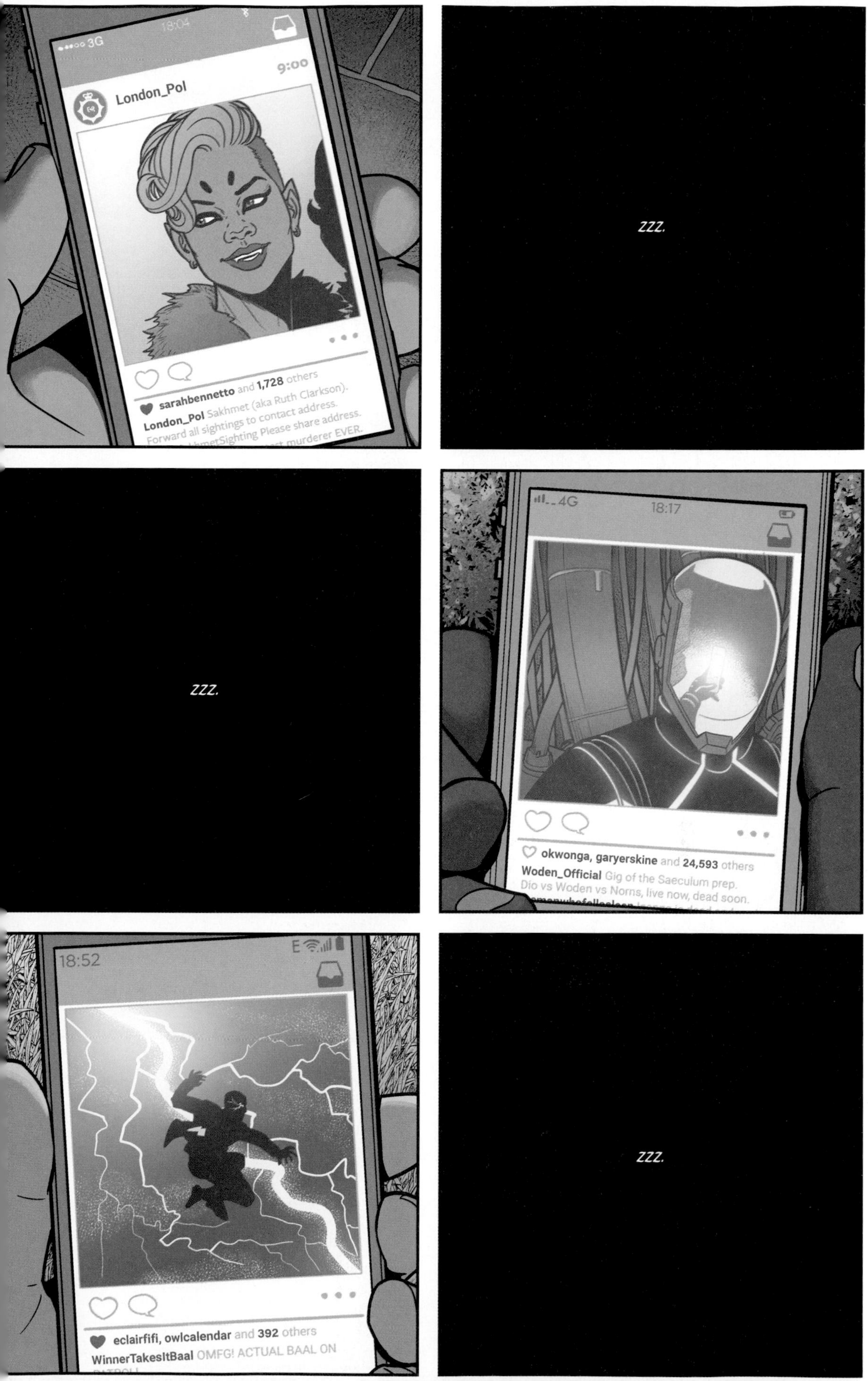

3G 18:04
9:00
London_Pol
sarahbennetto and 1,728 others
London_Pol Sakhmet (aka Ruth Clarkson).
Forward all sightings to contact address.
ZZZ.
ZZZ.
4G 18:17
okwonga, garyerskine and 24,593 others
Woden_Official Gig of the Saeculum prep.
Dio vs Woden vs Norns, live now, dead soon.
18:52
eclairfifi, owlcalendar and 392 others
WinnerTakesItBaal OMFG! ACTUAL BAAL ON
ZZZ.

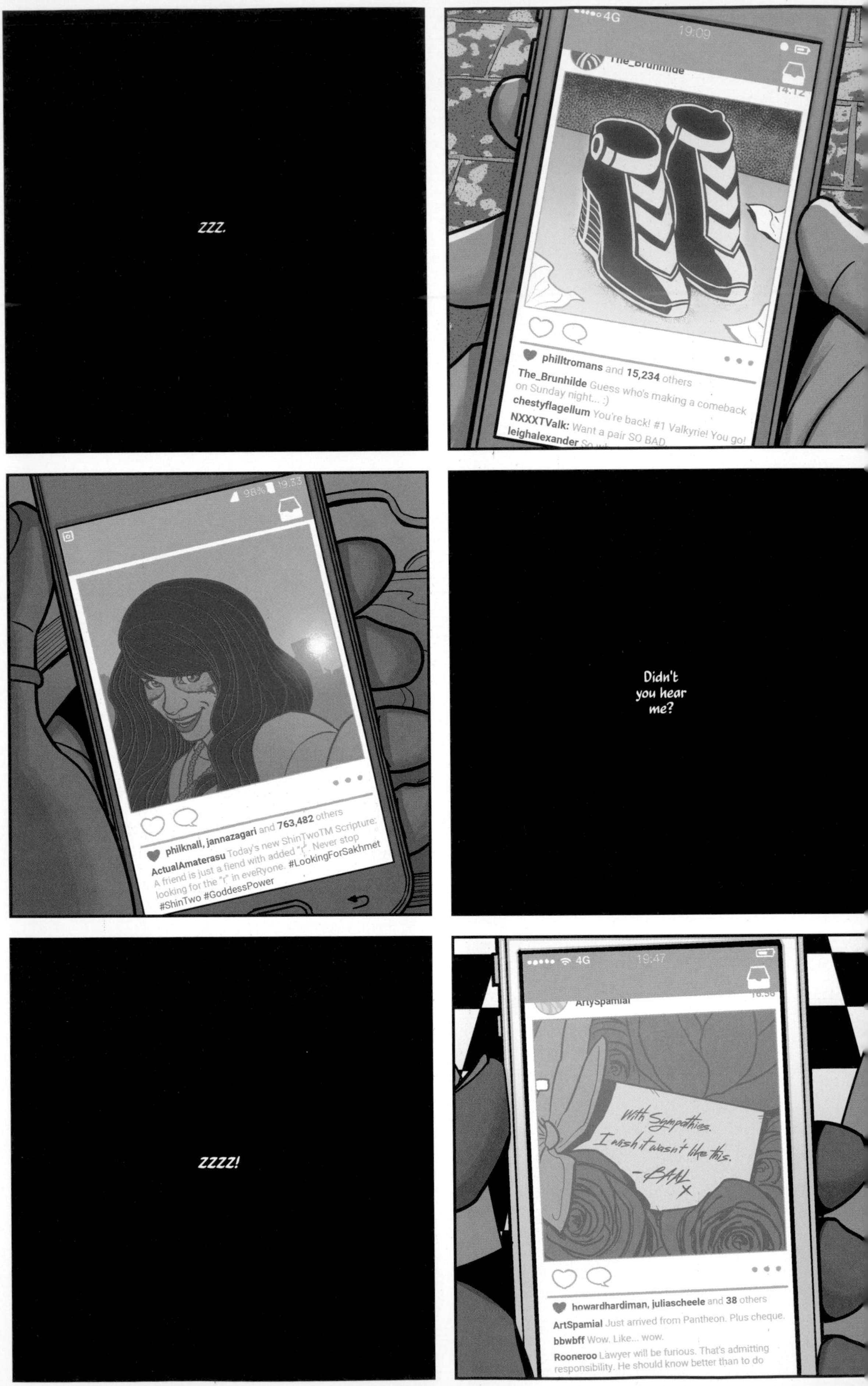
ZZZ.
4G
19:09
14:12
philltromans and 15,234 others
The_Brunhilde Guess who's making a comeback on Sunday night... :)
chestyflagellum You're back! #1 Valkyrie! You go!
NXXXTValk: Want a pair SO BAD.
leighalexander
98%
19:33
philknall, jannazagari and 763,482 others
ActualAmaterasu Today's new ShinTwoTM Scripture: A friend is just a fiend with added "r". Never stop looking for the "r" in eveRyone. #LookingForSakhmet #ShinTwo #GoddessPower
Didn't you hear me?
ZZZZ!
4G
19:47
With Sympathies.
I wish it wasn't like this.
-BAAL
howardhardiman, juliascheele and 38 others
ArtSpamial Just arrived from Pantheon. Plus cheque.
bbwbff Wow. Like... wow.
Rooneroo Lawyer will be furious. That's admitting responsibility. He should know better than to do

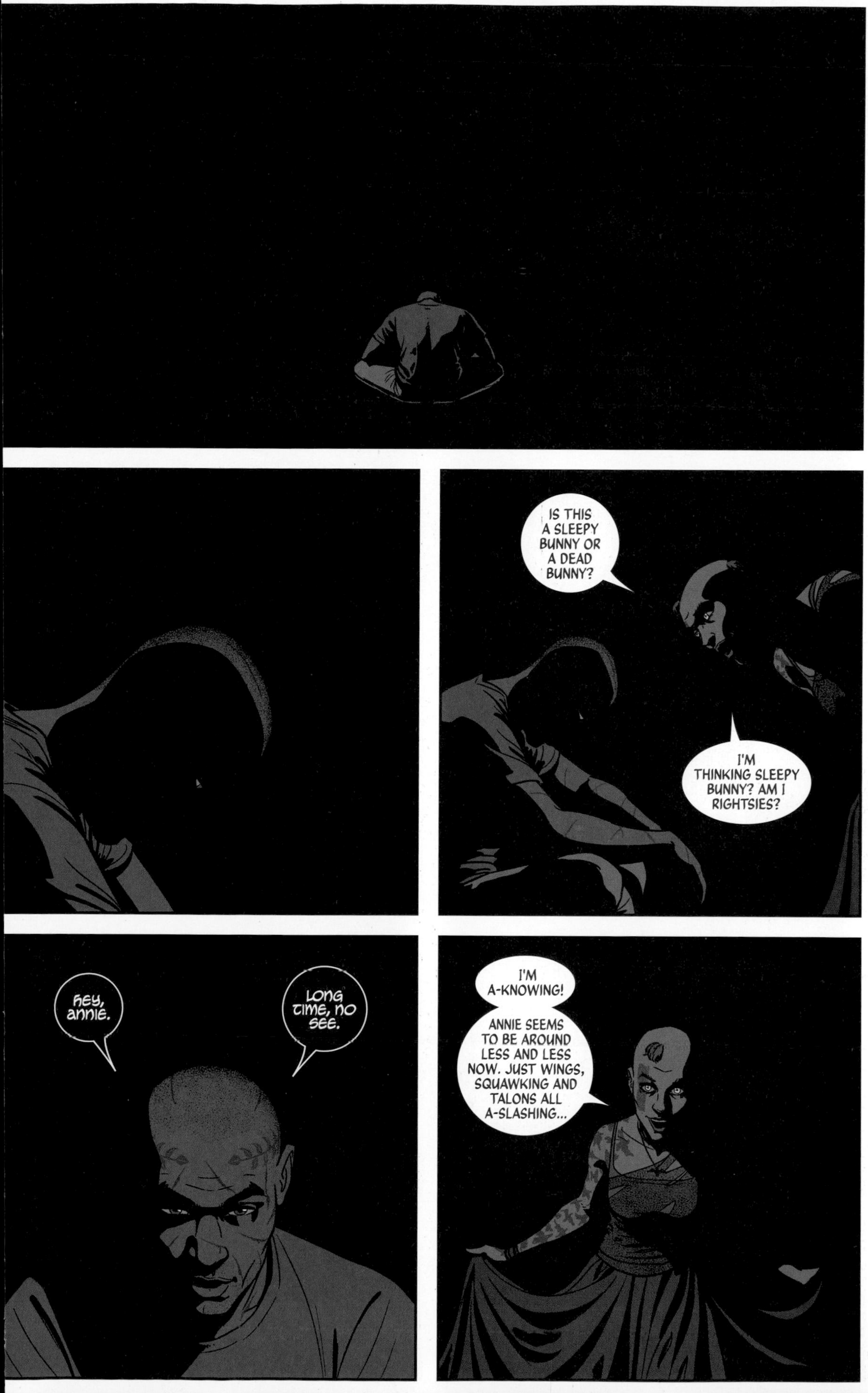
IS THIS A SLEEPY BUNNY OR A DEAD BUNNY?
I'M THINKING SLEEPY BUNNY? AM I RIGHTSIES?
HEY, ANNIE.
LONG TIME, NO SEE.
I'M A-KNOWING!
ANNIE SEEMS TO BE AROUND LESS AND LESS NOW. JUST WINGS, SQUAWKING AND TALONS ALL A-SLASHING...

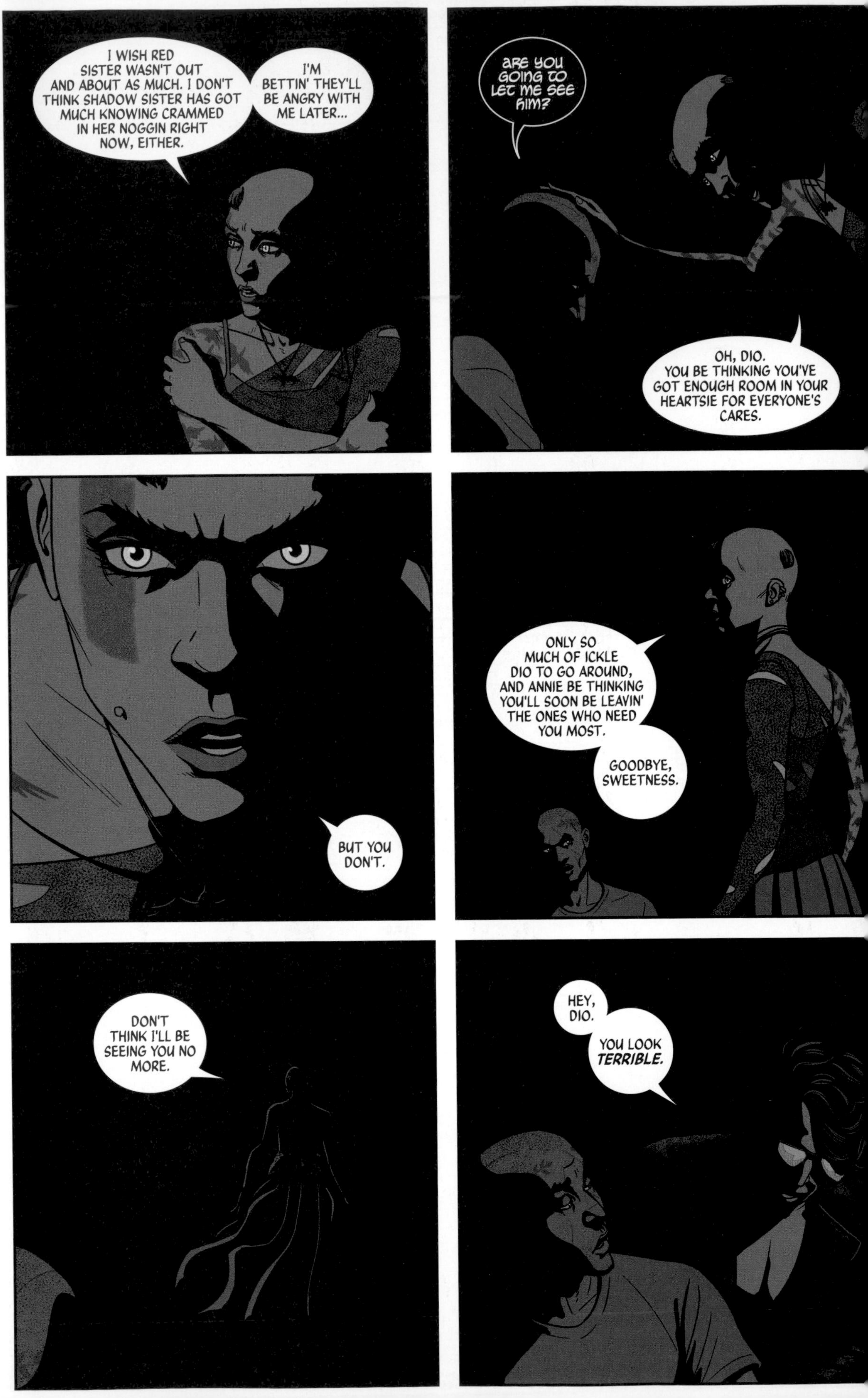
I WISH RED SISTER WASN'T OUT AND ABOUT AS MUCH. I DON'T THINK SHADOW SISTER HAS GOT MUCH KNOWING CRAMMED IN HER NOGGIN RIGHT NOW, EITHER.
I'M BETTIN' THEY'LL BE ANGRY WITH ME LATER...
ARE YOU GOING TO LET ME SEE HIM?
OH, DIO. YOU BE THINKING YOU'VE GOT ENOUGH ROOM IN YOUR HEARTSIE FOR EVERYONE'S CARES.
BUT YOU DON'T.
ONLY SO MUCH OF ICKLE DIO TO GO AROUND, AND ANNIE BE THINKING YOU'LL SOON BE LEAVIN' THE ONES WHO NEED YOU MOST.
GOODBYE, SWEETNESS.
DON'T THINK I'LL BE SEEING YOU NO MORE.
HEY, DIO.
YOU LOOK *TERRIBLE.*

OKAY, FOUR REPORTED SIGHTINGS OF SAKHMET ENTERING THE BUILDING.

ARE WE *SURE* IT'S HER?

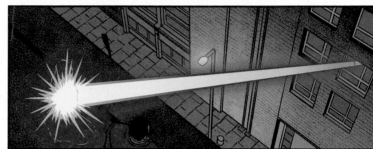

AS IF WE HAVE TIME TO GET THE NORNS TO DO A DIVINATION PEEK. I'M READY TO MAKE MY MOVE...

I'LL DO A FLYBY. TELL ME WHAT YOU SEE, MINERVA. IF IT'S BAD, STOP BAAL.

ABORT!

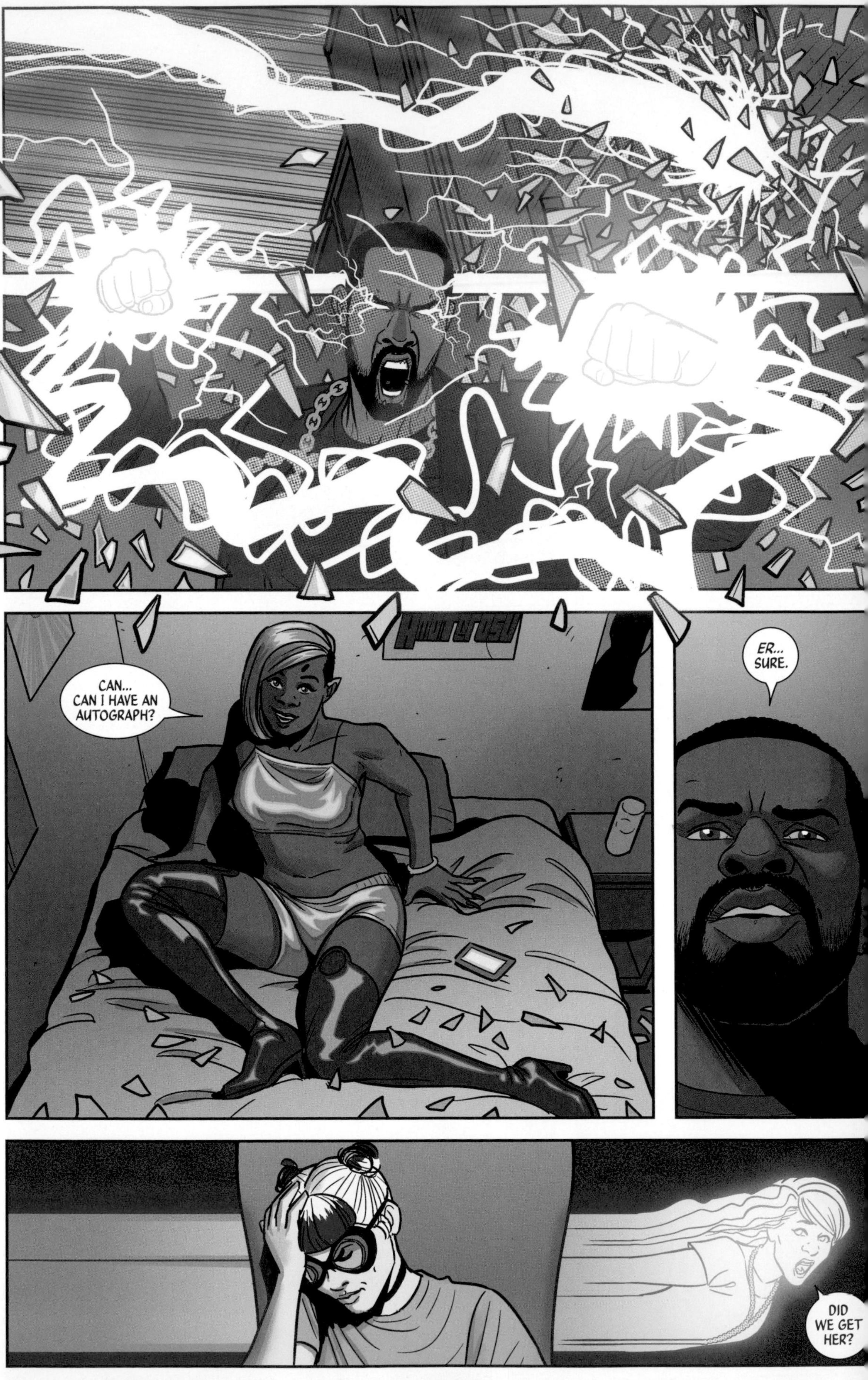
CAN... CAN I HAVE AN AUTOGRAPH?
ER... SURE.
DID WE GET HER?

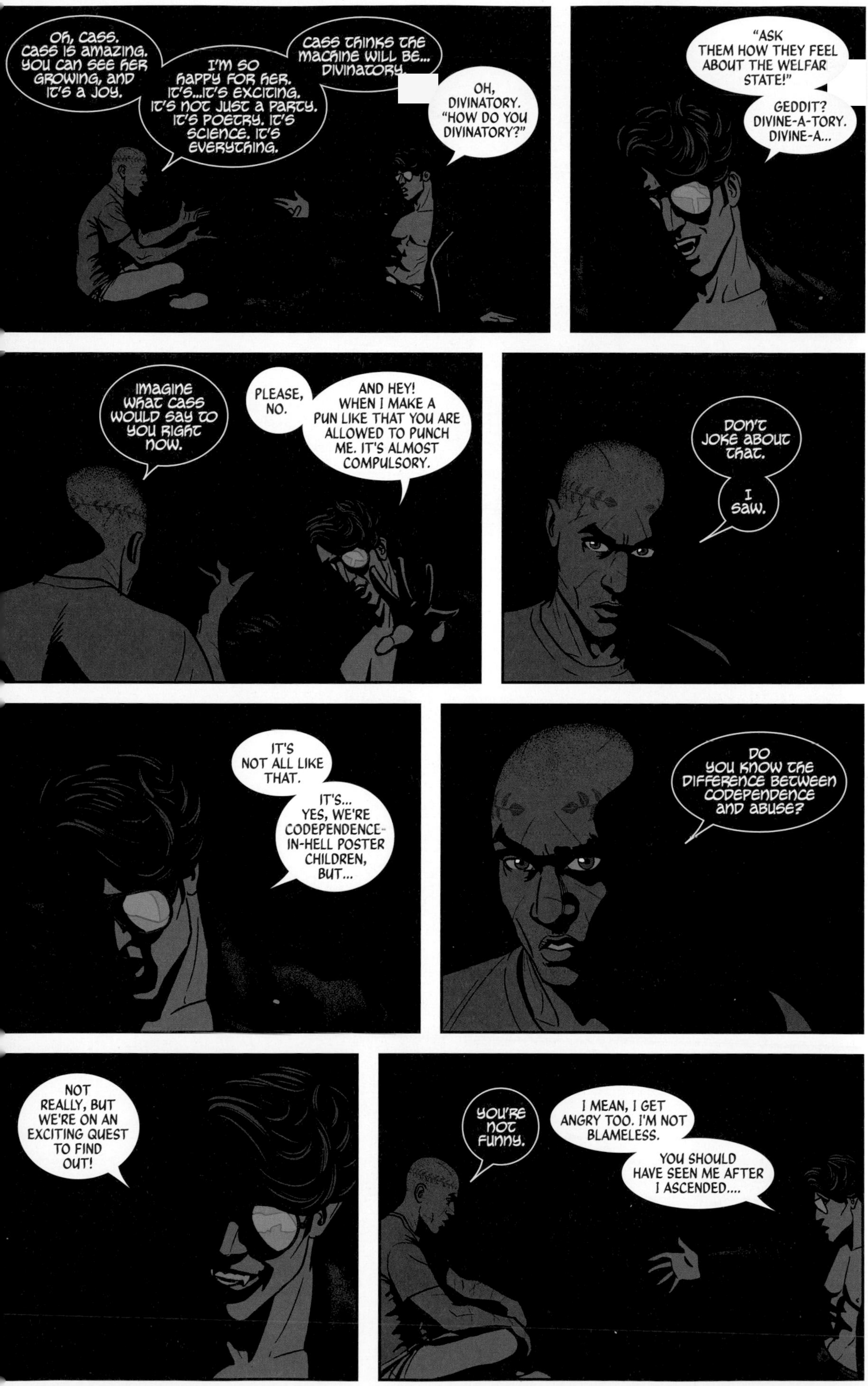
OH, CASS. CASS IS AMAZING. YOU CAN SEE HER GROWING, AND IT'S A JOY.
I'M SO HAPPY FOR HER. IT'S...IT'S EXCITING. IT'S NOT JUST A PARTY. IT'S POETRY. IT'S SCIENCE. IT'S EVERYTHING.
CASS THINKS THE MACHINE WILL BE... DIVINATORY.
OH, DIVINATORY. "HOW DO YOU DIVINATORY?"
"ASK THEM HOW THEY FEEL ABOUT THE WELFAR STATE!"
GEDDIT? DIVINE-A-TORY. DIVINE-A...
IMAGINE WHAT CASS WOULD SAY TO YOU RIGHT NOW.
PLEASE, NO.
AND HEY! WHEN I MAKE A PUN LIKE THAT YOU ARE ALLOWED TO PUNCH ME. IT'S ALMOST COMPULSORY.
DON'T JOKE ABOUT THAT.
I SAW.
IT'S NOT ALL LIKE THAT.
IT'S... YES, WE'RE CODEPENDENCE-IN-HELL POSTER CHILDREN, BUT...
DO YOU KNOW THE DIFFERENCE BETWEEN CODEPENDENCE AND ABUSE?
NOT REALLY, BUT WE'RE ON AN EXCITING QUEST TO FIND OUT!
YOU'RE NOT FUNNY.
I MEAN, I GET ANGRY TOO. I'M NOT BLAMELESS.
YOU SHOULD HAVE SEEN ME AFTER I ASCENDED....

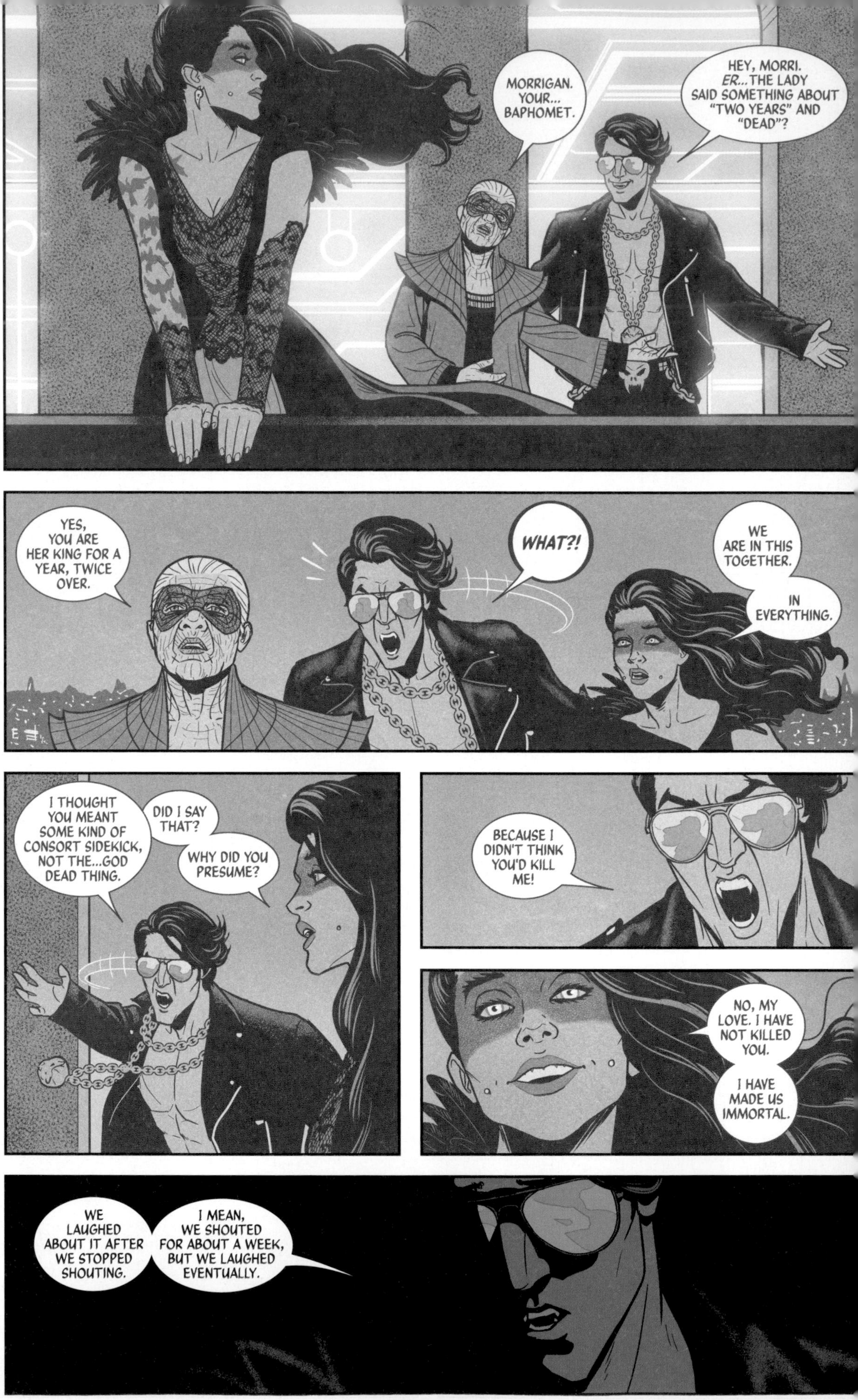
MORRIGAN. YOUR... BAPHOMET.
HEY, MORRI. *ER*... THE LADY SAID SOMETHING ABOUT "TWO YEARS" AND "DEAD"?
YES, YOU ARE HER KING FOR A YEAR, TWICE OVER.
WHAT?!
WE ARE IN THIS TOGETHER.
IN EVERYTHING.
I THOUGHT YOU MEANT SOME KIND OF CONSORT SIDEKICK, NOT THE...GOD DEAD THING.
DID I SAY THAT?
WHY DID YOU PRESUME?
BECAUSE I DIDN'T THINK YOU'D KILL ME!
NO, MY LOVE. I HAVE NOT KILLED YOU.
I HAVE MADE US IMMORTAL.
WE LAUGHED ABOUT IT AFTER WE STOPPED SHOUTING.
I MEAN, WE SHOUTED FOR ABOUT A WEEK, BUT WE LAUGHED EVENTUALLY.

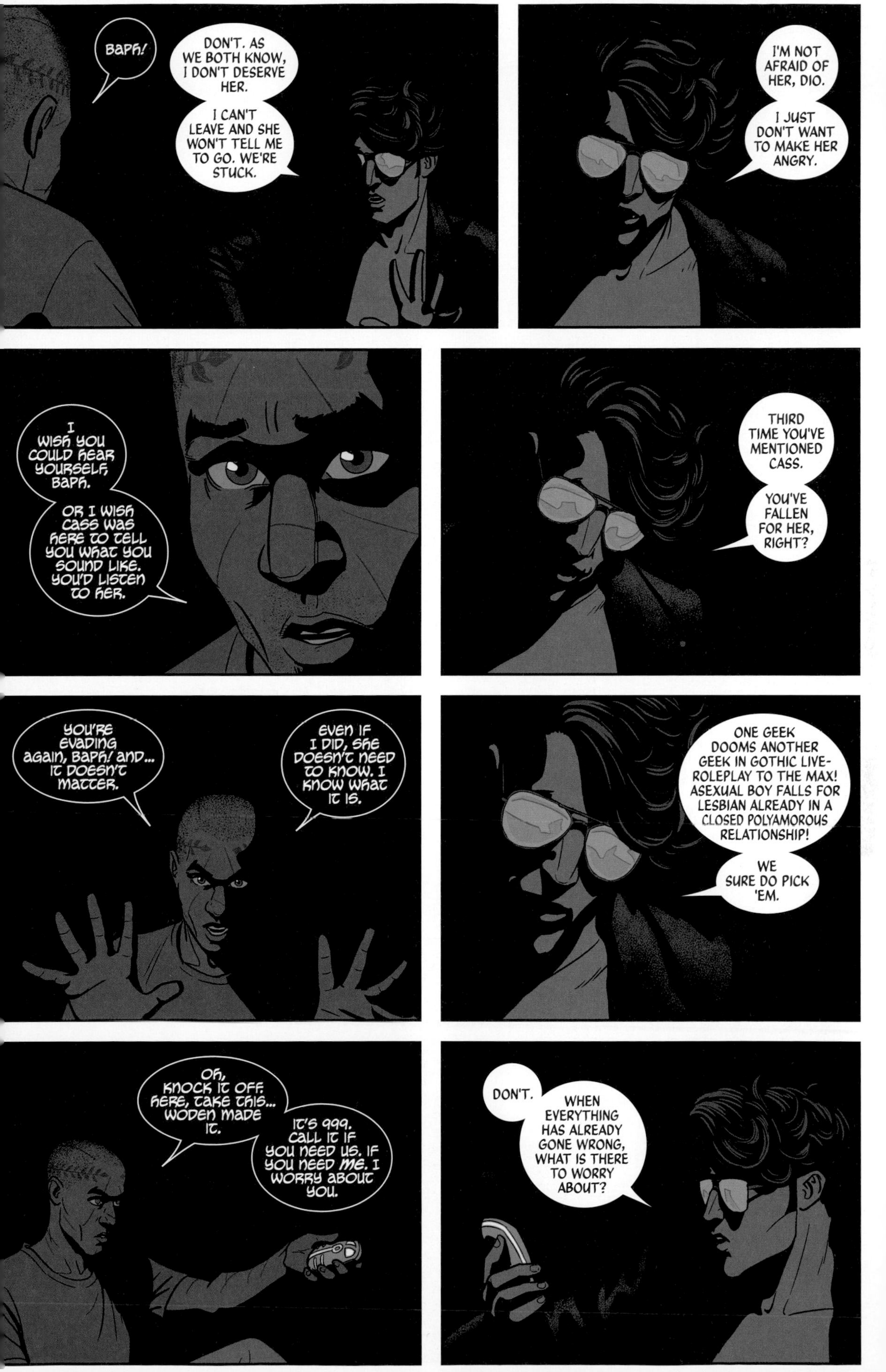
BAPH!
DON'T. AS WE BOTH KNOW, I DON'T DESERVE HER.
I CAN'T LEAVE AND SHE WON'T TELL ME TO GO. WE'RE STUCK.
I'M NOT AFRAID OF HER, DIO.
I JUST DON'T WANT TO MAKE HER ANGRY.
I WISH YOU COULD HEAR YOURSELF, BAPH.
OR I WISH CASS WAS HERE TO TELL YOU WHAT YOU SOUND LIKE. YOU'D LISTEN TO HER.
THIRD TIME YOU'VE MENTIONED CASS.
YOU'VE FALLEN FOR HER, RIGHT?
YOU'RE EVADING AGAIN, BAPH! AND... IT DOESN'T MATTER.
EVEN IF I DID, SHE DOESN'T NEED TO KNOW. I KNOW WHAT IT IS.
ONE GEEK DOOMS ANOTHER GEEK IN GOTHIC LIVE-ROLEPLAY TO THE MAX! ASEXUAL BOY FALLS FOR LESBIAN ALREADY IN A CLOSED POLYAMOROUS RELATIONSHIP!
WE SURE DO PICK 'EM.
OH, KNOCK IT OFF. HERE, TAKE THIS... WODEN MADE IT.
IT'S 999. CALL IT IF YOU NEED US. IF YOU NEED *ME*. I WORRY ABOUT YOU.
DON'T.
WHEN EVERYTHING HAS ALREADY GONE WRONG, WHAT IS THERE TO WORRY ABOUT?

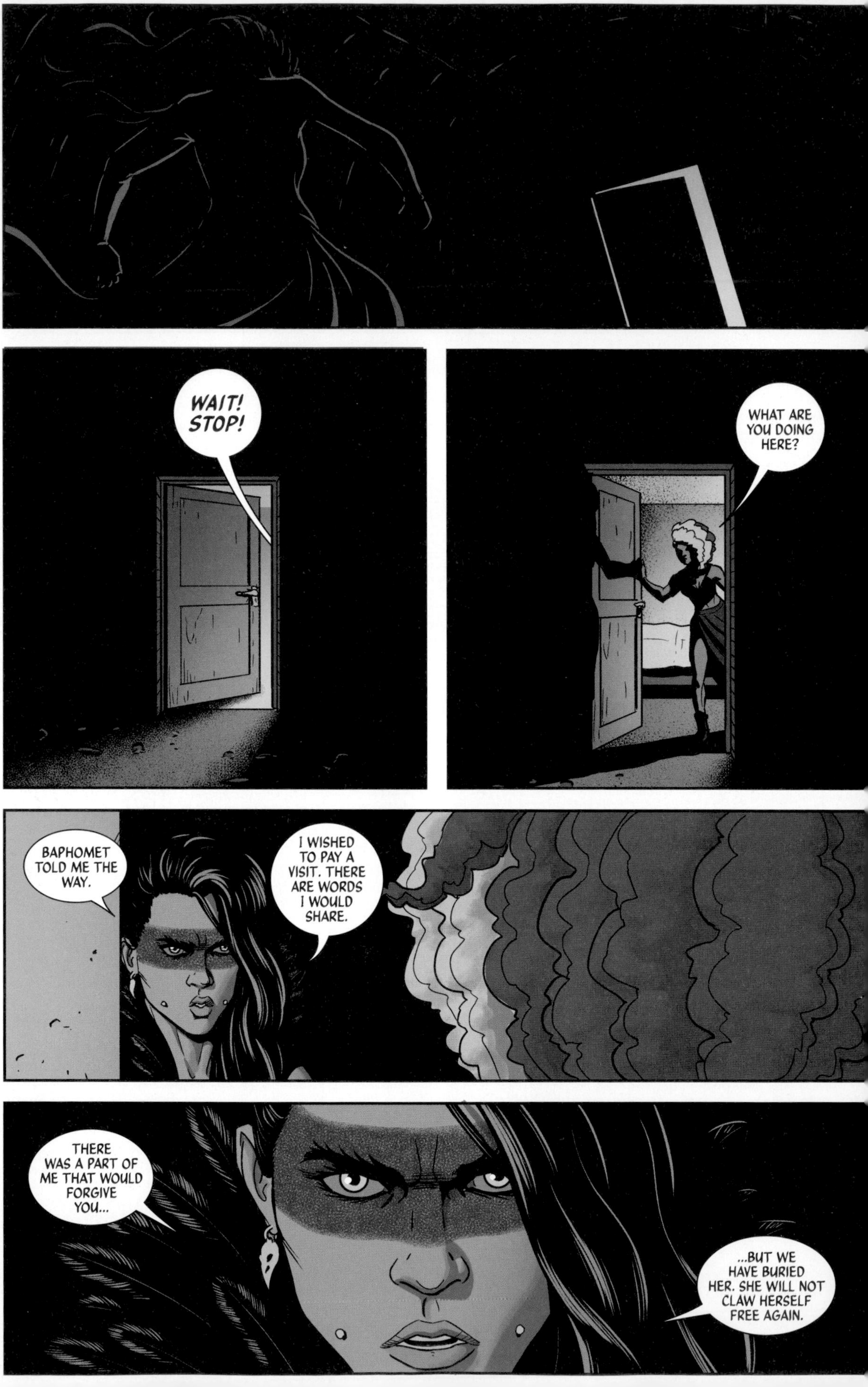
WAIT! STOP!
WHAT ARE YOU DOING HERE?
BAPHOMET TOLD ME THE WAY.
I WISHED TO PAY A VISIT. THERE ARE WORDS I WOULD SHARE.
THERE WAS A PART OF ME THAT WOULD FORGIVE YOU...
...BUT WE HAVE BURIED HER. SHE WILL NOT CLAW HERSELF FREE AGAIN.

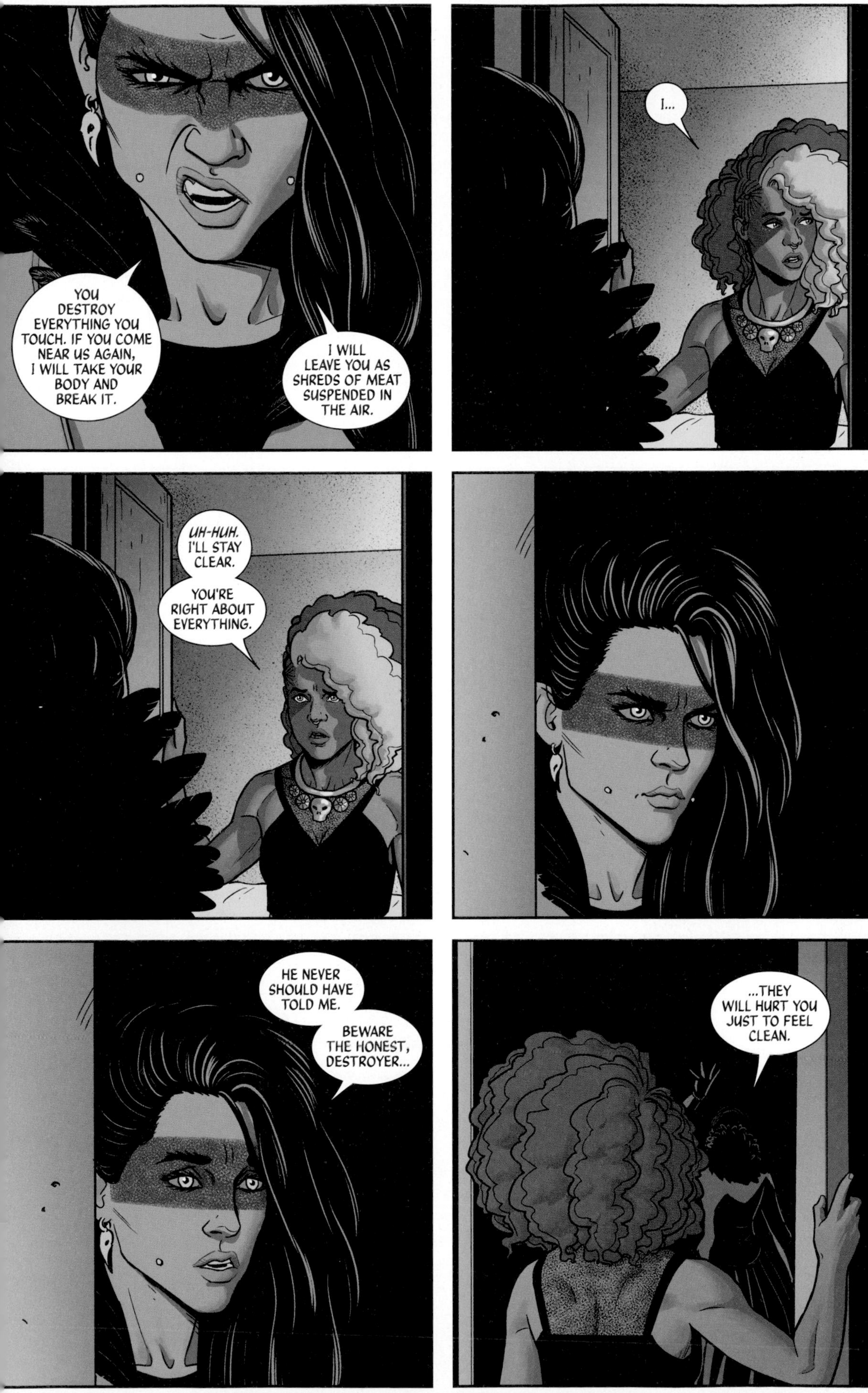
YOU DESTROY EVERYTHING YOU TOUCH. IF YOU COME NEAR US AGAIN, I WILL TAKE YOUR BODY AND BREAK IT.
I WILL LEAVE YOU AS SHREDS OF MEAT SUSPENDED IN THE AIR.
I...
UH-HUH. I'LL STAY CLEAR.
YOU'RE RIGHT ABOUT EVERYTHING.
HE NEVER SHOULD HAVE TOLD ME.
BEWARE THE HONEST, DESTROYER...
...THEY WILL HURT YOU JUST TO FEEL CLEAN.

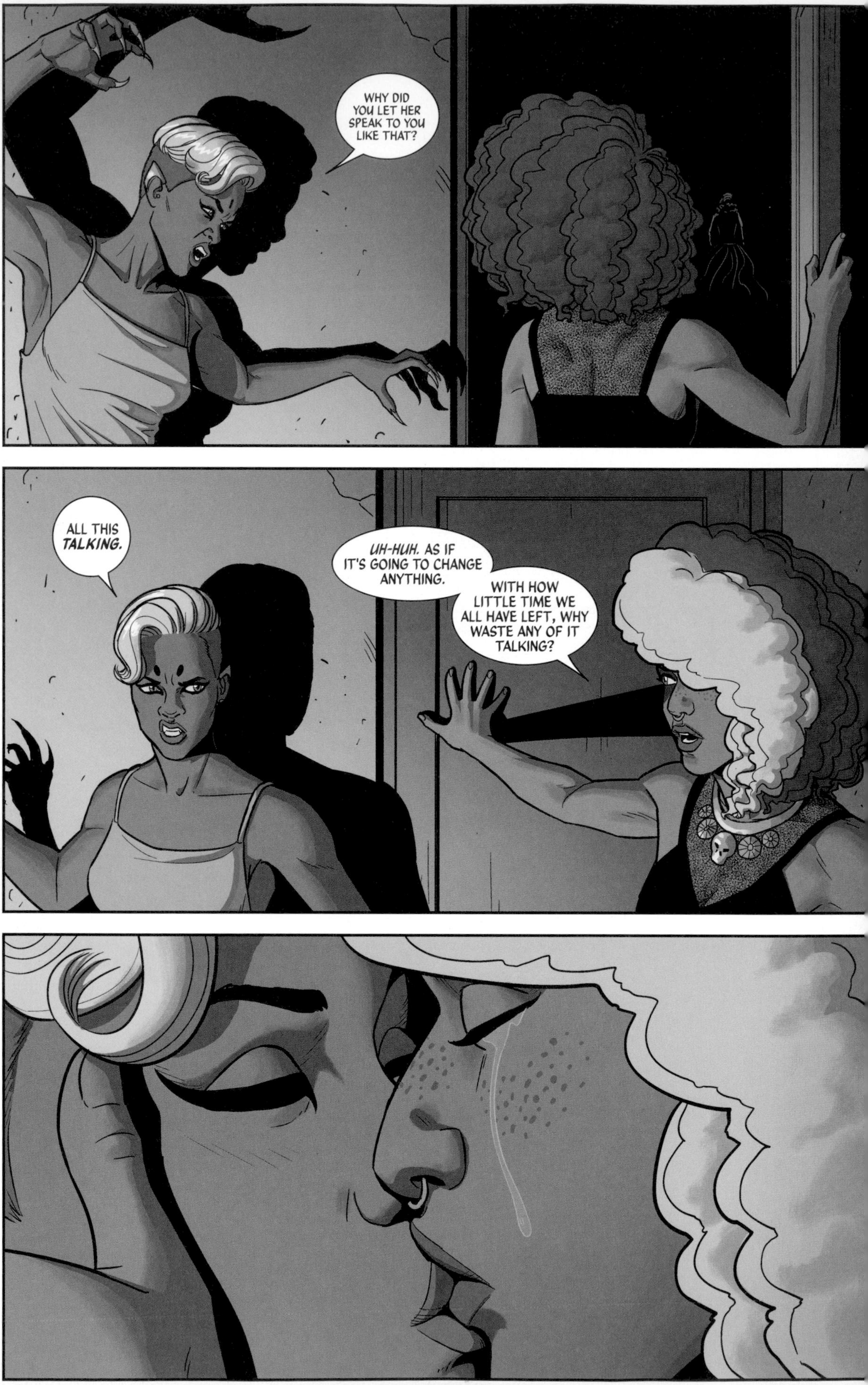
WHY DID YOU LET HER SPEAK TO YOU LIKE THAT?
ALL THIS *TALKING.*
UH-HUH. AS IF IT'S GOING TO CHANGE ANYTHING.
WITH HOW LITTLE TIME WE ALL HAVE LEFT, WHY WASTE ANY OF IT TALKING?

MY ALIGNMENT IS
CHAOTIC FUCK-UP

8 MARCH 2015

31

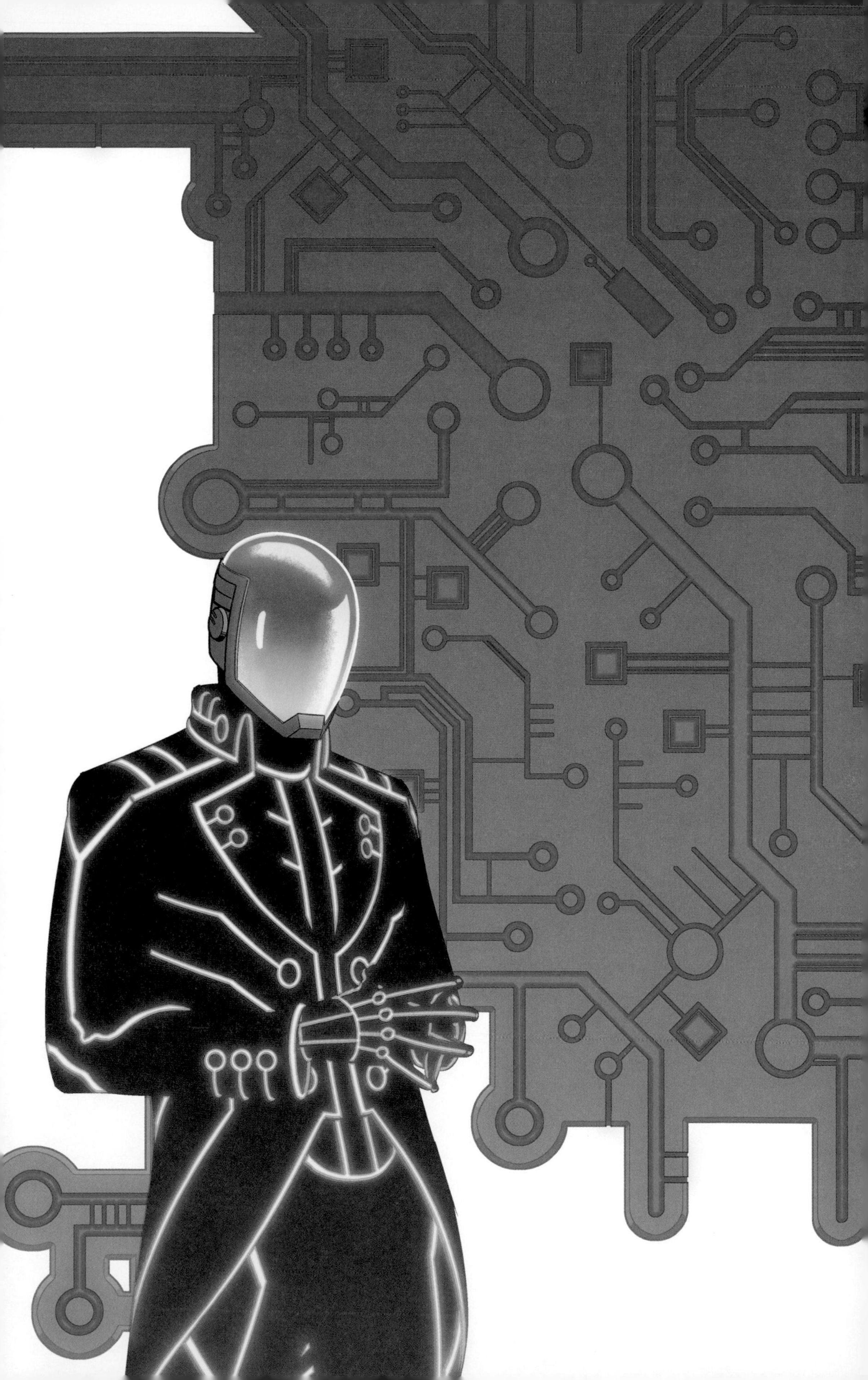

THE
WICKED
+
THE DIVINE

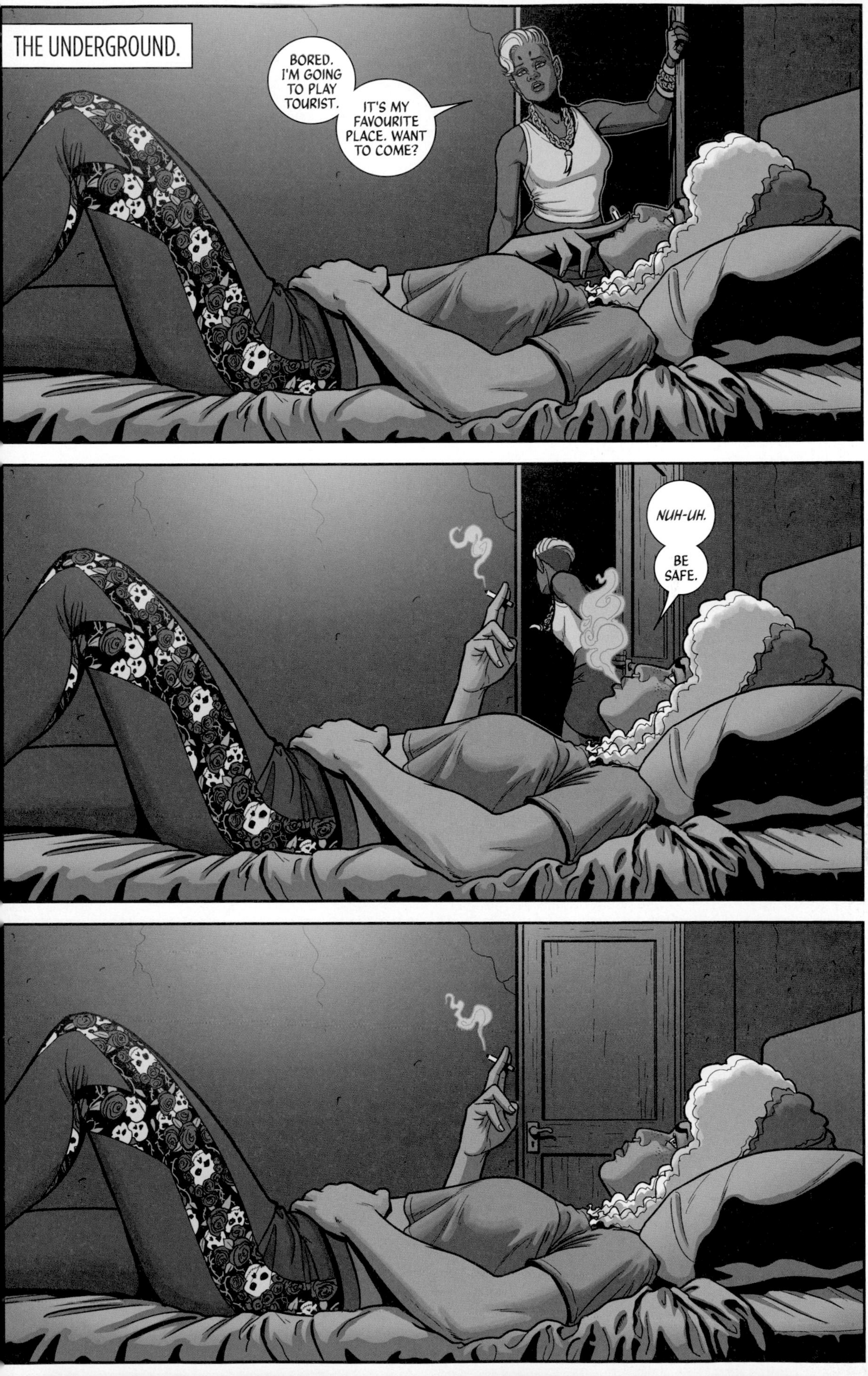
THE UNDERGROUND.
BORED. I'M GOING TO PLAY TOURIST.
IT'S MY FAVOURITE PLACE. WANT TO COME?
NUH-UH.
BE SAFE.

I DON'T
LOVE ANYONE

8 MARCH 2015

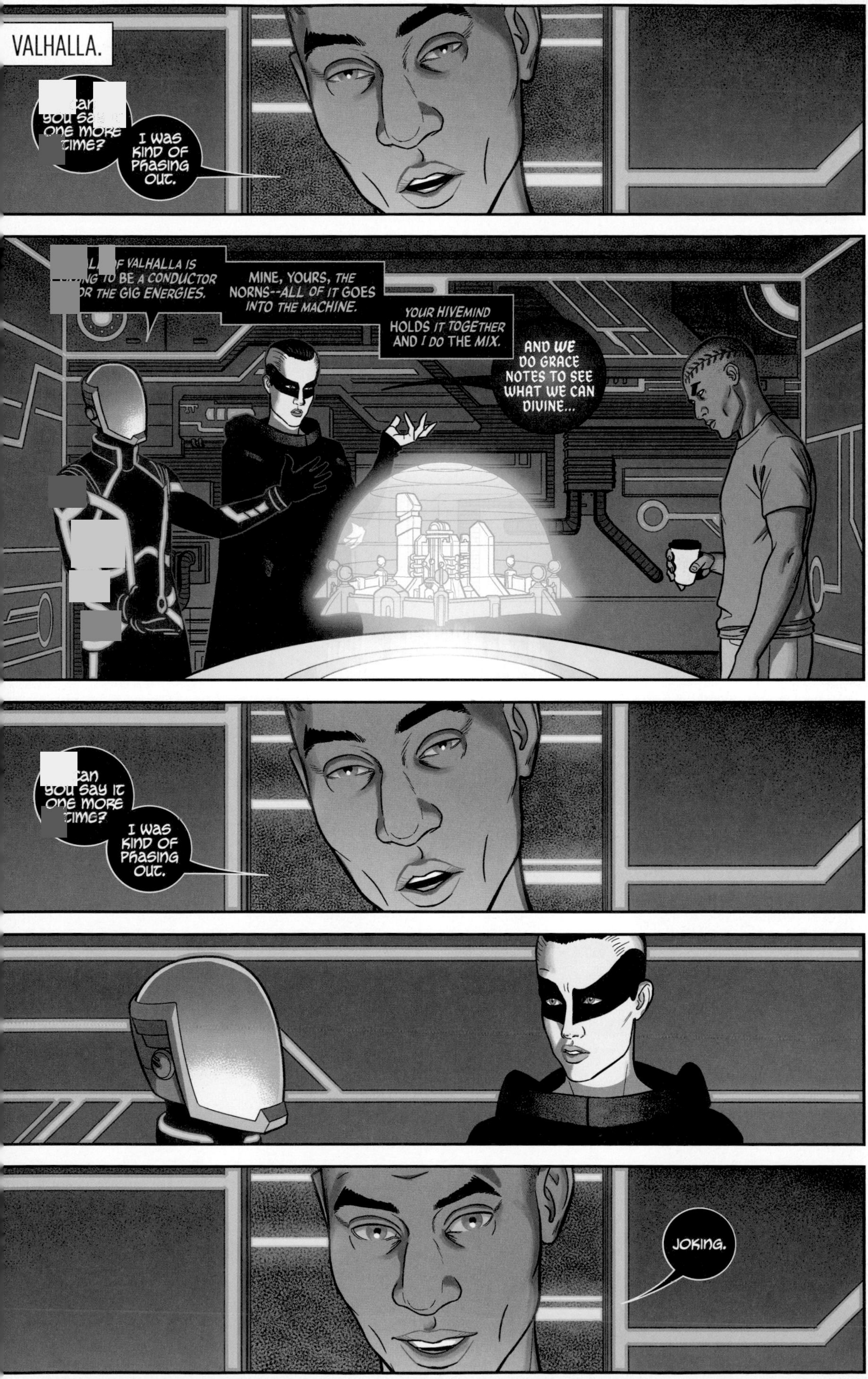
VALHALLA.
can you say one more time?
I was kind of phasing out.
of Valhalla is to be a conductor for the gig energies.
Mine, yours, the Norns--all of it goes into the machine.
Your hivemind holds it together and I do the mix.
And we do grace notes to see what we can divine...
can you say it one more time?
I was kind of phasing out.
Joking.

JOKING-NOT-JOKING! YOU ARE FUCKED, DIO!
WE SHOULD CALL OFF THE GIG.
IT'D MEAN STARTING EVERYTHING OVER FROM SCRATCH. EVEN JUST ARRANGING THE CROWD WASN'T EASY.
BUT IF WE HAVE TO, WE--
I'M FINE.
I CAN SLEEP WHEN I'M DEAD.
GREAT, BUT IDEALLY THAT WOULD NOT BE THIS EVENING!
I'LL SHOWER AND GET READY.
IT'LL BE OKAY.
I DON'T KNOW WHY HE DOES IT.
I DO.
NO. NO. NO.

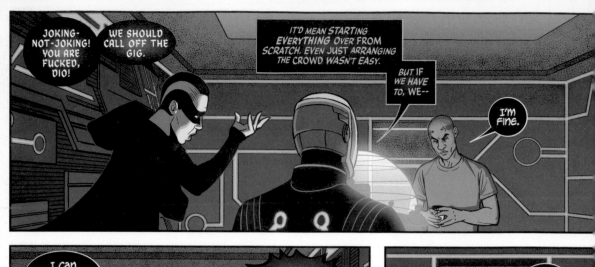

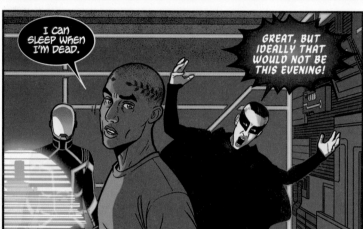

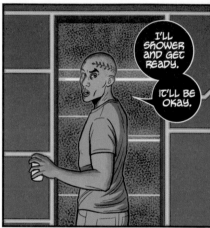

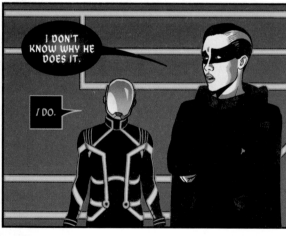

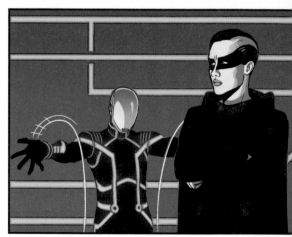

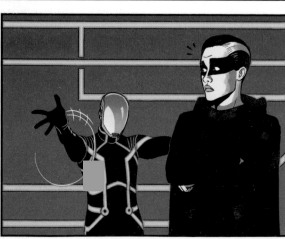

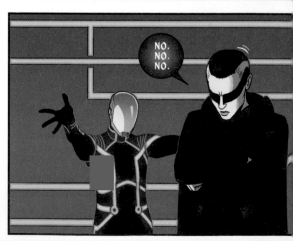

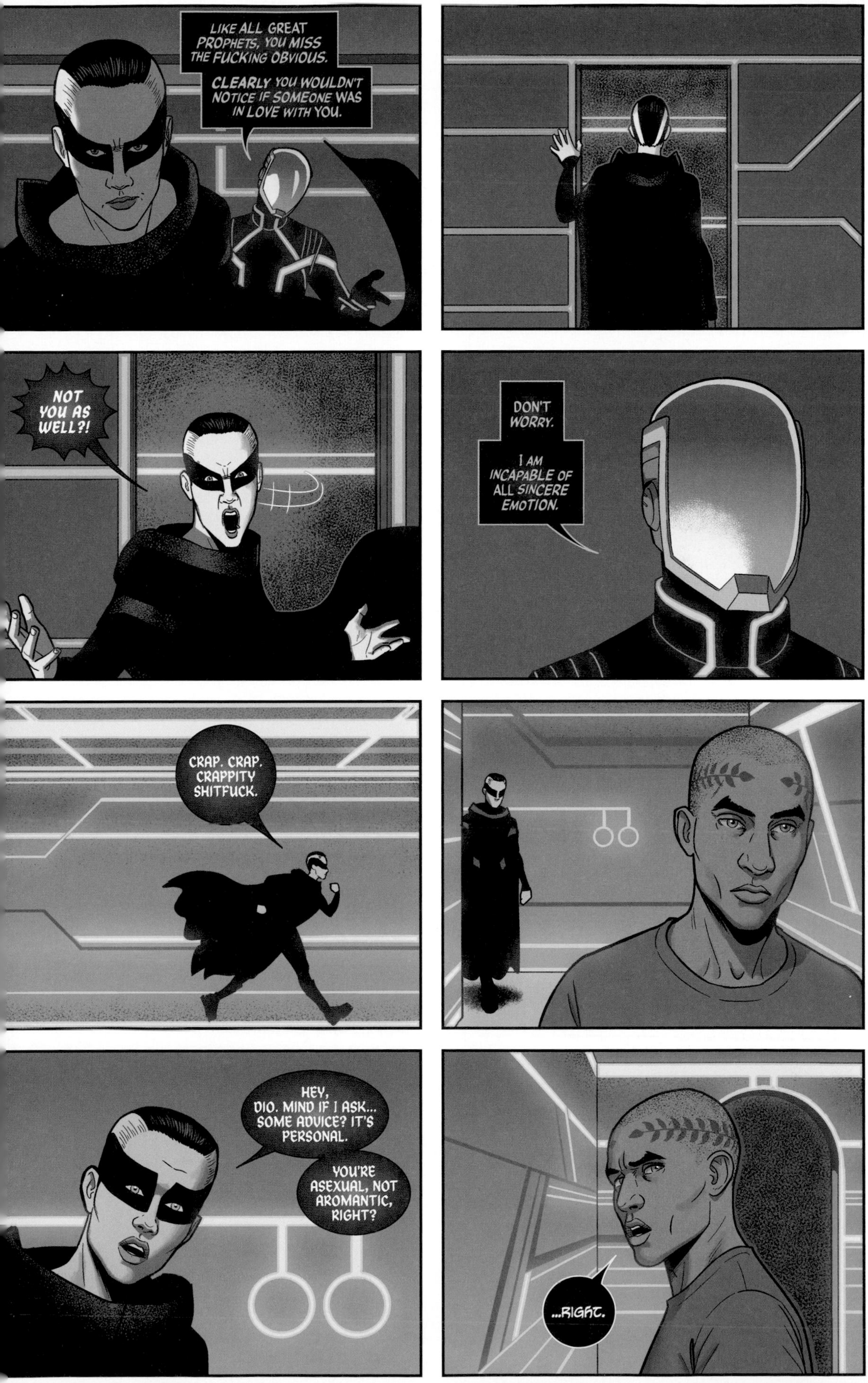
LIKE ALL GREAT PROPHETS, YOU MISS THE FUCKING OBVIOUS.
CLEARLY YOU WOULDN'T NOTICE IF SOMEONE WAS IN LOVE WITH YOU.
NOT YOU AS WELL?!
DON'T WORRY.
I AM INCAPABLE OF ALL SINCERE EMOTION.
CRAP. CRAP. CRAPPITY SHITFUCK.
HEY, DIO. MIND IF I ASK... SOME ADVICE? IT'S PERSONAL.
YOU'RE ASEXUAL, NOT AROMANTIC, RIGHT?
...RIGHT.

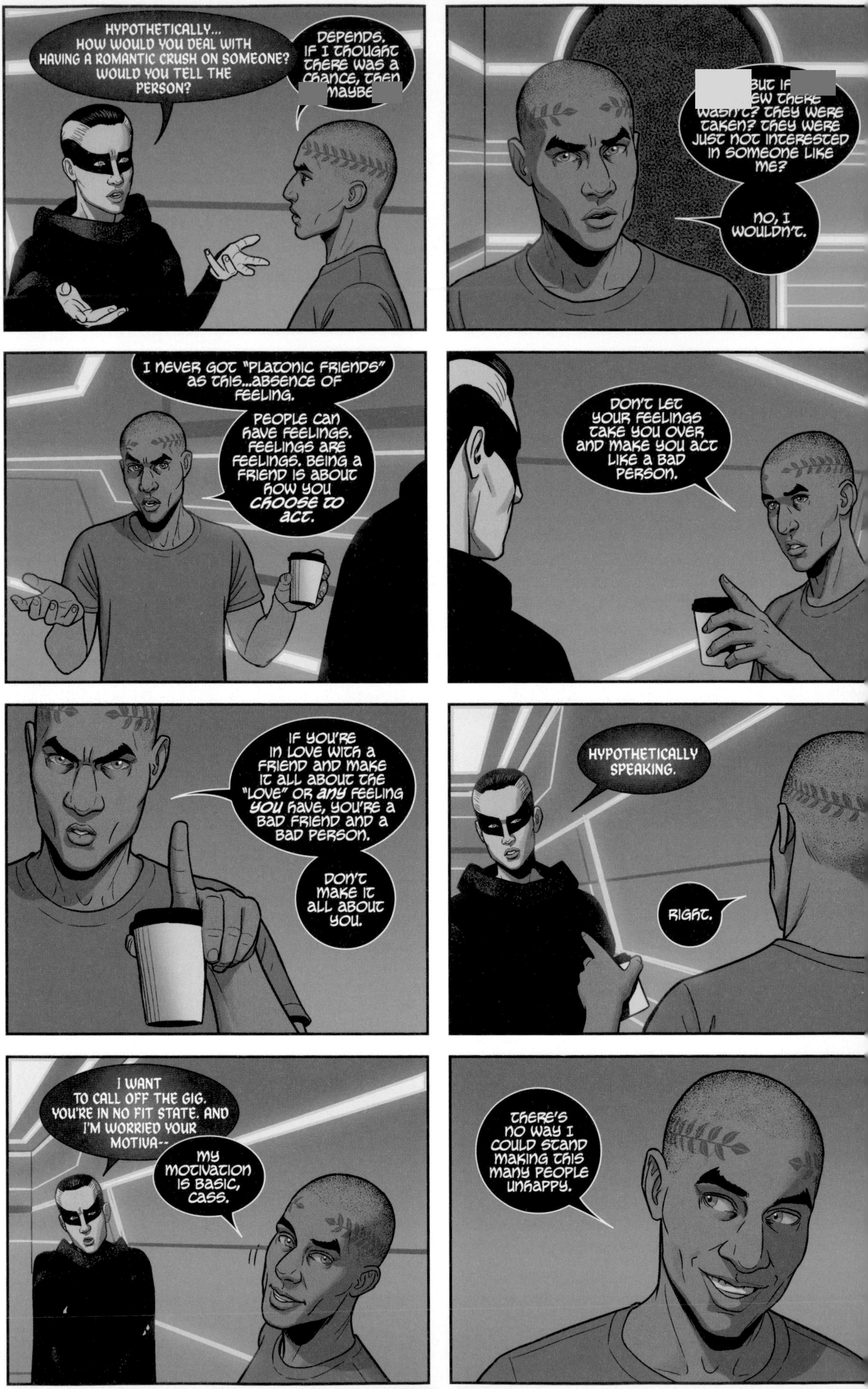
HYPOTHETICALLY... HOW WOULD YOU DEAL WITH HAVING A ROMANTIC CRUSH ON SOMEONE? WOULD YOU TELL THE PERSON?
DEPENDS. IF I THOUGHT THERE WAS A CHANCE, THEN [redacted] MAYBE [redacted]
[redacted] BUT IF [redacted]EW THERE WASN'T? THEY WERE TAKEN? THEY WERE JUST NOT INTERESTED IN SOMEONE LIKE ME?
NO, I WOULDN'T.
I NEVER GOT "PLATONIC FRIENDS" AS THIS...ABSENCE OF FEELING.
PEOPLE CAN HAVE FEELINGS. FEELINGS ARE FEELINGS. BEING A FRIEND IS ABOUT HOW YOU CHOOSE TO ACT.
DON'T LET YOUR FEELINGS TAKE YOU OVER AND MAKE YOU ACT LIKE A BAD PERSON.
IF YOU'RE IN LOVE WITH A FRIEND AND MAKE IT ALL ABOUT THE "LOVE" OR ANY FEELING YOU HAVE, YOU'RE A BAD FRIEND AND A BAD PERSON.
DON'T MAKE IT ALL ABOUT YOU.
HYPOTHETICALLY SPEAKING.
RIGHT.
I WANT TO CALL OFF THE GIG. YOU'RE IN NO FIT STATE. AND I'M WORRIED YOUR MOTIVA--
MY MOTIVATION IS BASIC, CASS.
THERE'S NO WAY I COULD STAND MAKING THIS MANY PEOPLE UNHAPPY.

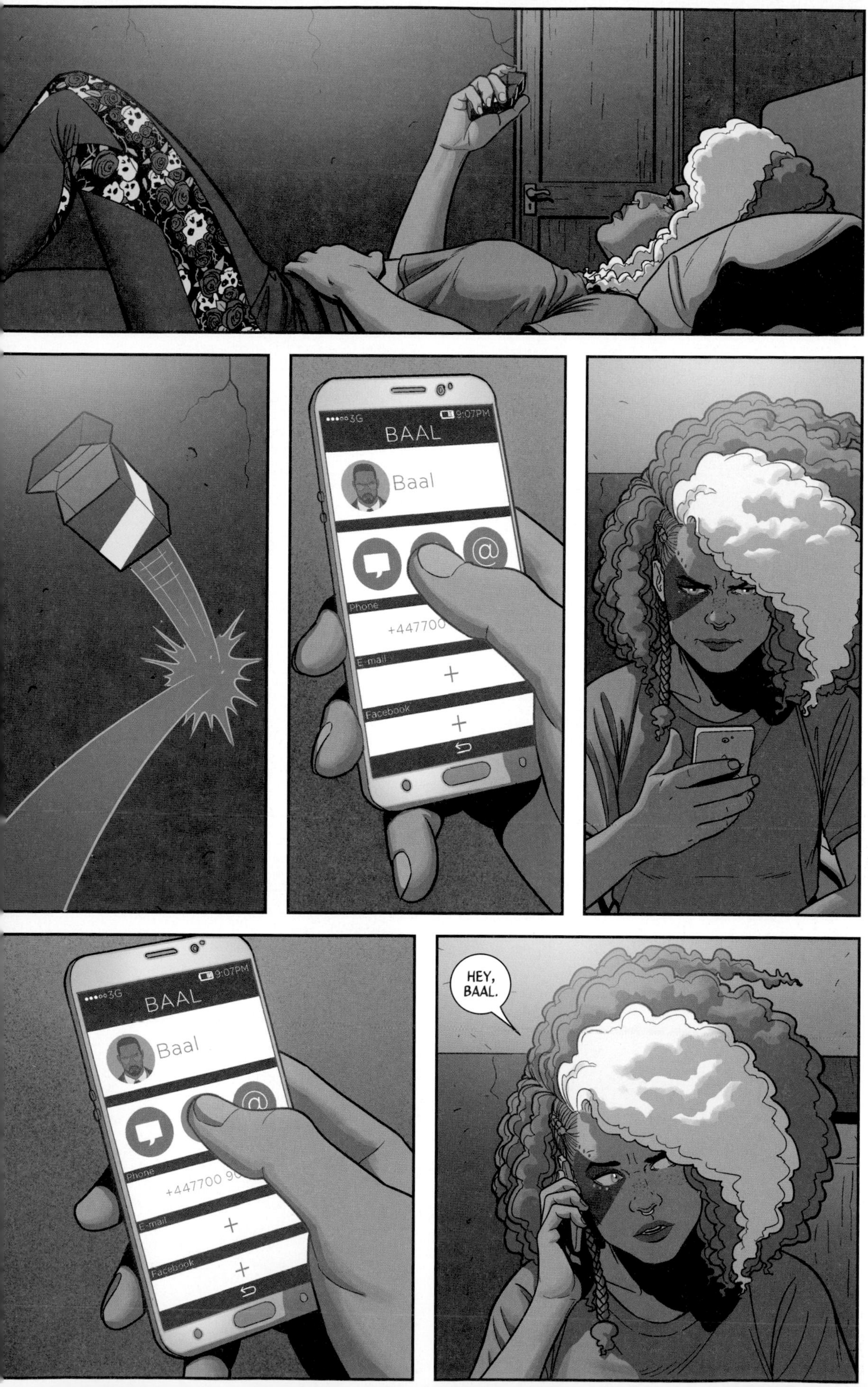
3G
9:07PM
BAAL
Baal
Phone
+447700
E-mail
Facebook
3G
9:07PM
BAAL
Baal
Phone
+447700 90
E-mail
Facebook
HEY, BAAL.

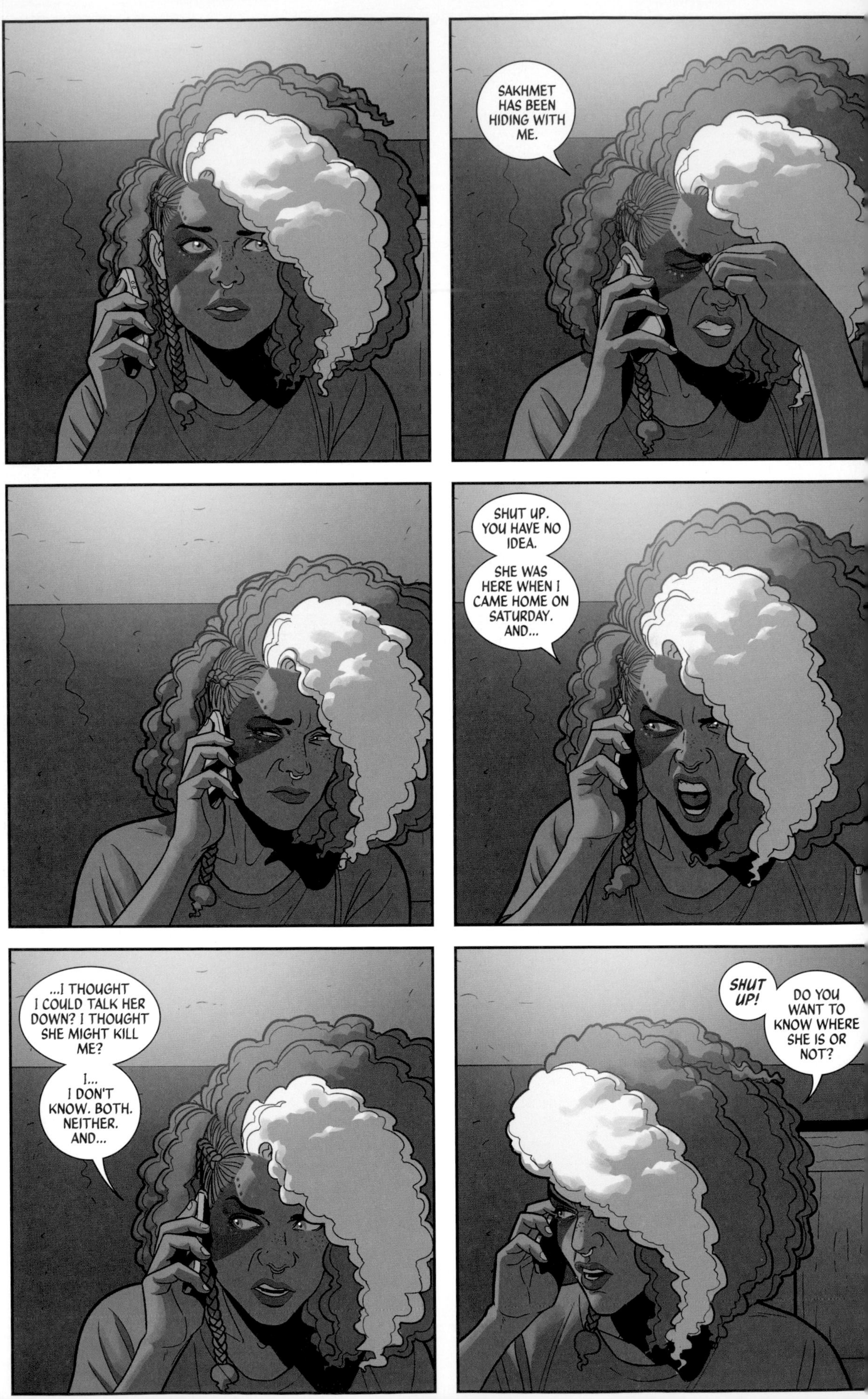
SAKHMET HAS BEEN HIDING WITH ME.
SHUT UP. YOU HAVE NO IDEA.
SHE WAS HERE WHEN I CAME HOME ON SATURDAY. AND...
...I THOUGHT I COULD TALK HER DOWN? I THOUGHT SHE MIGHT KILL ME?
I... I DON'T KNOW. BOTH. NEITHER. AND...
SHUT UP!
DO YOU WANT TO KNOW WHERE SHE IS OR NOT?

"OKAY, HERE WE GO..."

YOU'RE UP.

GOOD LUCK.

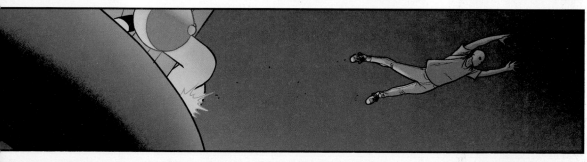

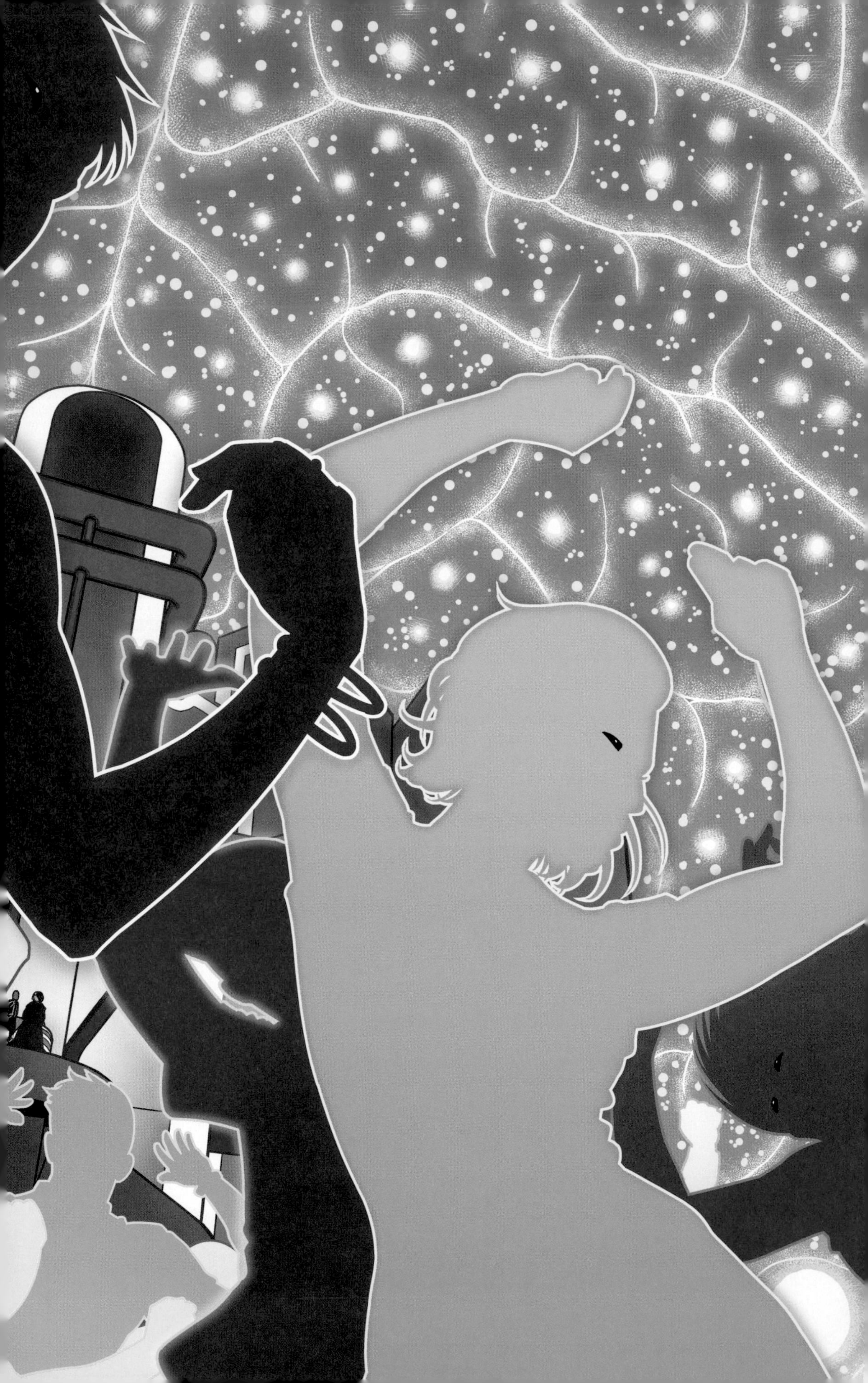

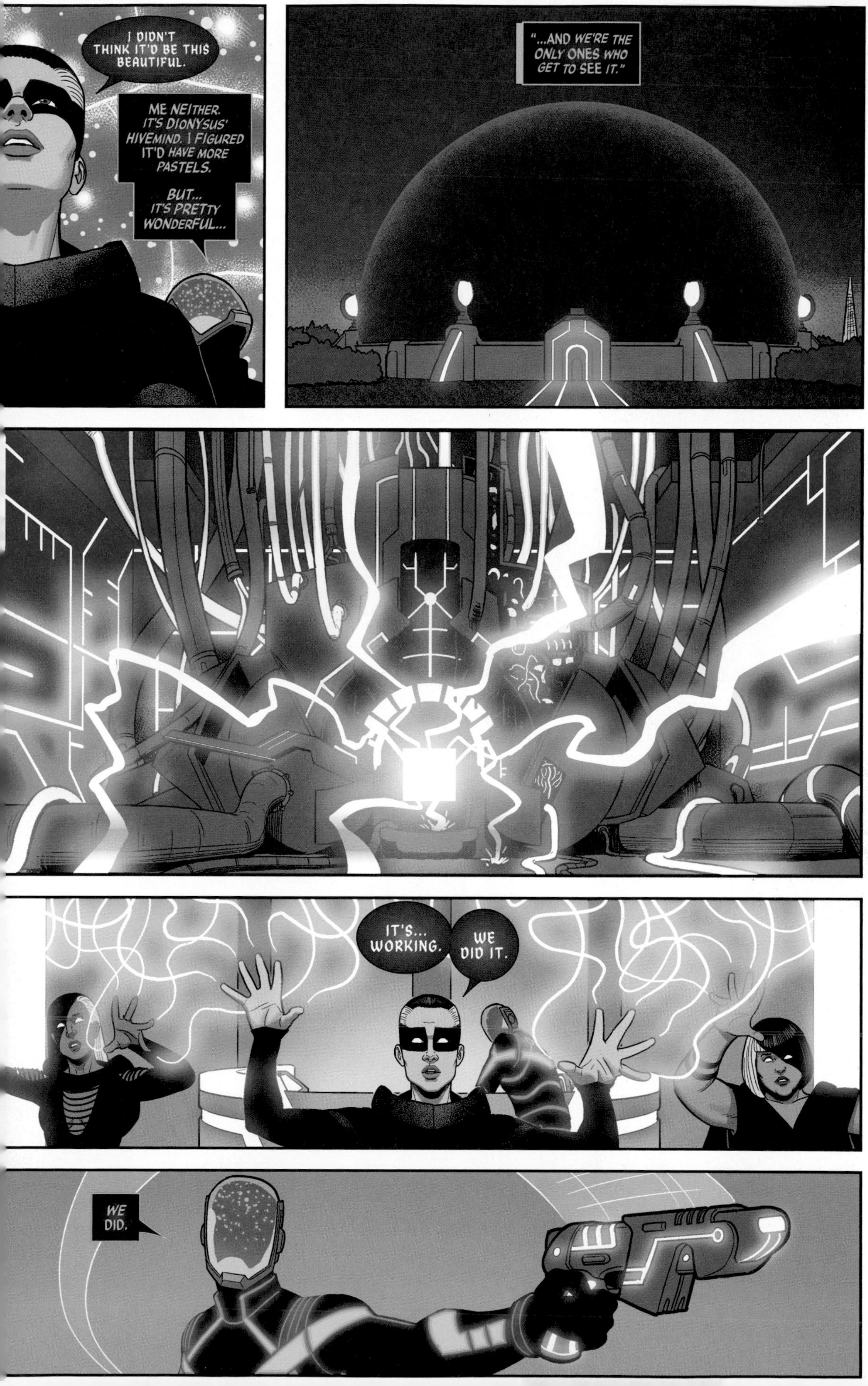

I DIDN'T THINK IT'D BE THIS BEAUTIFUL.
ME NEITHER. IT'S DIONYSUS' HIVEMIND. I FIGURED IT'D HAVE MORE PASTELS.
BUT... IT'S PRETTY WONDERFUL...
"...AND WE'RE THE ONLY ONES WHO GET TO SEE IT."
IT'S... WORKING.
WE DID IT.
WE DID.

THE BRITISH
MUSEUM.

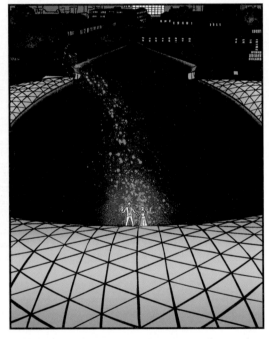

LET OWLY IN AND I'LL
LOOK FOR HER...

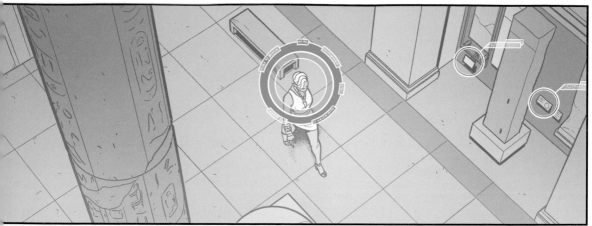

FOUND HER.

THIS IS AS GOOD AS IT GETS. NO ONE'S AROUND.

AT LEAST WE'RE NOT GOING TO ENDANGER A CIVILIAN...

...AND MAKE CASSANDRA PHONE UP AND SHOUT AT US AGAIN.

SHE IS VERY MEAN.

YEAH, BUT SHE WAS RIGHT.

WHAT IS SAKHMET *DOING* HERE?

WHO KNOWS? PERSEPHONE SAYS SHE ALWAYS LIKES TO WANDER LATE AT NIGHT. THE SECRET LIFE OF CATS.

OKAY. PUSS IN THIGH BOOTS GOES DOWN.

WE DON'T NEED TO PUNCH HER. I CAN *PERFORM*. I'M THE BEST PERFORMER.

CALM HER. LIKE I DID WITH LUCIFER.

THAT DIDN'T WORK!

BECAUSE *YOU* PUNCHED HER IN THE HEAD. AND HEY!

IF IT GOES WRONG, I CAN RUN. I AM *ALSO* THE BEST AT RUNNING.

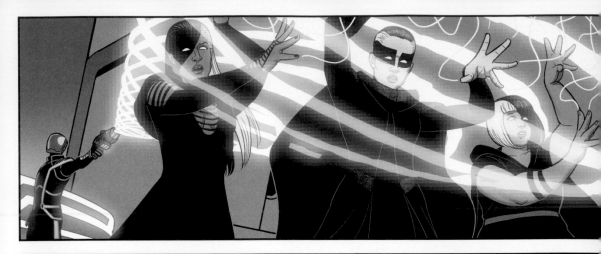

WHAT ARE YOU--

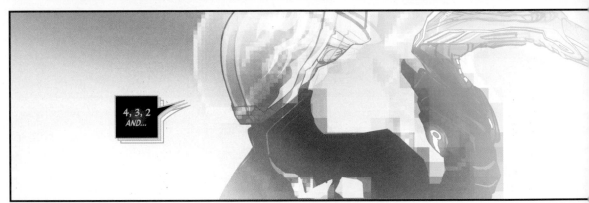

4, 3, 2 AND...

SEER. ONE WHO SEES.

THE VOLUME'S BEEN TURNED UP ON YOUR POWERS AND...WELL, YOU CAN HAVE A REST.

OH, CASS. YOU AND YOUR MACHINE.

AS IF THAT WAS THE ONLY MYSTERY.

OKAY...ONE HIVEMIND...

MAPPING...

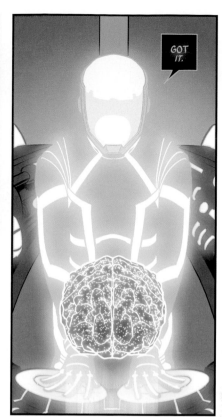

GOT IT.

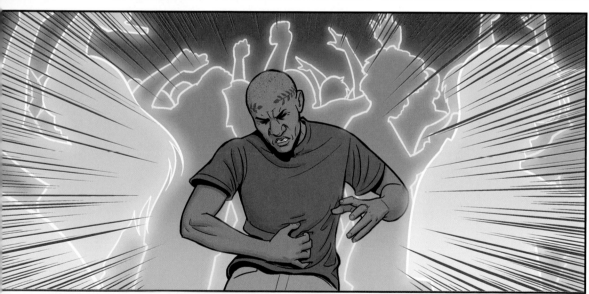

WHAT--

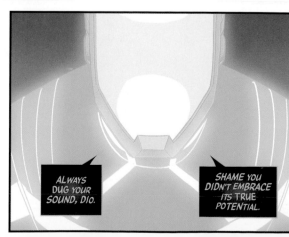

ALWAYS DUG YOUR SOUND, DIO.

SHAME YOU DIDN'T EMBRACE ITS TRUE POTENTIAL.

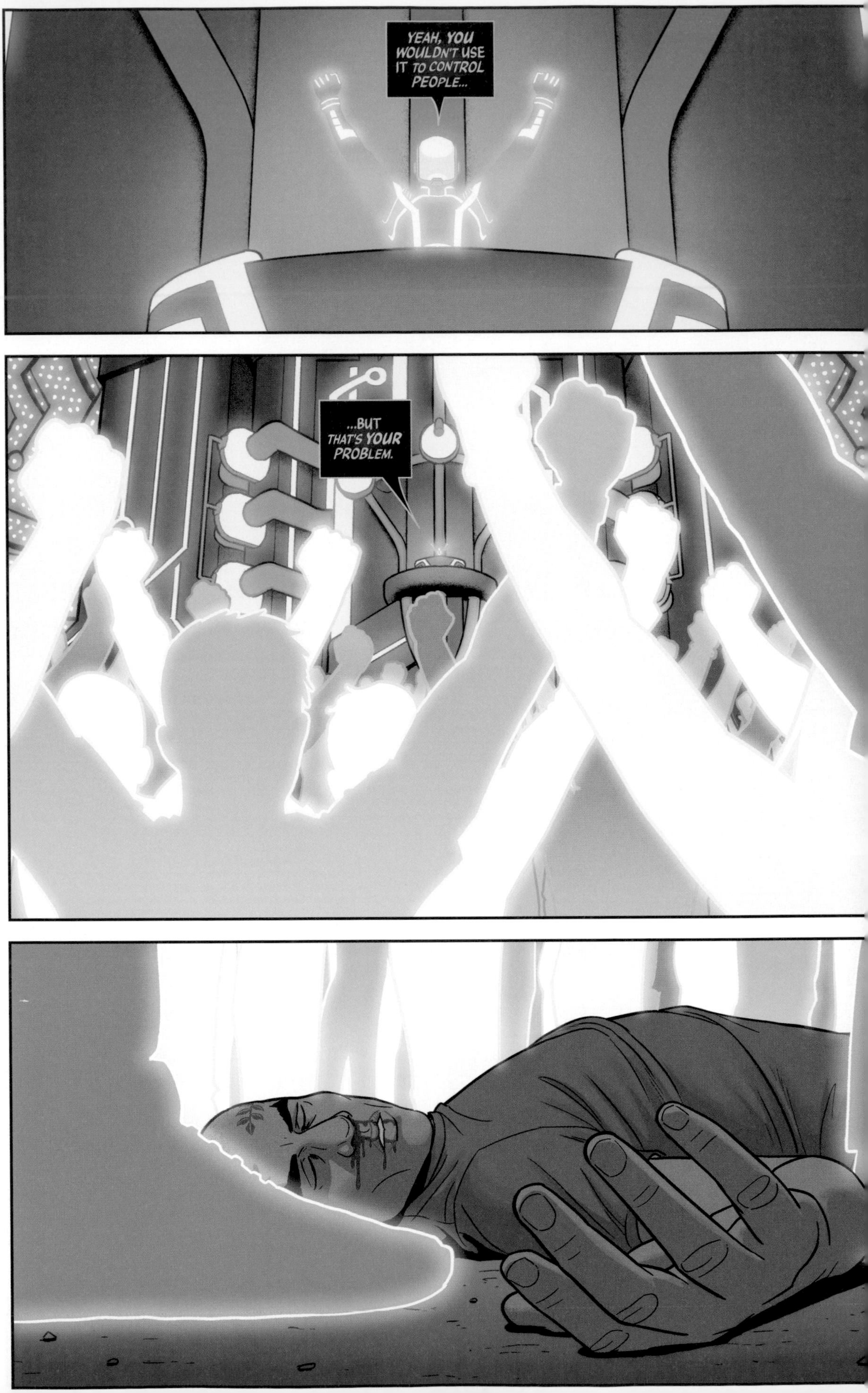
YEAH, YOU WOULDN'T USE IT TO CONTROL PEOPLE...
...BUT THAT'S YOUR PROBLEM.

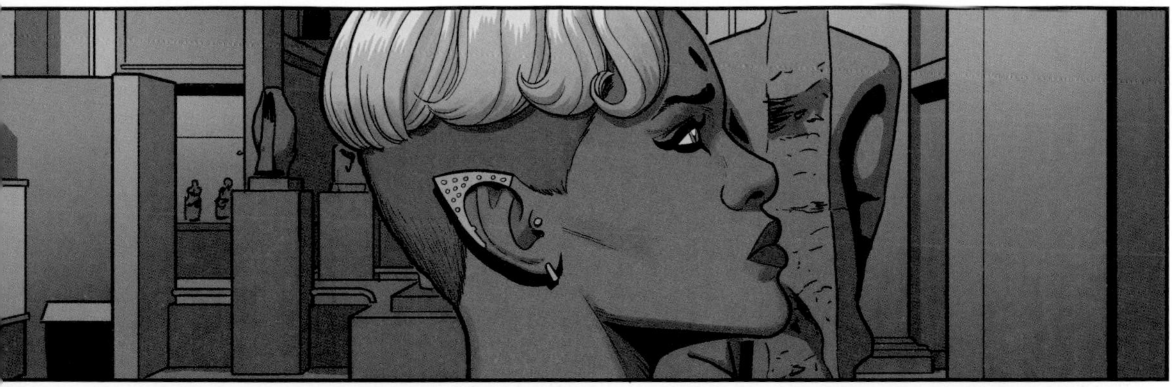

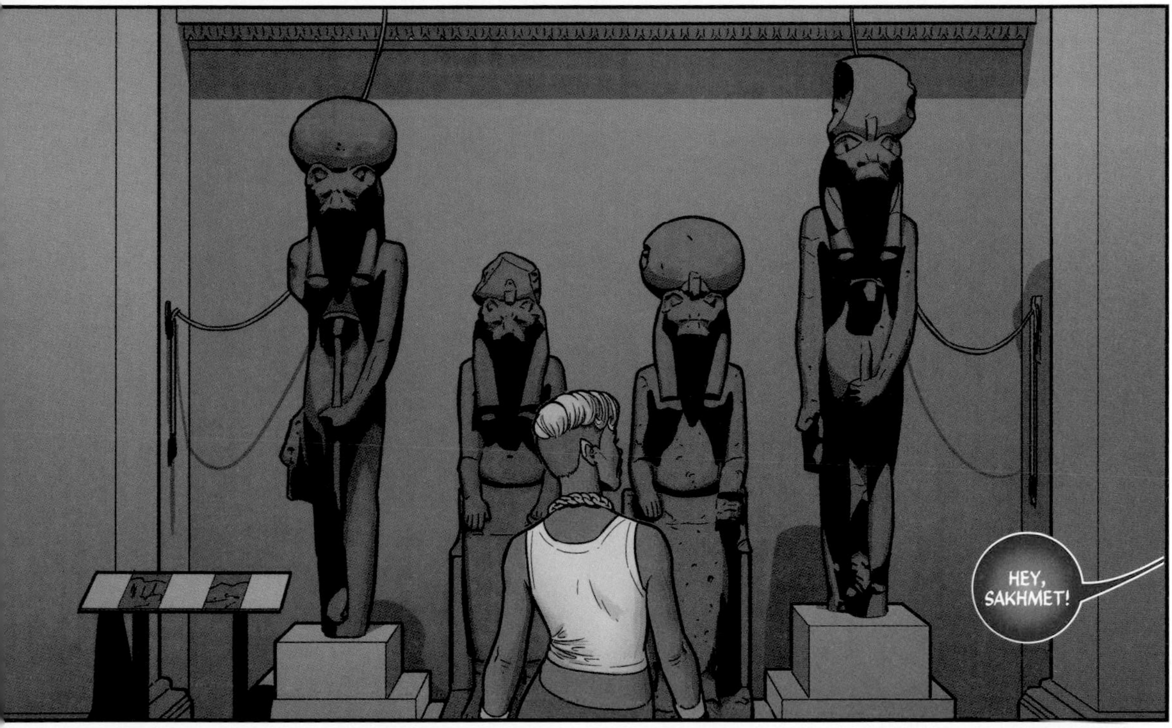
HEY, SAKHMET!

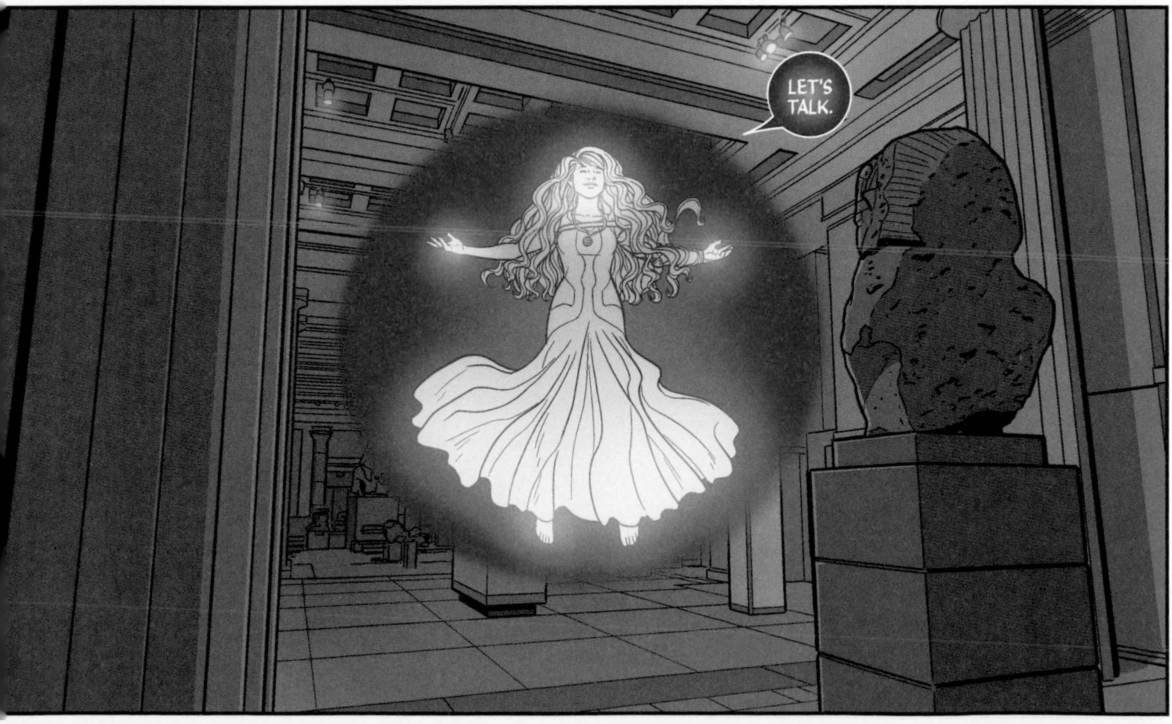
LET'S TALK.

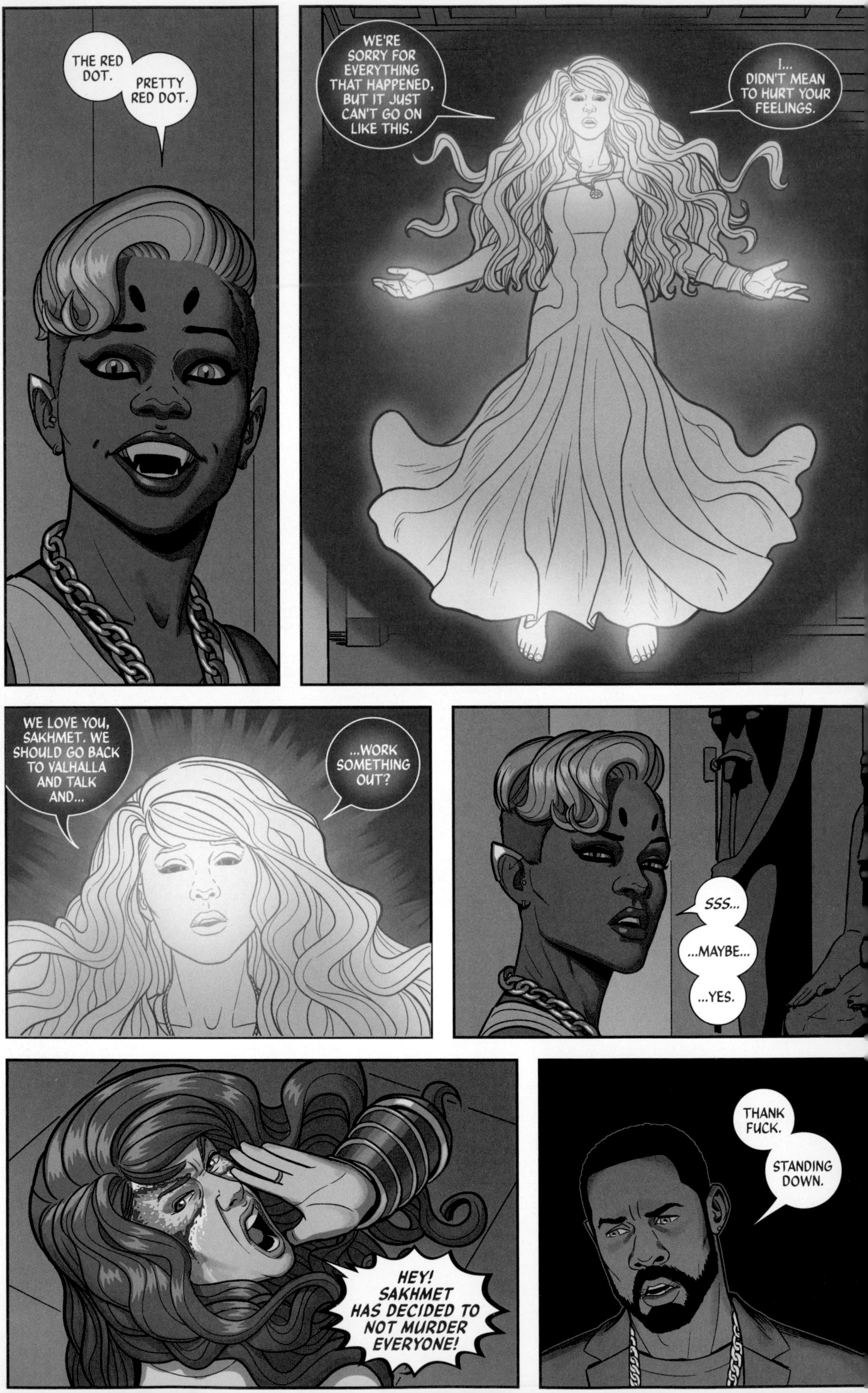
THE RED DOT.
PRETTY RED DOT.
WE'RE SORRY FOR EVERYTHING THAT HAPPENED, BUT IT JUST CAN'T GO ON LIKE THIS.
I... DIDN'T MEAN TO HURT YOUR FEELINGS.
WE LOVE YOU, SAKHMET. WE SHOULD GO BACK TO VALHALLA AND TALK AND...
...WORK SOMETHING OUT?
SSS...
...MAYBE...
...YES.
HEY! SAKHMET HAS DECIDED TO NOT MURDER EVERYONE!
THANK FUCK.
STANDING DOWN.

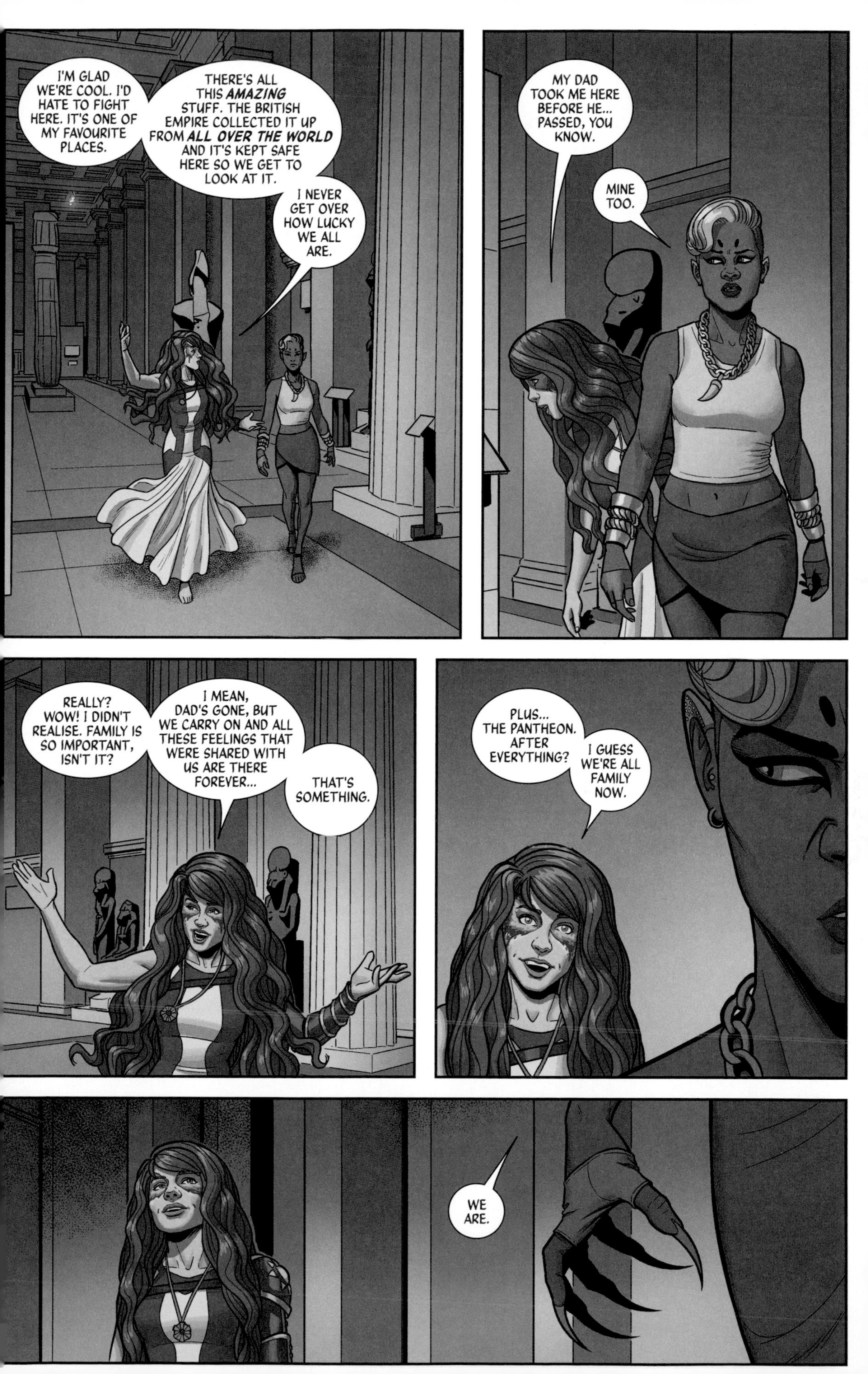
I'M GLAD WE'RE COOL. I'D HATE TO FIGHT HERE. IT'S ONE OF MY FAVOURITE PLACES.
THERE'S ALL THIS *AMAZING* STUFF. THE BRITISH EMPIRE COLLECTED IT UP FROM *ALL OVER THE WORLD* AND IT'S KEPT SAFE HERE SO WE GET TO LOOK AT IT.
I NEVER GET OVER HOW LUCKY WE ALL ARE.
MY DAD TOOK ME HERE BEFORE HE... PASSED, YOU KNOW.
MINE TOO.
REALLY? WOW! I DIDN'T REALISE. FAMILY IS SO IMPORTANT, ISN'T IT?
I MEAN, DAD'S GONE, BUT WE CARRY ON AND ALL THESE FEELINGS THAT WERE SHARED WITH US ARE THERE FOREVER...
THAT'S SOMETHING.
PLUS... THE PANTHEON. AFTER EVERYTHING?
I GUESS WE'RE ALL FAMILY NOW.
WE ARE.

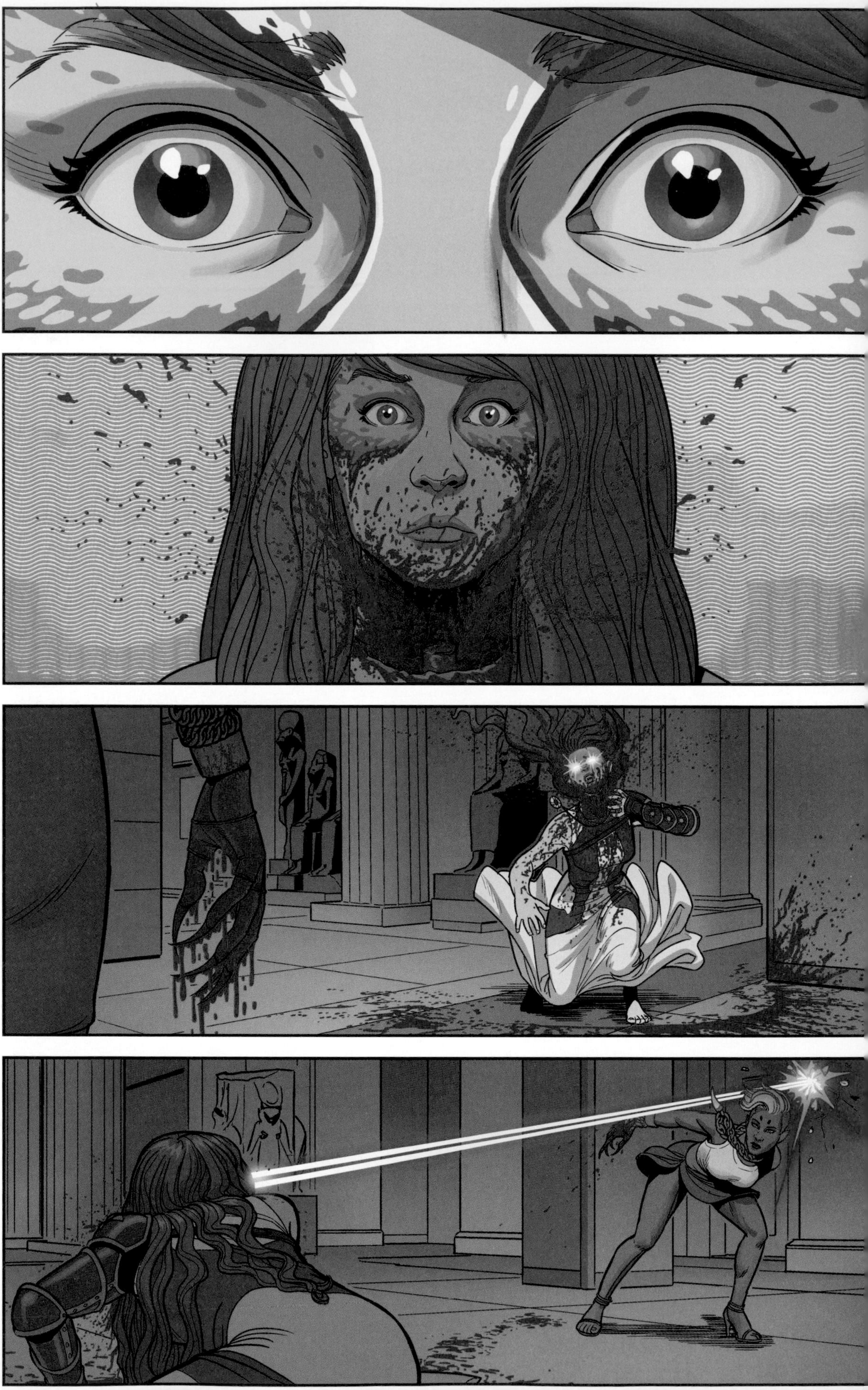

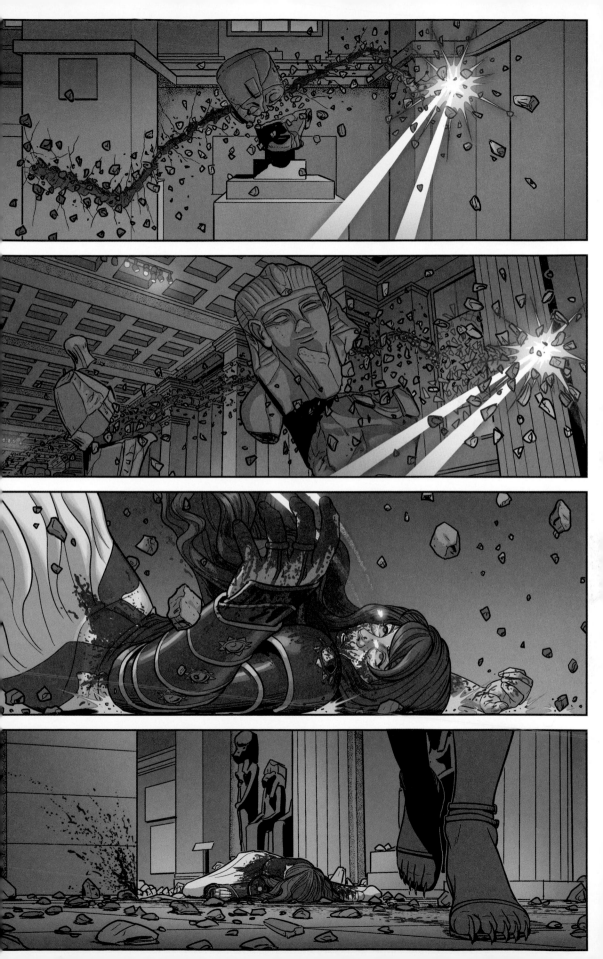

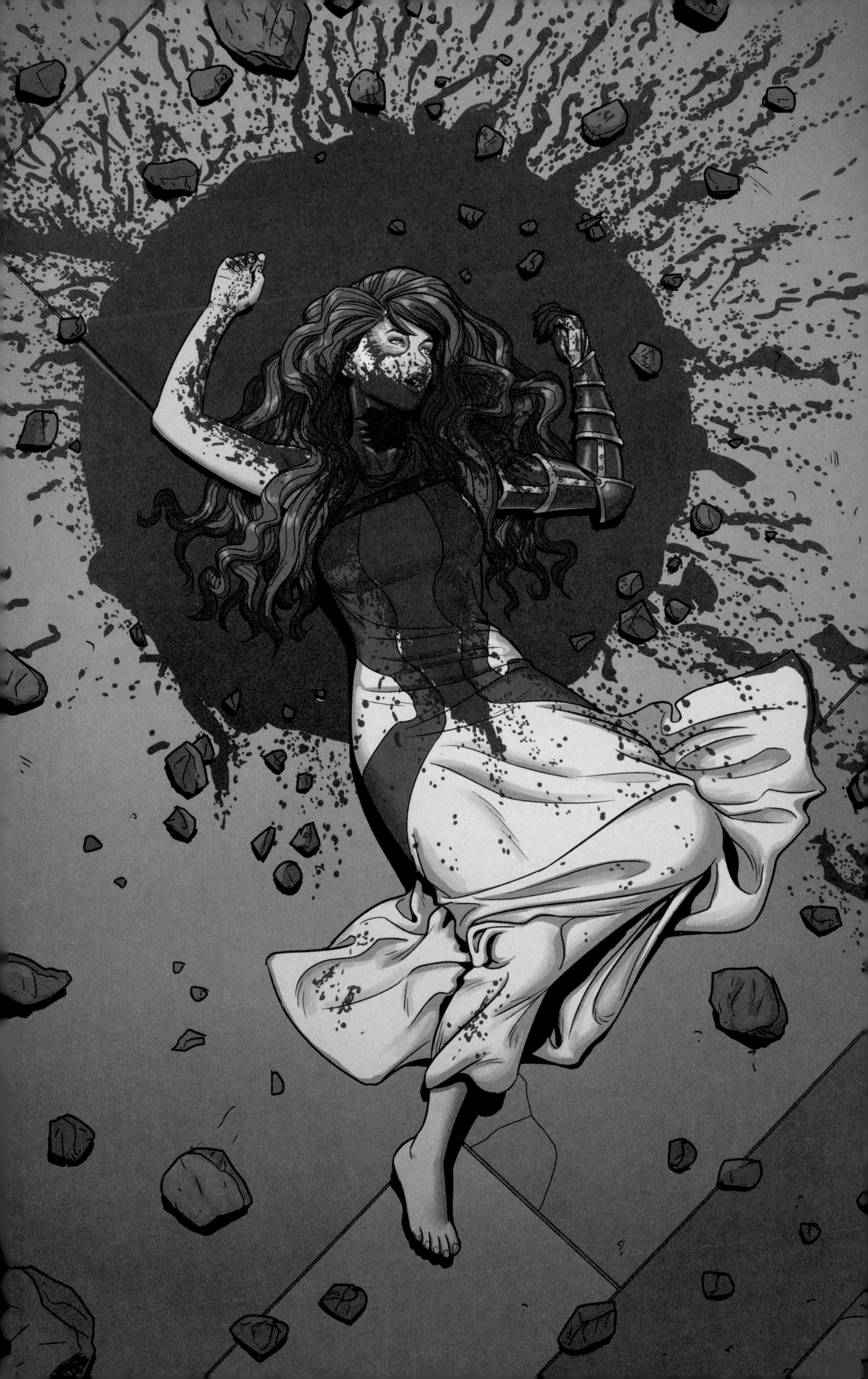

GENIUS STEALS.
AS DO THIEVES.

8 MARCH 2015

32

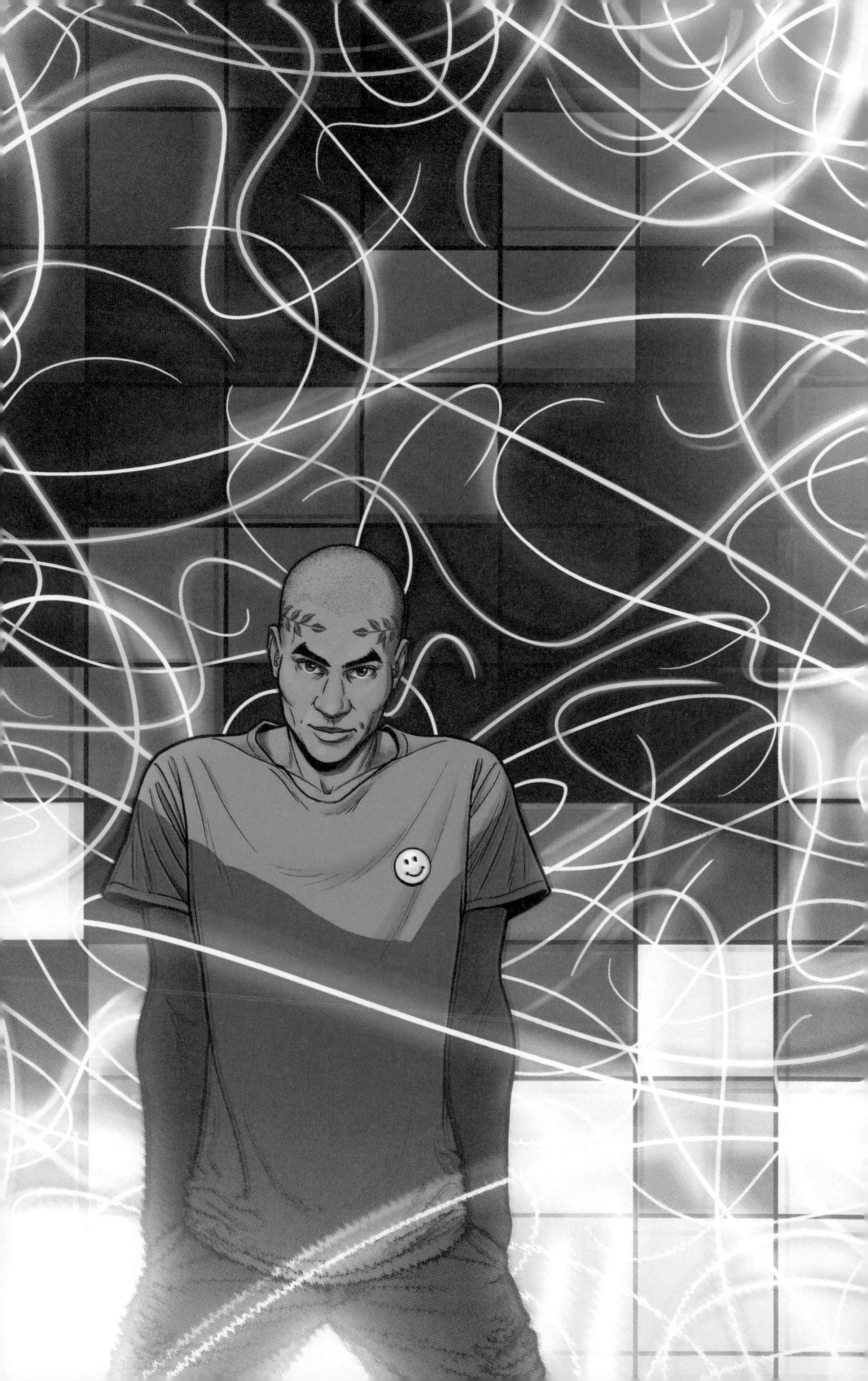

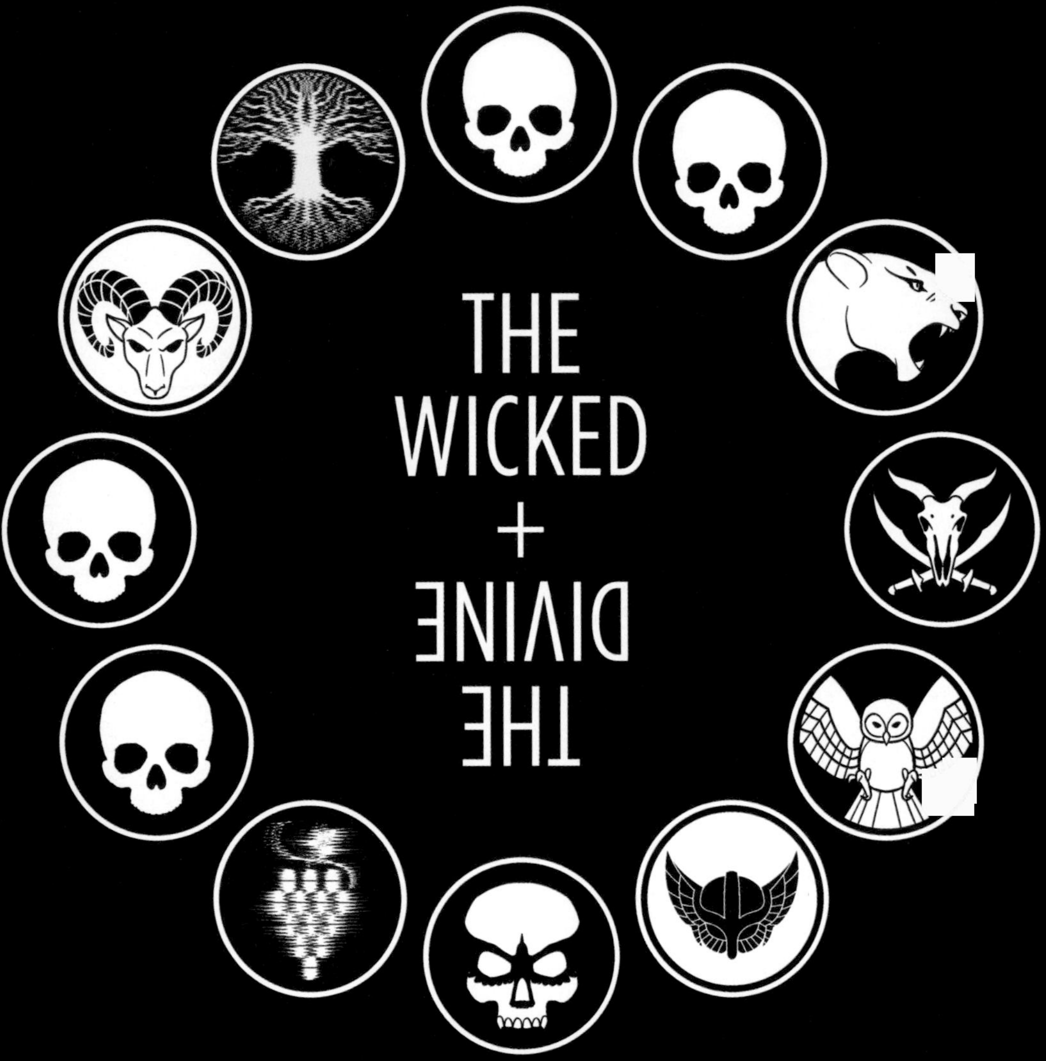
THE
WICKED
+
THE
DIVINE

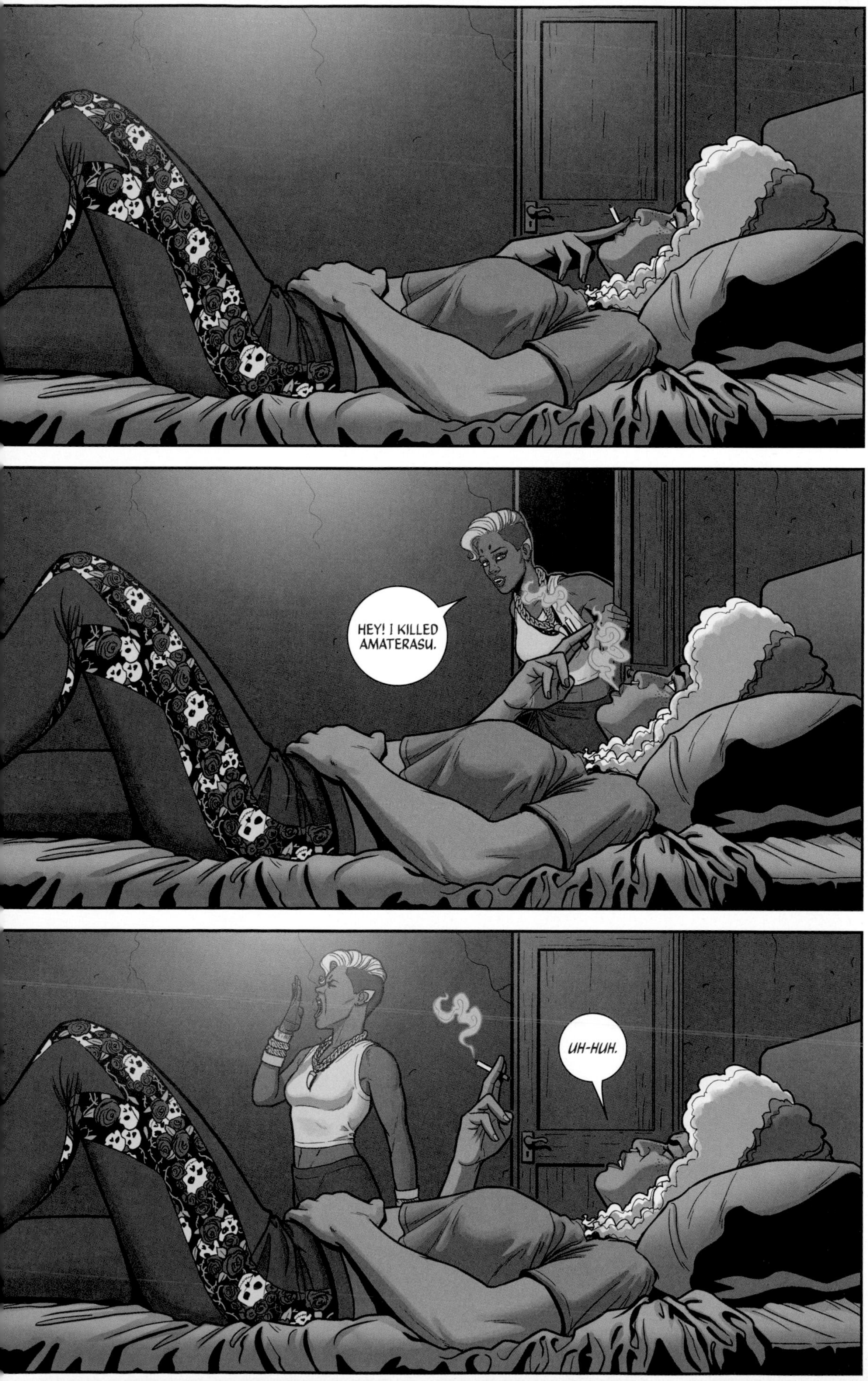
HEY! I KILLED AMATERASU.
UH-HUH.

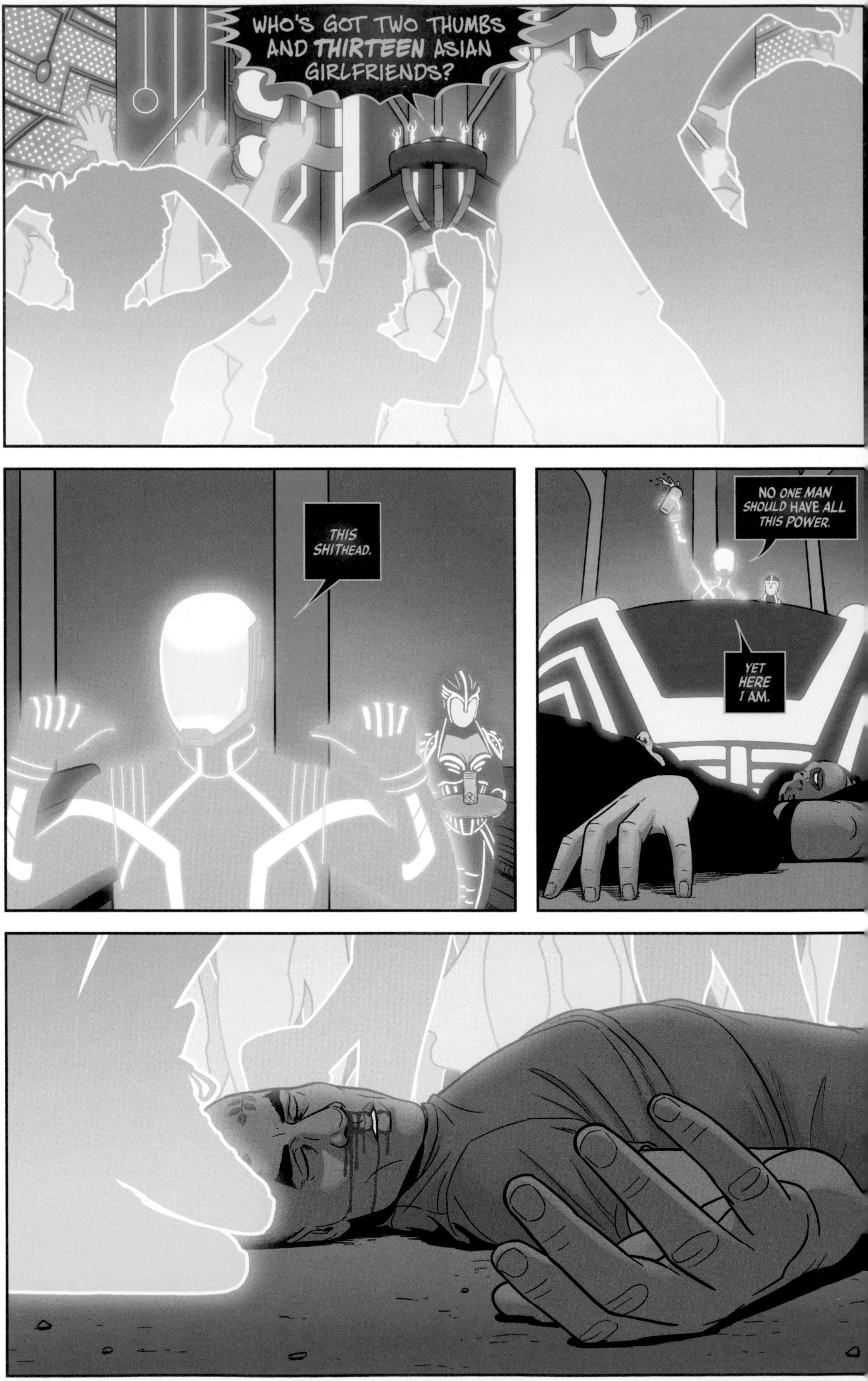
WHO'S GOT TWO THUMBS AND THIRTEEN ASIAN GIRLFRIENDS?
THIS SHITHEAD.
NO ONE MAN SHOULD HAVE ALL THIS POWER.
YET HERE I AM.

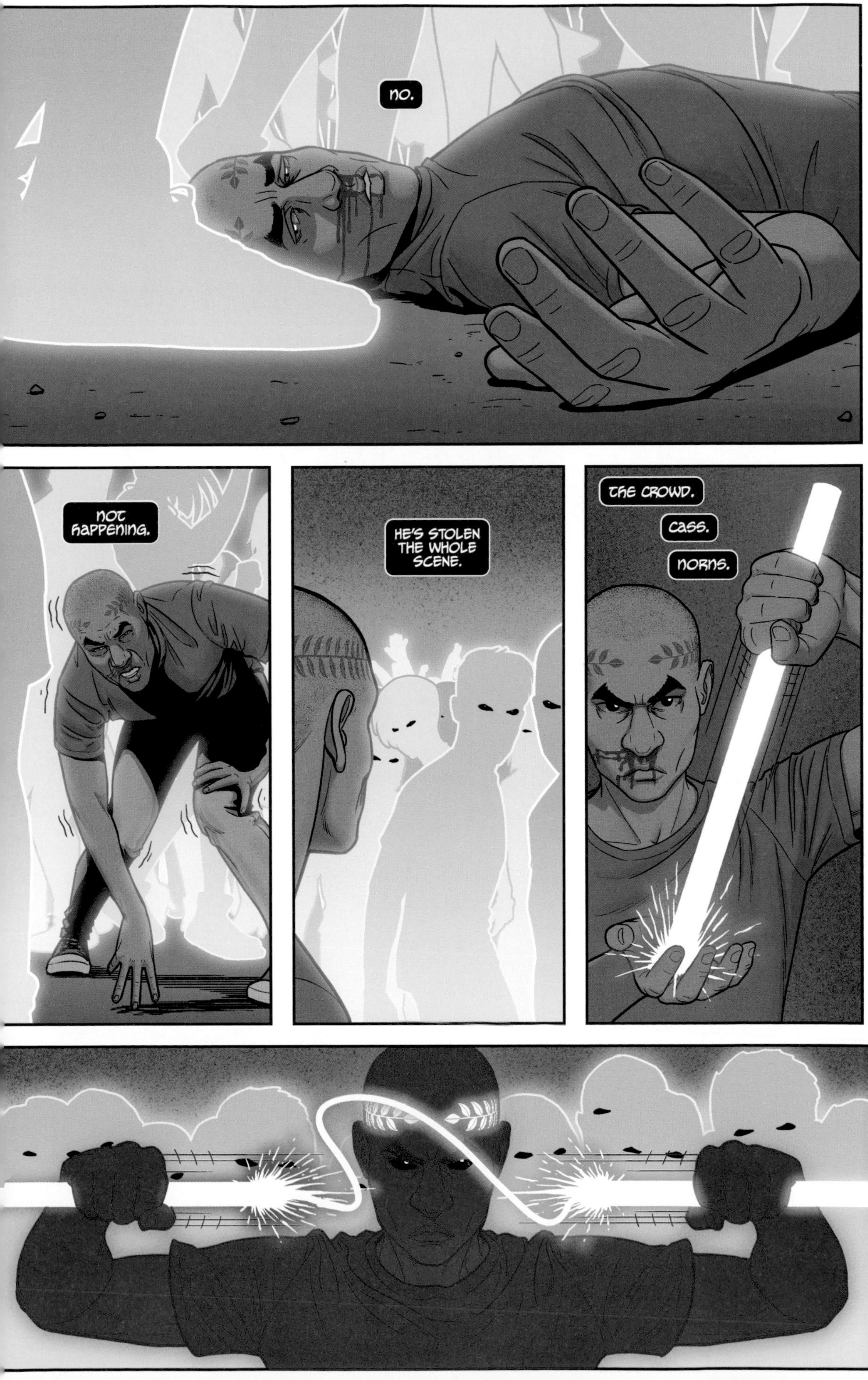
no.
not happening.
He's stolen the whole scene.
The crowd.
cass.
norns.

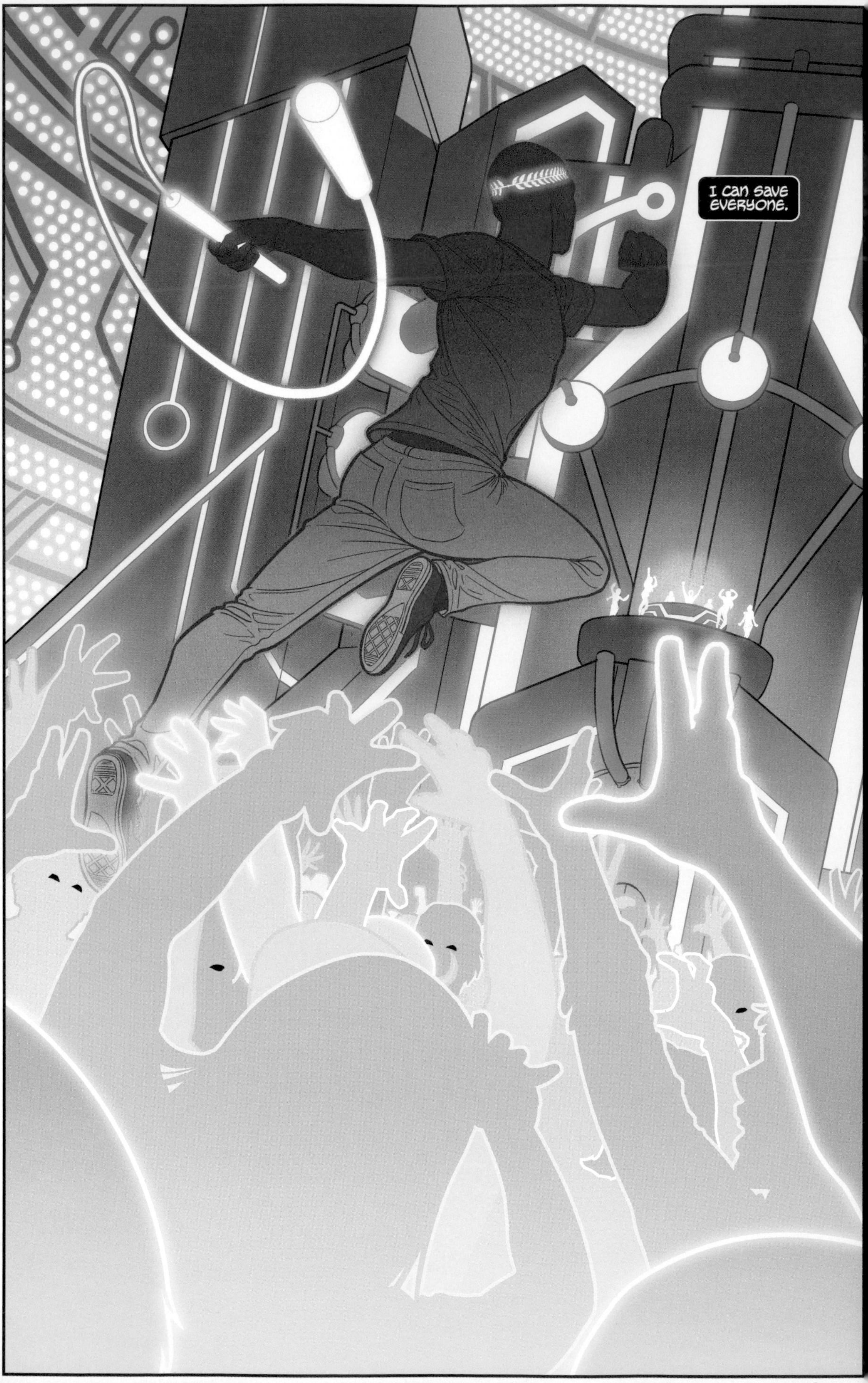
I CAN SAVE EVERYONE.

THE RED SHOES

8 MARCH 2015

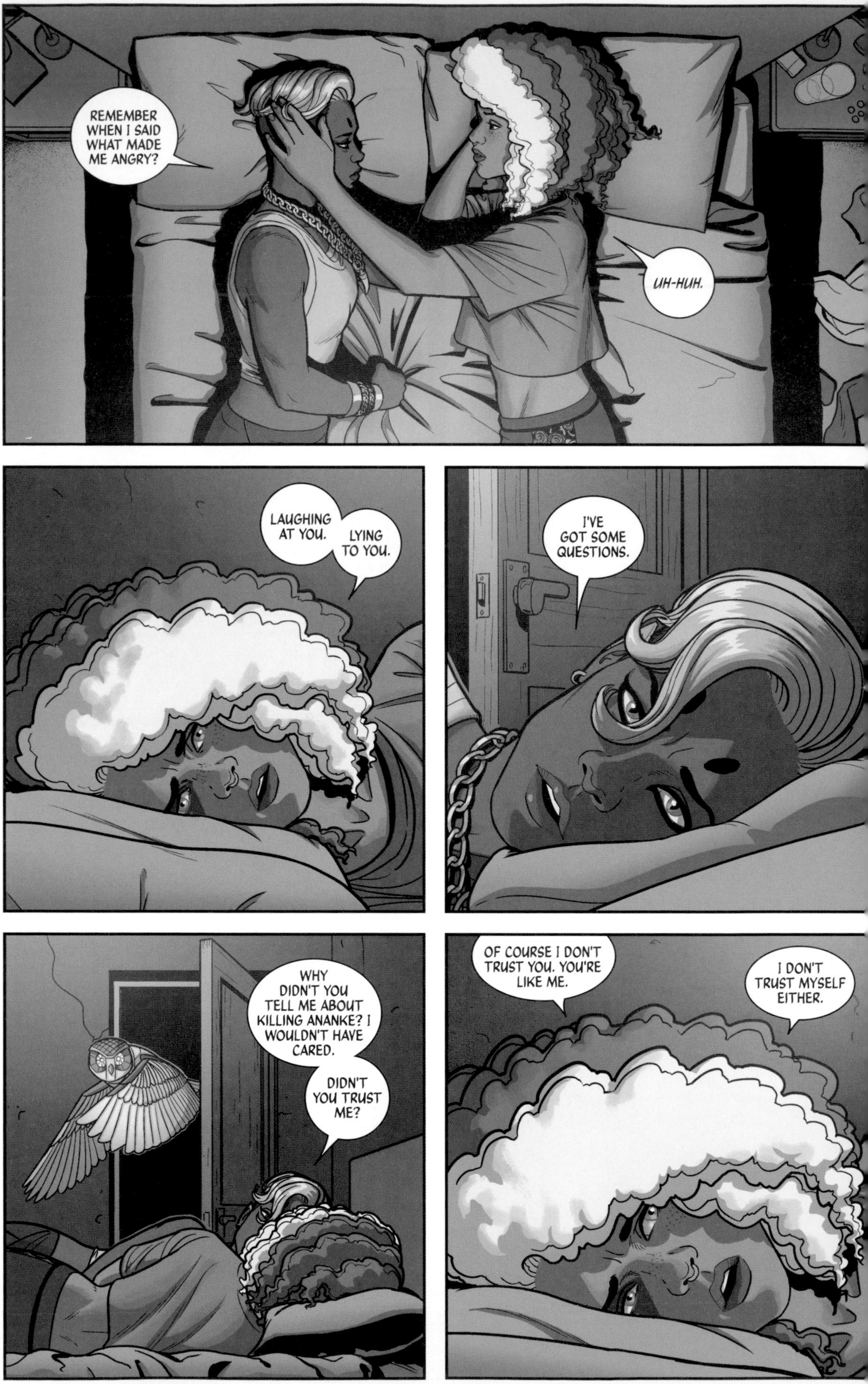
REMEMBER WHEN I SAID WHAT MADE ME ANGRY?
UH-HUH.
LAUGHING AT YOU.
LYING TO YOU.
I'VE GOT SOME QUESTIONS.
WHY DIDN'T YOU TELL ME ABOUT KILLING ANANKE? I WOULDN'T HAVE CARED.
DIDN'T YOU TRUST ME?
OF COURSE I DON'T TRUST YOU. YOU'RE LIKE ME.
I DON'T TRUST MYSELF EITHER.

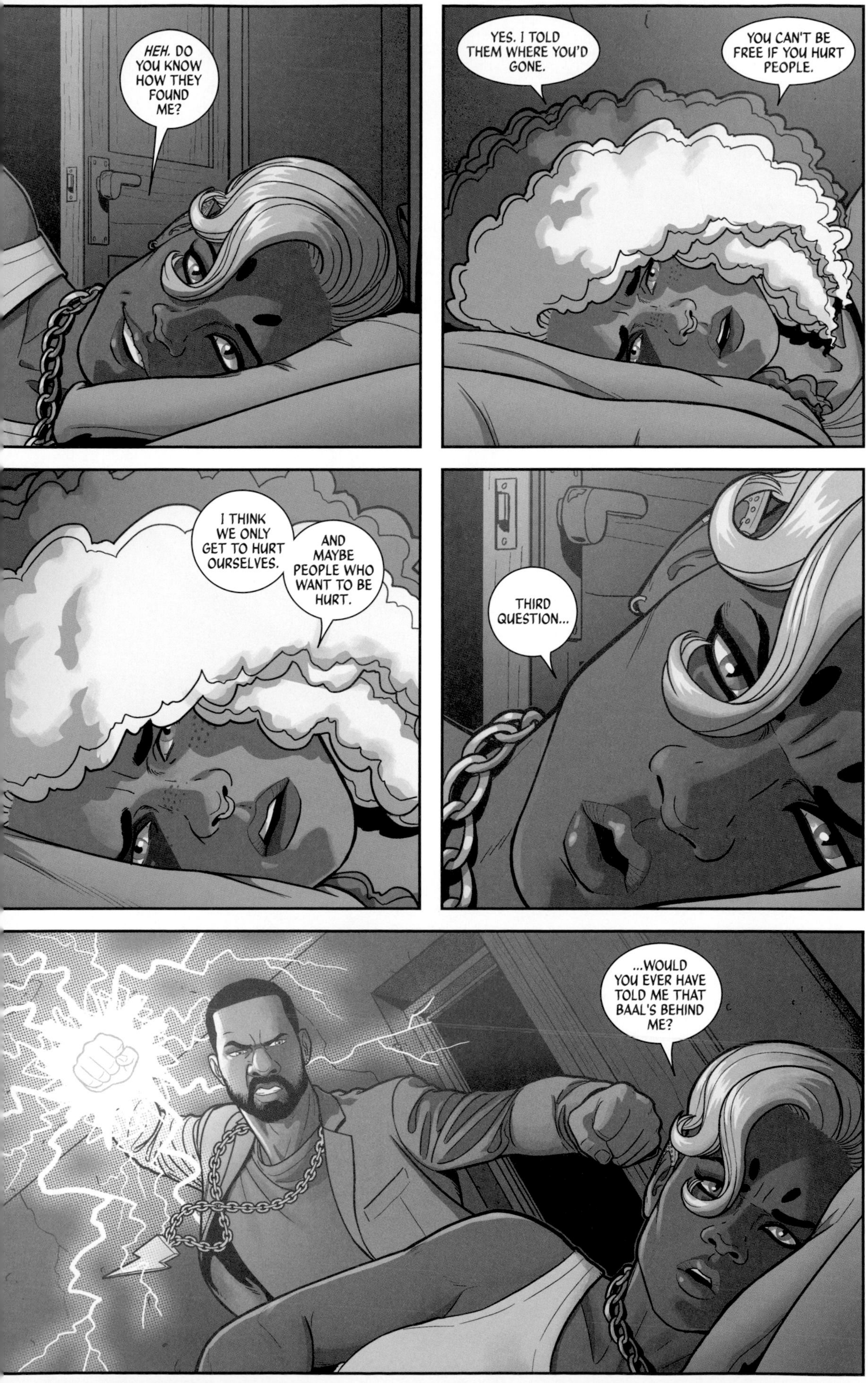
HEH. DO YOU KNOW HOW THEY FOUND ME?
YES. I TOLD THEM WHERE YOU'D GONE.
YOU CAN'T BE FREE IF YOU HURT PEOPLE.
I THINK WE ONLY GET TO HURT OURSELVES.
AND MAYBE PEOPLE WHO WANT TO BE HURT.
THIRD QUESTION...
...WOULD YOU EVER HAVE TOLD ME THAT BAAL'S BEHIND ME?

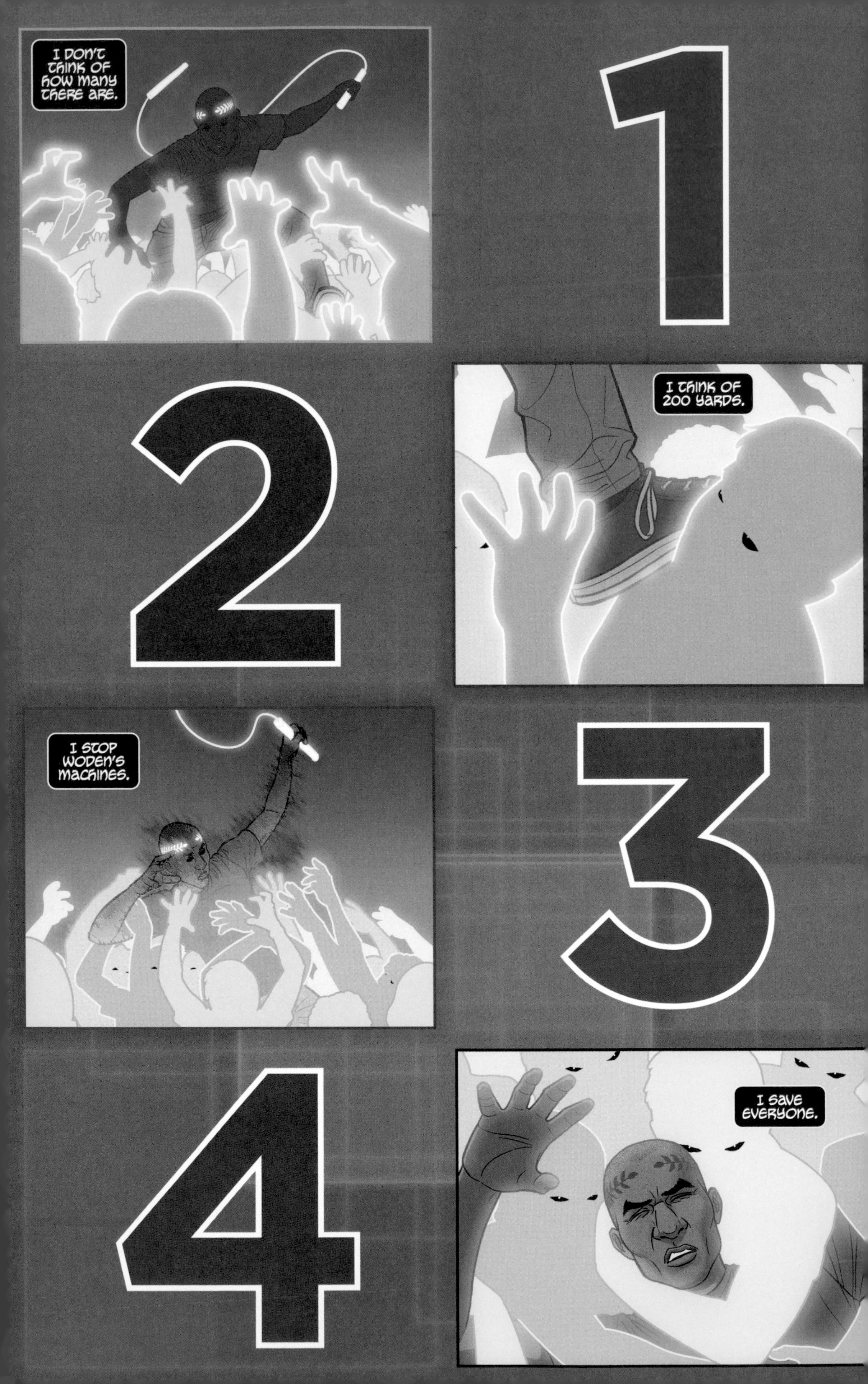
I DON'T THINK OF HOW MANY THERE ARE.
1
I THINK OF 200 YARDS.
2
I STOP WODEN'S MACHINES.
3
I SAVE EVERYONE.
4

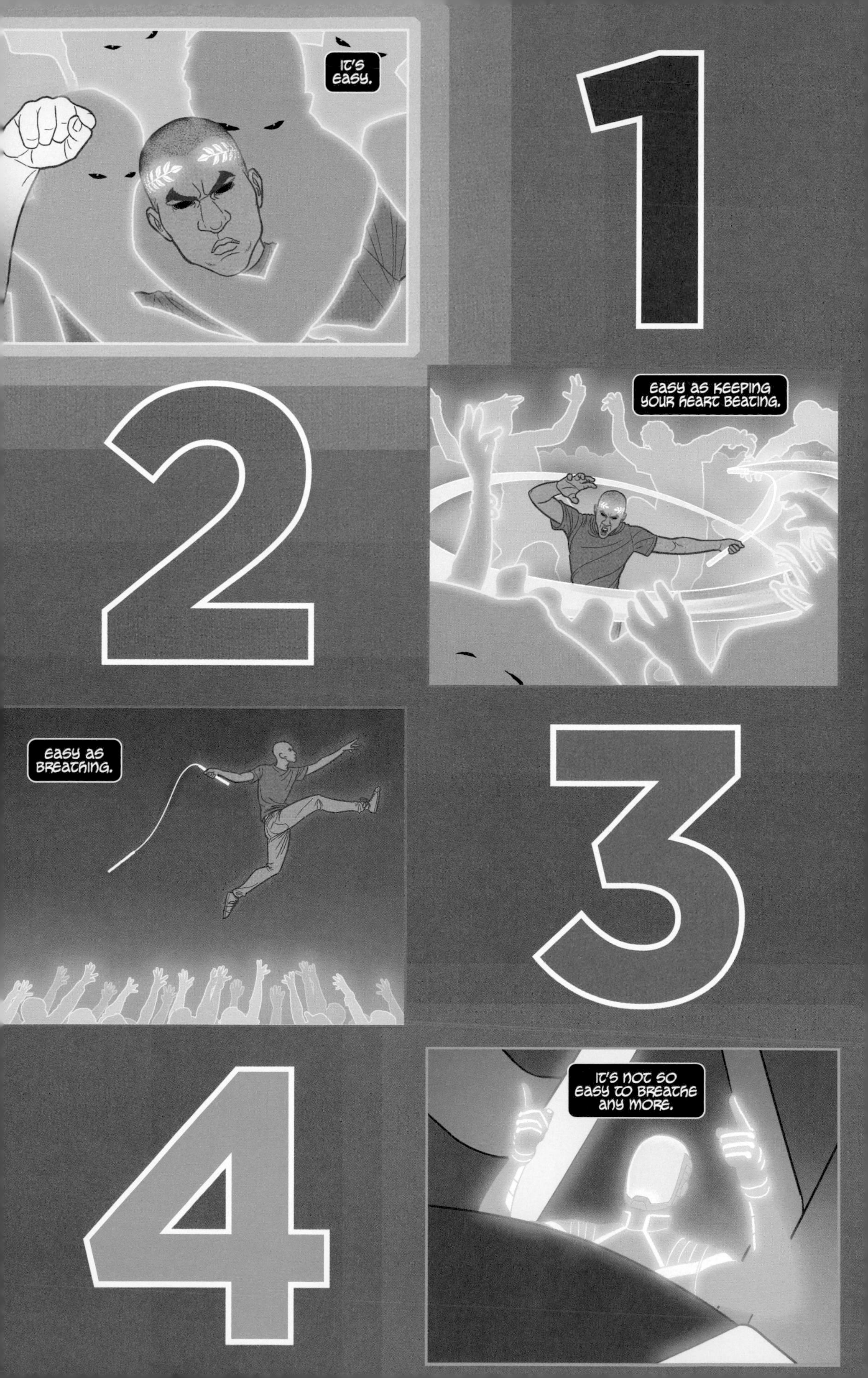
IT'S EASY.
1
2
EASY AS KEEPING YOUR HEART BEATING.
EASY AS BREATHING.
3
4
IT'S NOT SO EASY TO BREATHE ANY MORE.

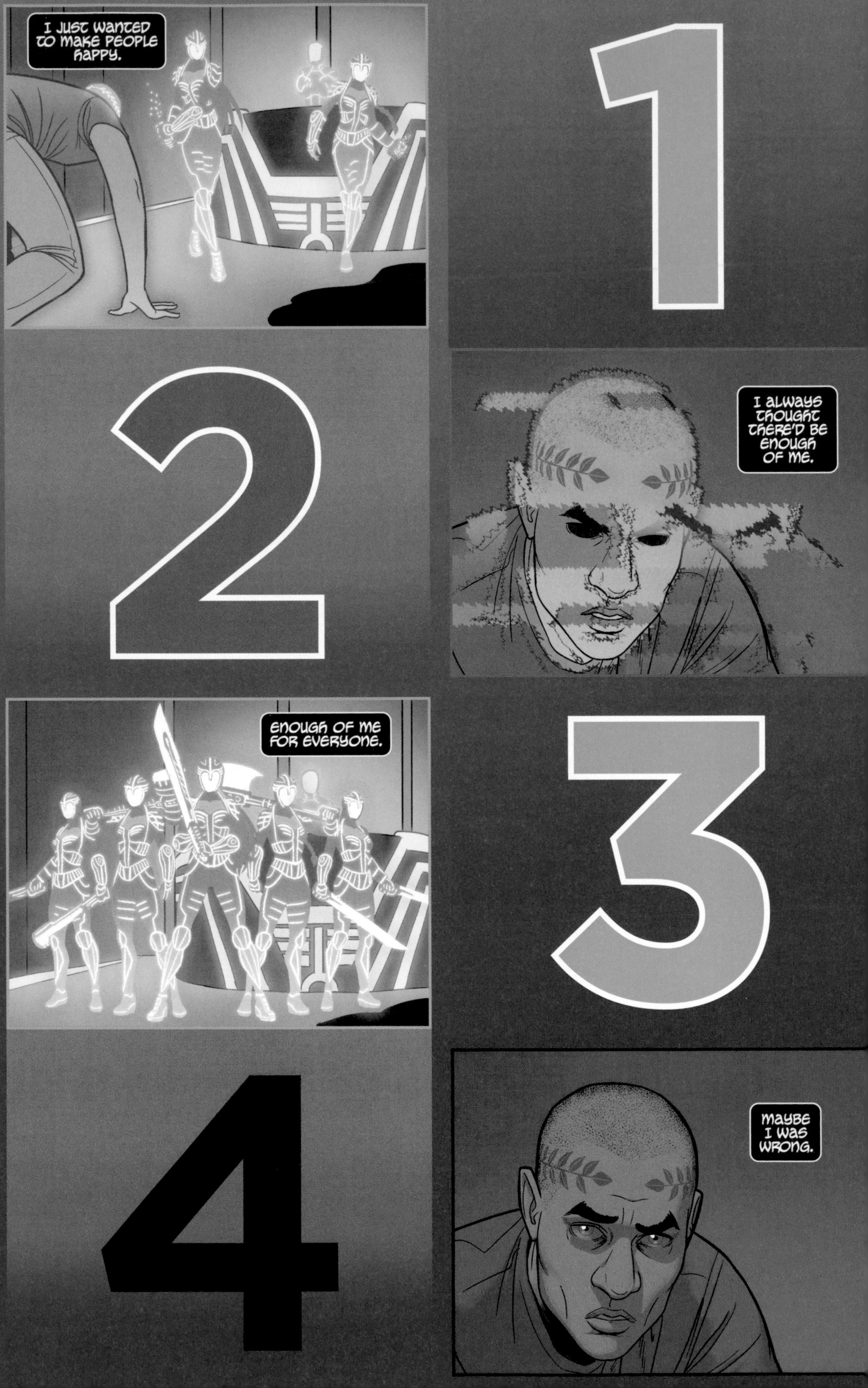
I JUST WANTED TO MAKE PEOPLE HAPPY.
1
2
I ALWAYS THOUGHT THERE'D BE ENOUGH OF ME.
ENOUGH OF ME FOR EVERYONE.
3
4
MAYBE I WAS WRONG.

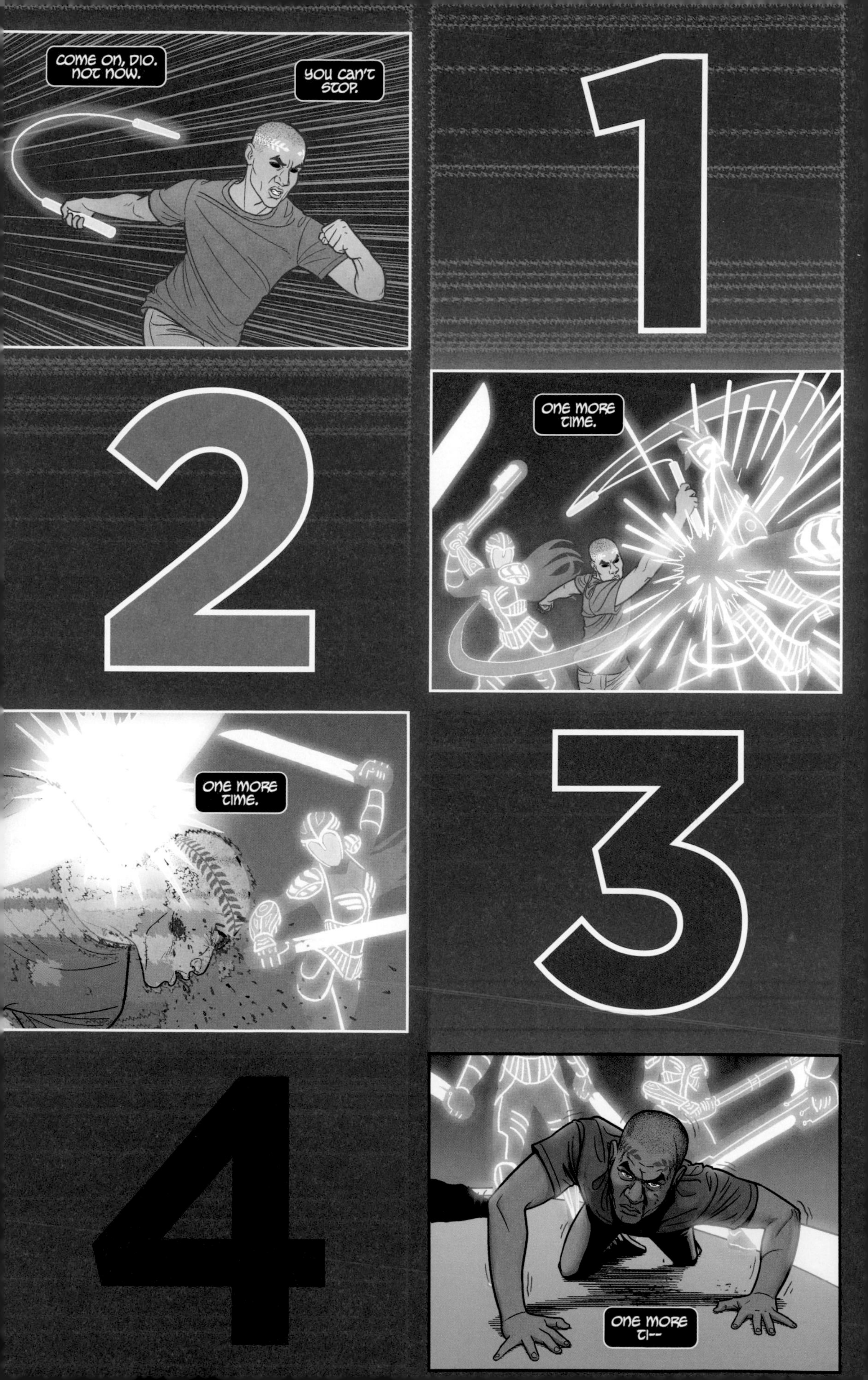
COME ON, DIO. NOT NOW.
YOU CAN'T STOP.
1
2
ONE MORE TIME.
ONE MORE TIME.
3
4
ONE MORE TI--

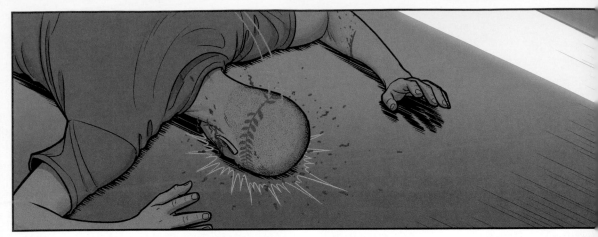

WOW. WHAT AN ASTOUNDING ACT OF ALTRUISTIC YET FUTILE HEROISM!

HEY, THE NORNS ARE AWAKE. WELCOME TO THE VALKYRIES.

NOW WE START THE REAL WORK. YOU NEED TO--

YOU

DUMB

FUCK.

I'M A FUCKING CRITIC!

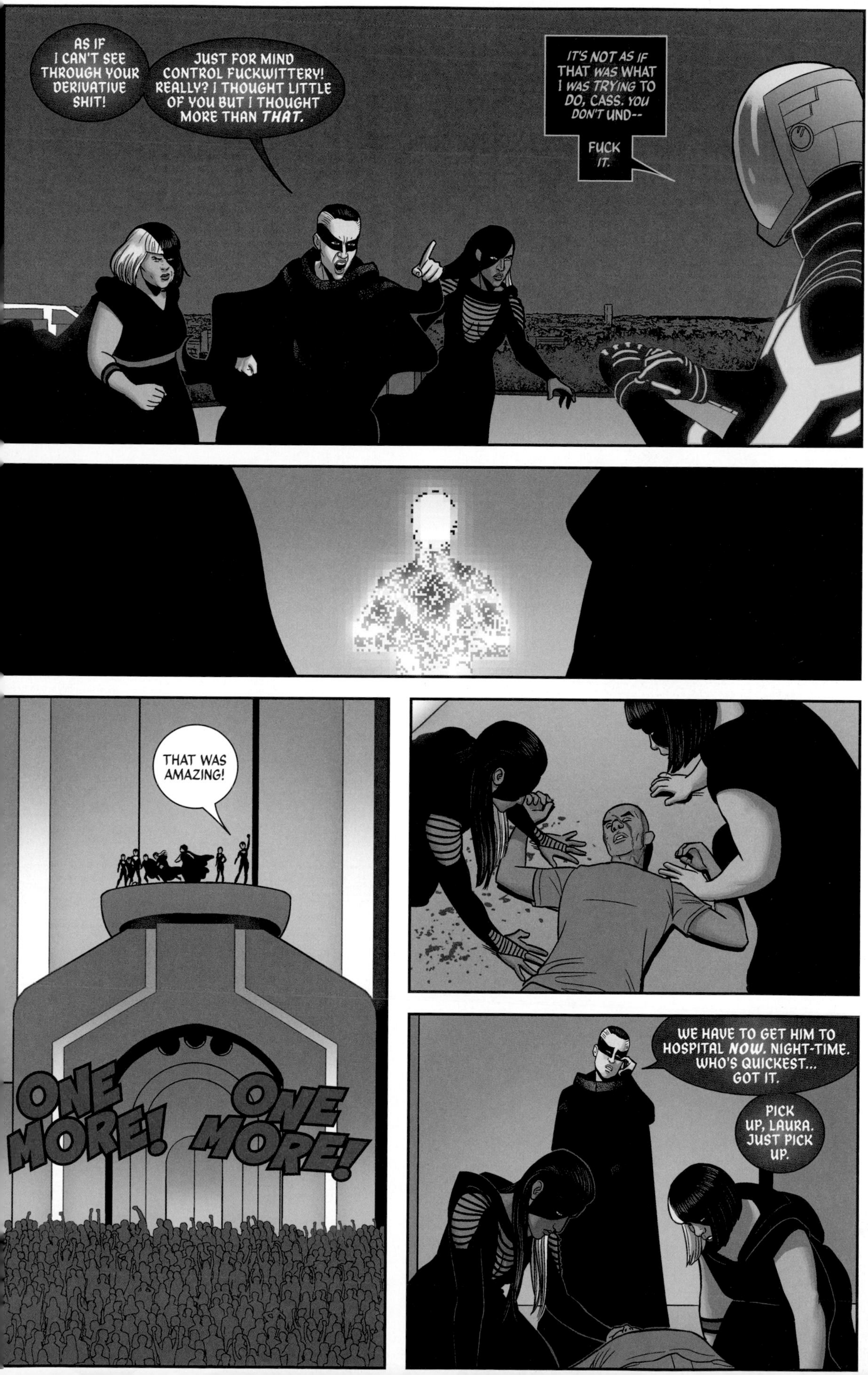
AS IF I CAN'T SEE THROUGH YOUR DERIVATIVE SHIT!
JUST FOR MIND CONTROL FUCKWITTERY! REALLY? I THOUGHT LITTLE OF YOU BUT I THOUGHT MORE THAN THAT.
IT'S NOT AS IF THAT WAS WHAT I WAS TRYING TO DO, CASS. YOU DON'T UND--
FUCK IT.
THAT WAS AMAZING!
ONE MORE! ONE MORE!
WE HAVE TO GET HIM TO HOSPITAL NOW. NIGHT-TIME. WHO'S QUICKEST... GOT IT.
PICK UP, LAURA. JUST PICK UP.

〈DEFAULT ELEUSINIA RINGTONE!〉

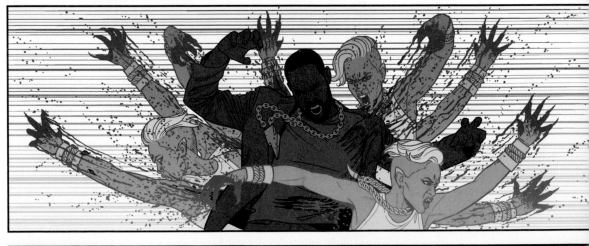

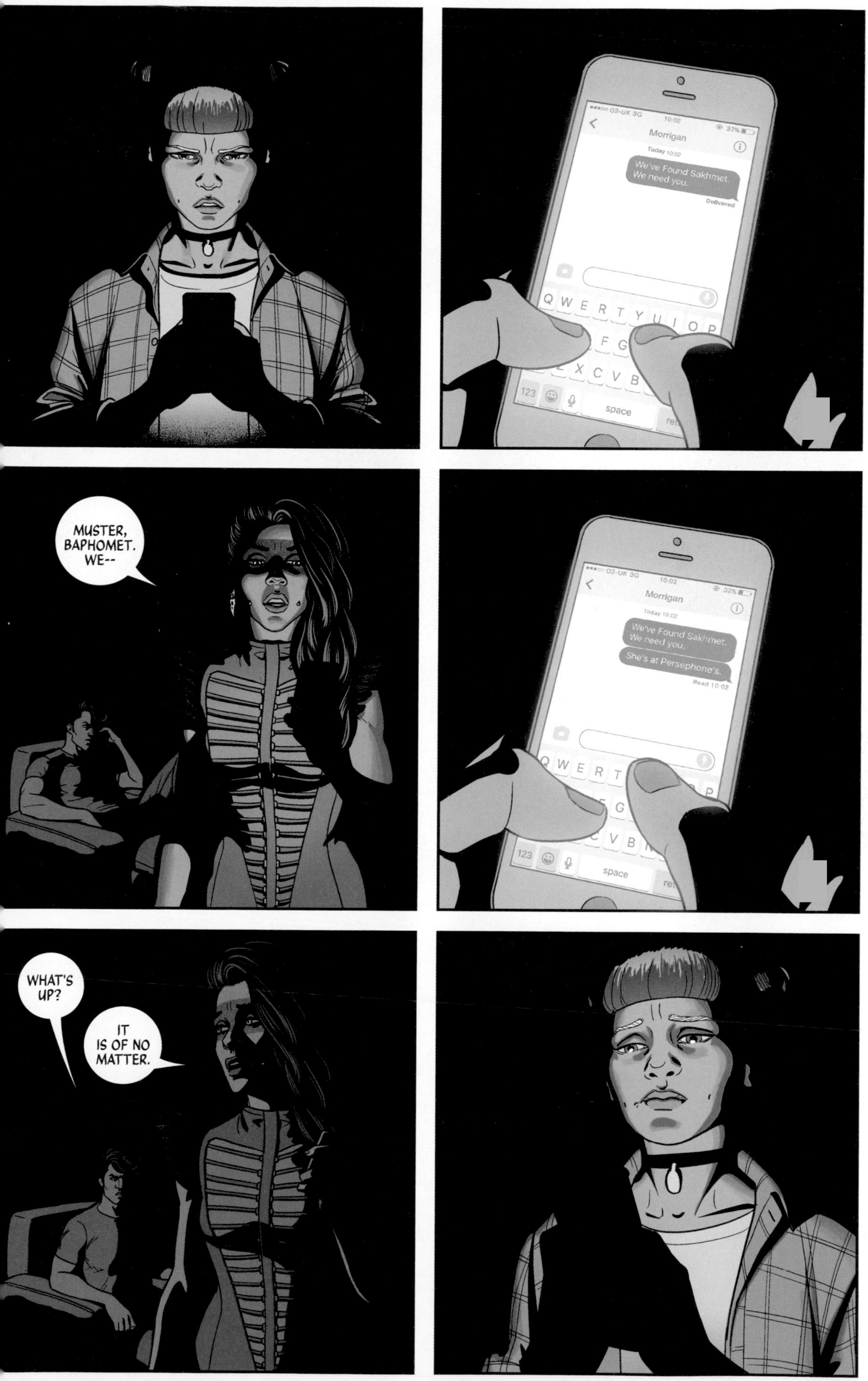

O2-UK 3G
10:02
32%
Morrigan
Today 10:02
We've Found Sakhmet. We need you.
Delivered
space
MUSTER, BAPHOMET. WE--
O2-UK 3G
10:03
32%
Morrigan
Today 10:02
We've Found Sakhmet. We need you.
She's at Persephone's.
Read 10:02
space
WHAT'S UP?
IT IS OF NO MATTER.

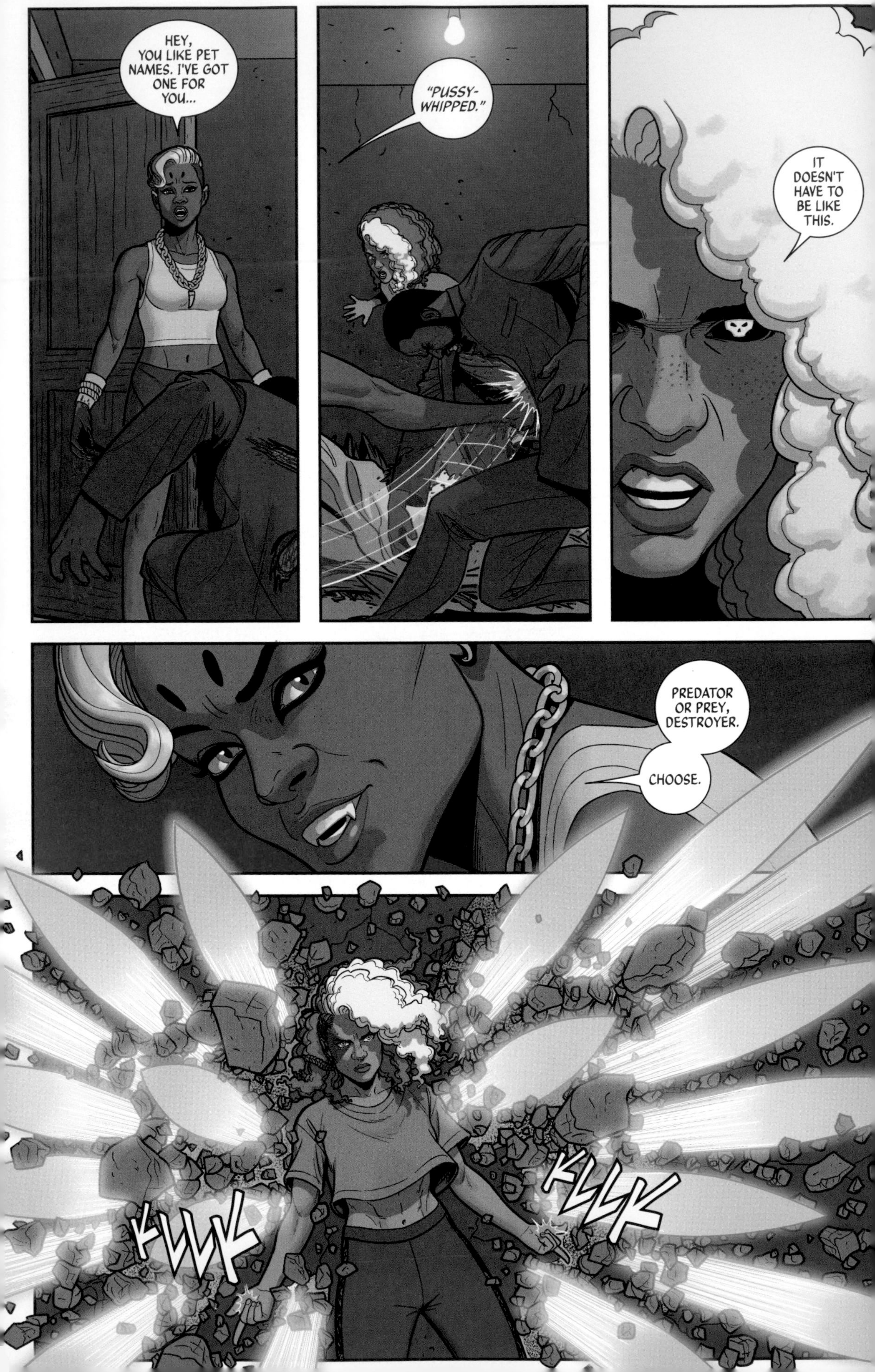
HEY, YOU LIKE PET NAMES. I'VE GOT ONE FOR YOU...
"PUSSY-WHIPPED."
IT DOESN'T HAVE TO BE LIKE THIS.
PREDATOR OR PREY, DESTROYER.
CHOOSE.
KLLK
KLLK

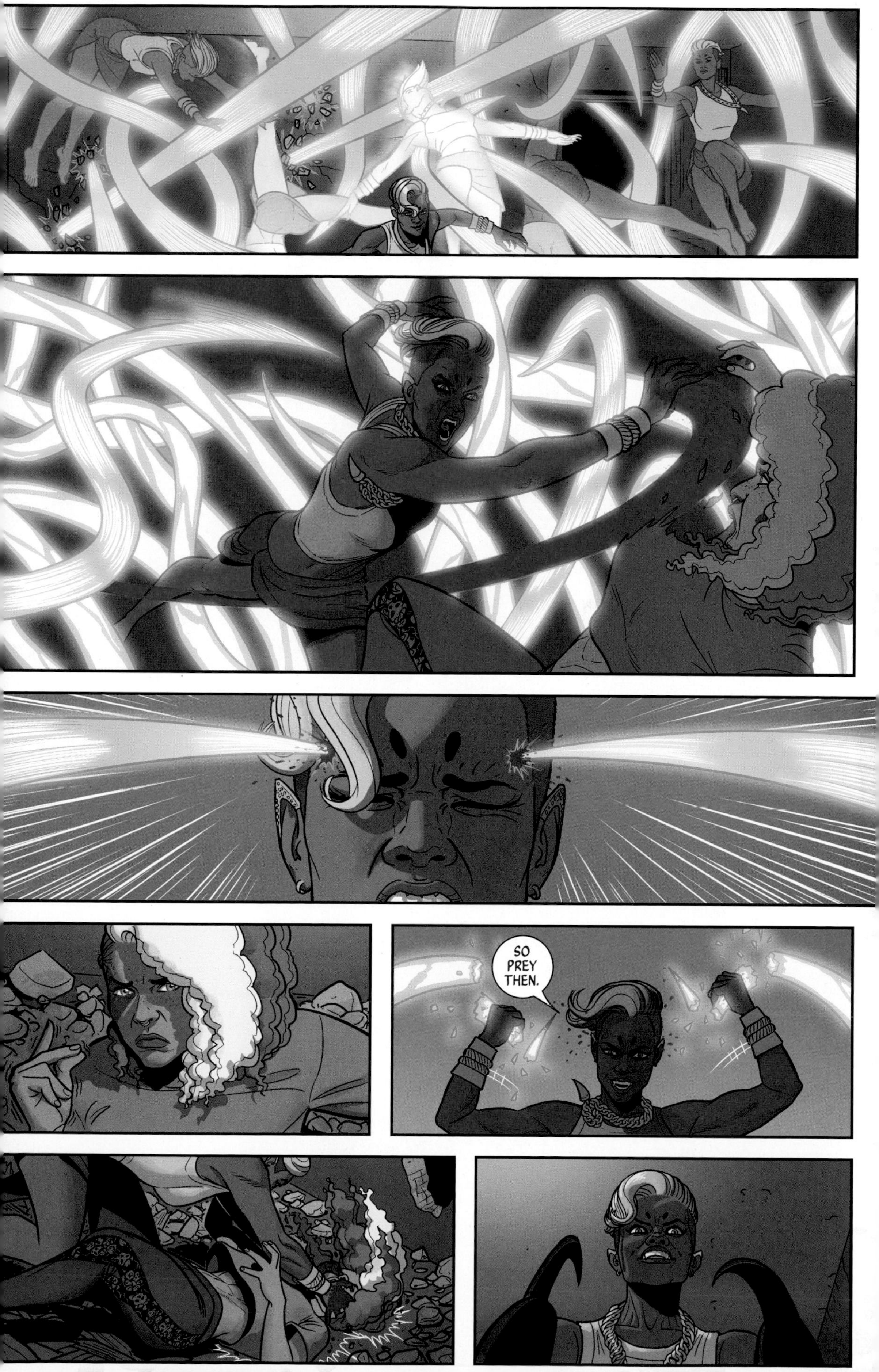
SO PREY THEN.

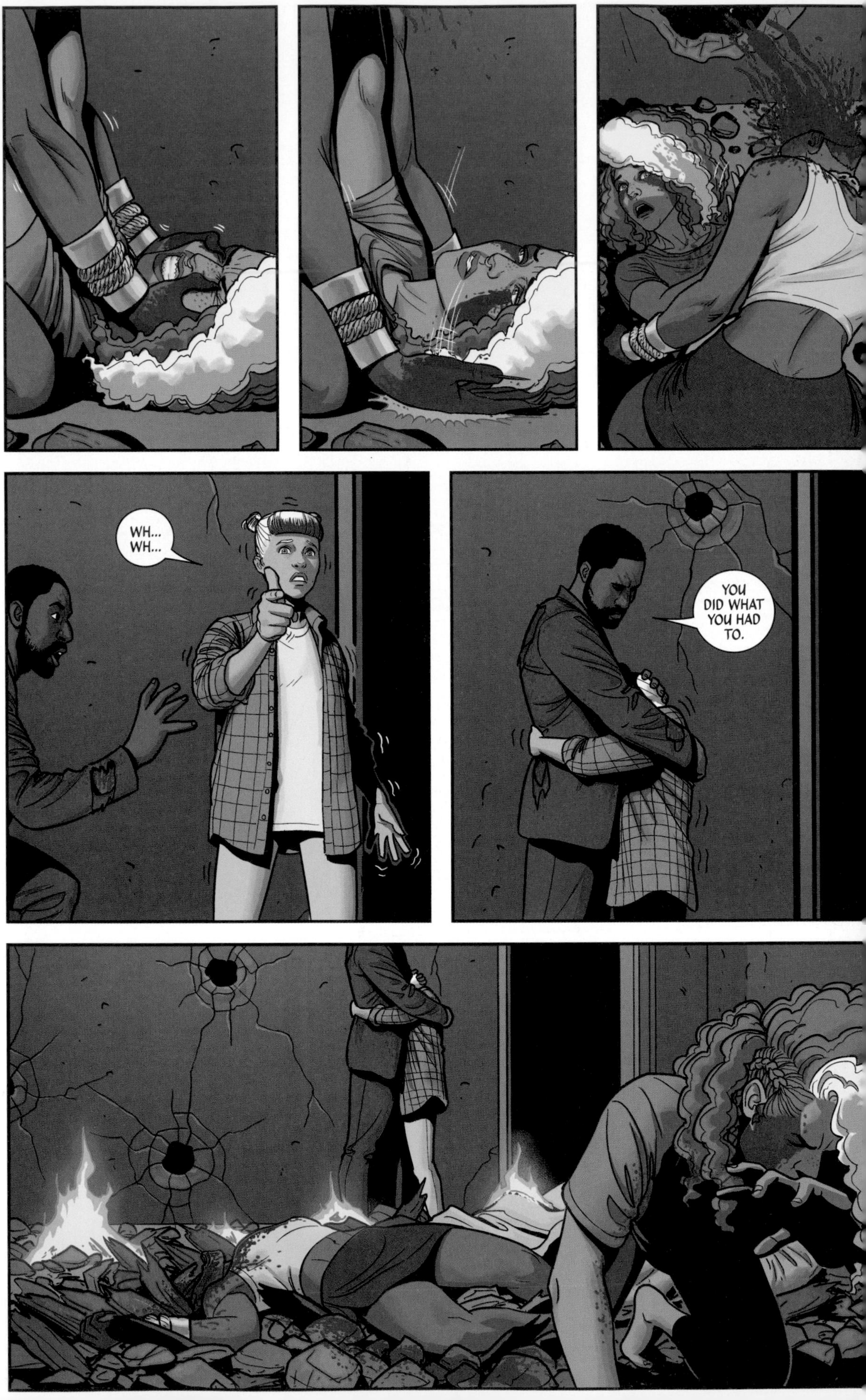
WH... WH...
YOU DID WHAT YOU HAD TO.

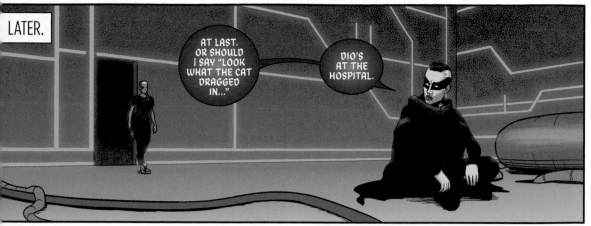

LATER.

AT LAST. OR SHOULD I SAY "LOOK WHAT THE CAT DRAGGED IN..."

DIO'S AT THE HOSPITAL.

HE'S ALIVE?

THEY CAN KEEP HIM BREATHING. BUT HE'S BRAIN DEAD. HE'S GONE.

IF HE HAD GOT TO THE HOSPITAL QUICKER...

ALL FOR FUCK ALL. I DUNNO WHAT WODEN WAS *REALLY* UP TO OR THE MACHINE OR...ANYTHING. I'VE GOT A BUNCH OF DATA, BUT...IT'S TEA LEAVES.

I'M SEEING PATTERNS, BUT THEY'RE THE PATTERNS I *SEE*. I CAN'T BE SURE IF THERE'S ANYTHING REALLY THERE.

POOR DIO.

HE NEVER STOPPED BELIEVING HE COULD HELP PEOPLE.

I DON'T THINK *WE* CAN HELP ANYONE.

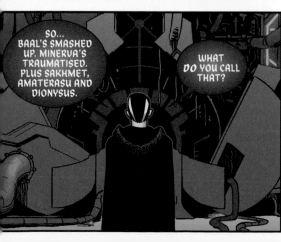

SO... BAAL'S SMASHED UP. MINERVA'S TRAUMATISED. PLUS SAKHMET, AMATERASU AND DIONYSUS.

WHAT *DO* YOU CALL THAT?

A NICE NIGHT'S WORK IF YOU'RE THE DESTROYER, RIGHT?

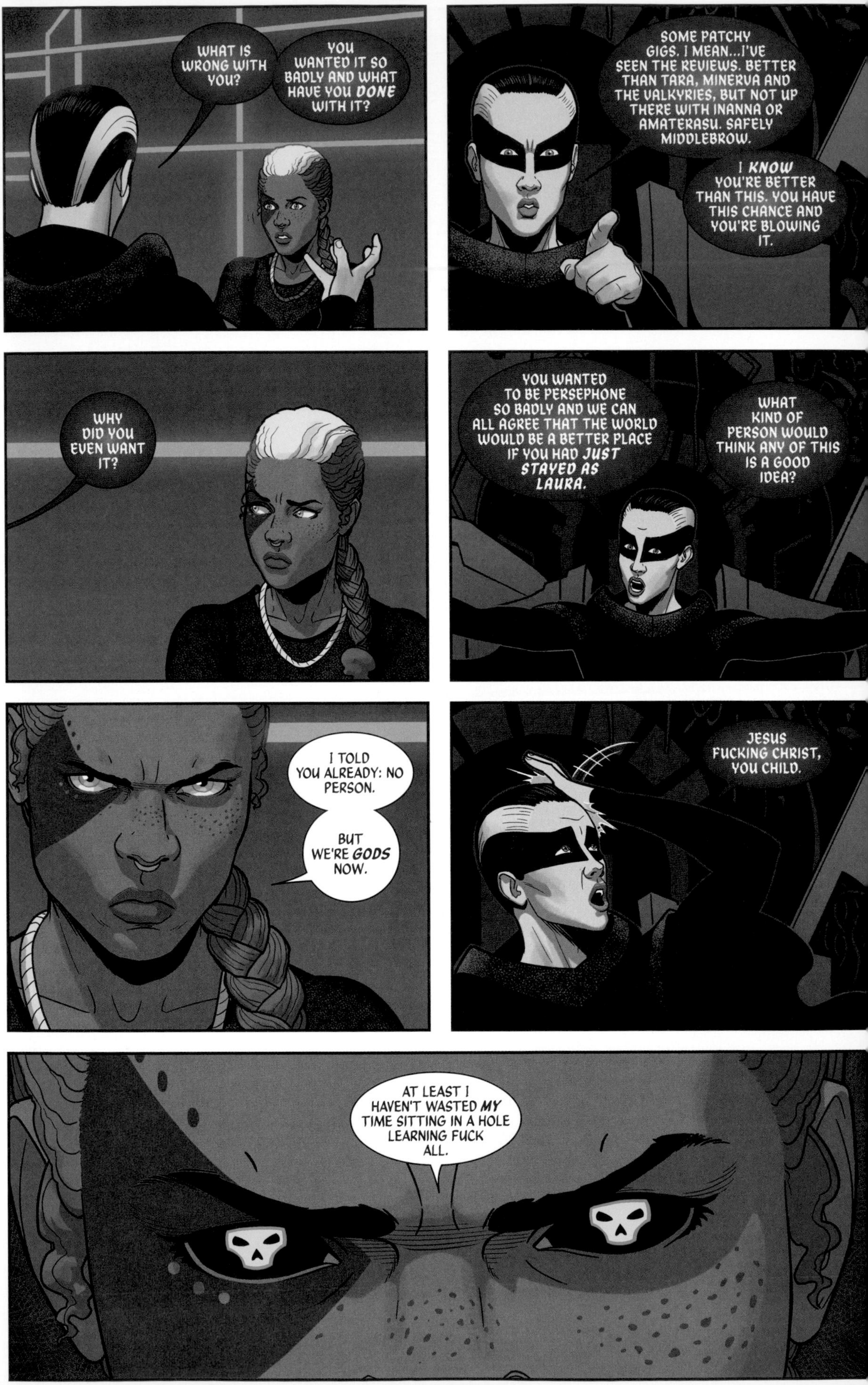
WHAT IS WRONG WITH YOU?
YOU WANTED IT SO BADLY AND WHAT HAVE YOU *DONE* WITH IT?
SOME PATCHY GIGS. I MEAN...I'VE SEEN THE REVIEWS. BETTER THAN TARA, MINERVA AND THE VALKYRIES, BUT NOT UP THERE WITH INANNA OR AMATERASU. SAFELY MIDDLEBROW.
I *KNOW* YOU'RE BETTER THAN THIS. YOU HAVE THIS CHANCE AND YOU'RE BLOWING IT.
WHY DID YOU EVEN WANT IT?
YOU WANTED TO BE PERSEPHONE SO BADLY AND WE CAN ALL AGREE THAT THE WORLD WOULD BE A BETTER PLACE IF YOU HAD *JUST STAYED AS LAURA.*
WHAT KIND OF PERSON WOULD THINK ANY OF THIS IS A GOOD IDEA?
I TOLD YOU ALREADY: NO PERSON.
BUT WE'RE *GODS* NOW.
JESUS FUCKING CHRIST, YOU CHILD.
AT LEAST I HAVEN'T WASTED *MY* TIME SITTING IN A HOLE LEARNING FUCK ALL.

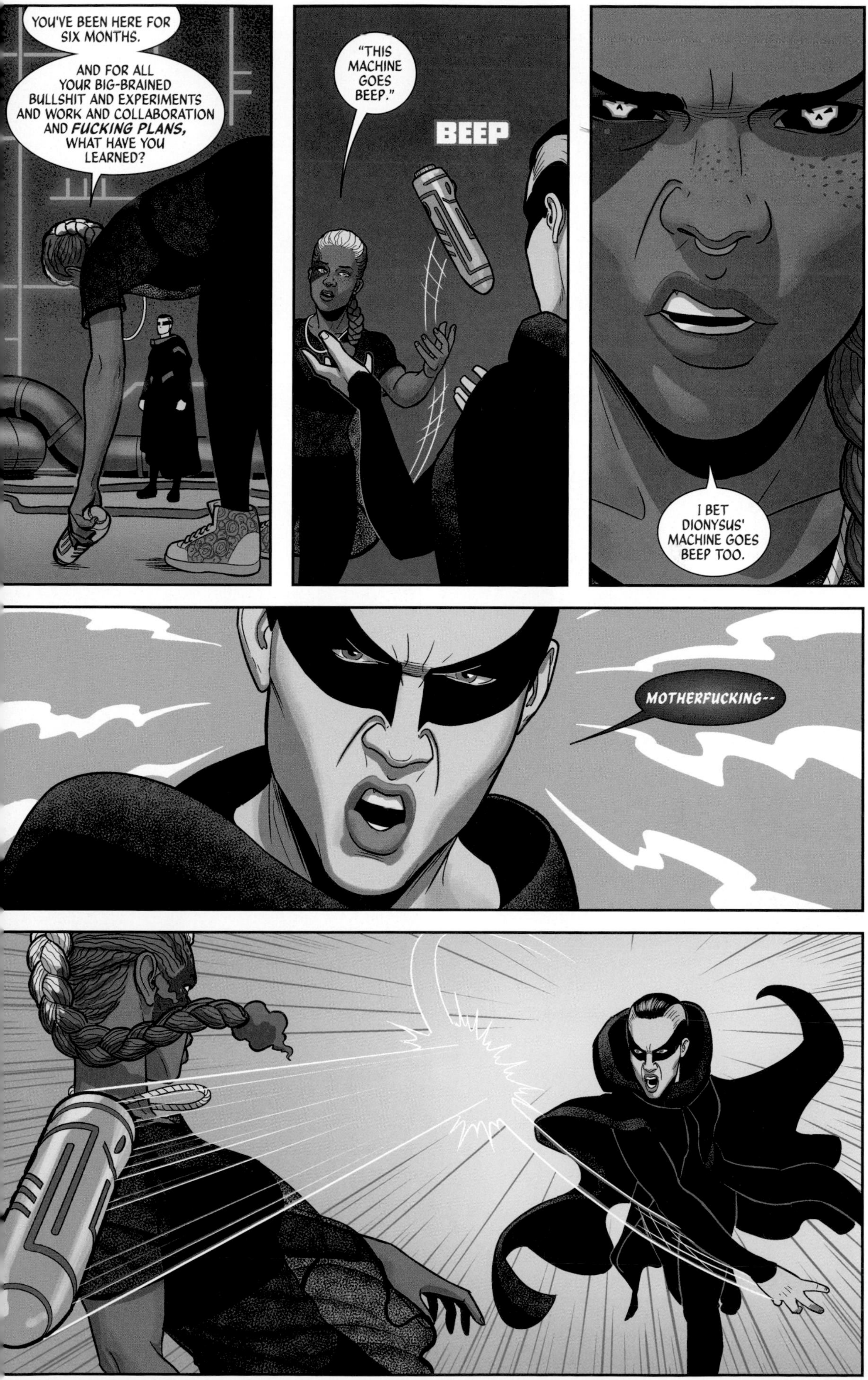
YOU'VE BEEN HERE FOR SIX MONTHS.
AND FOR ALL YOUR BIG-BRAINED BULLSHIT AND EXPERIMENTS AND WORK AND COLLABORATION AND FUCKING PLANS, WHAT HAVE YOU LEARNED?
"THIS MACHINE GOES BEEP."
BEEP
I BET DIONYSUS' MACHINE GOES BEEP TOO.
MOTHERFUCKING--

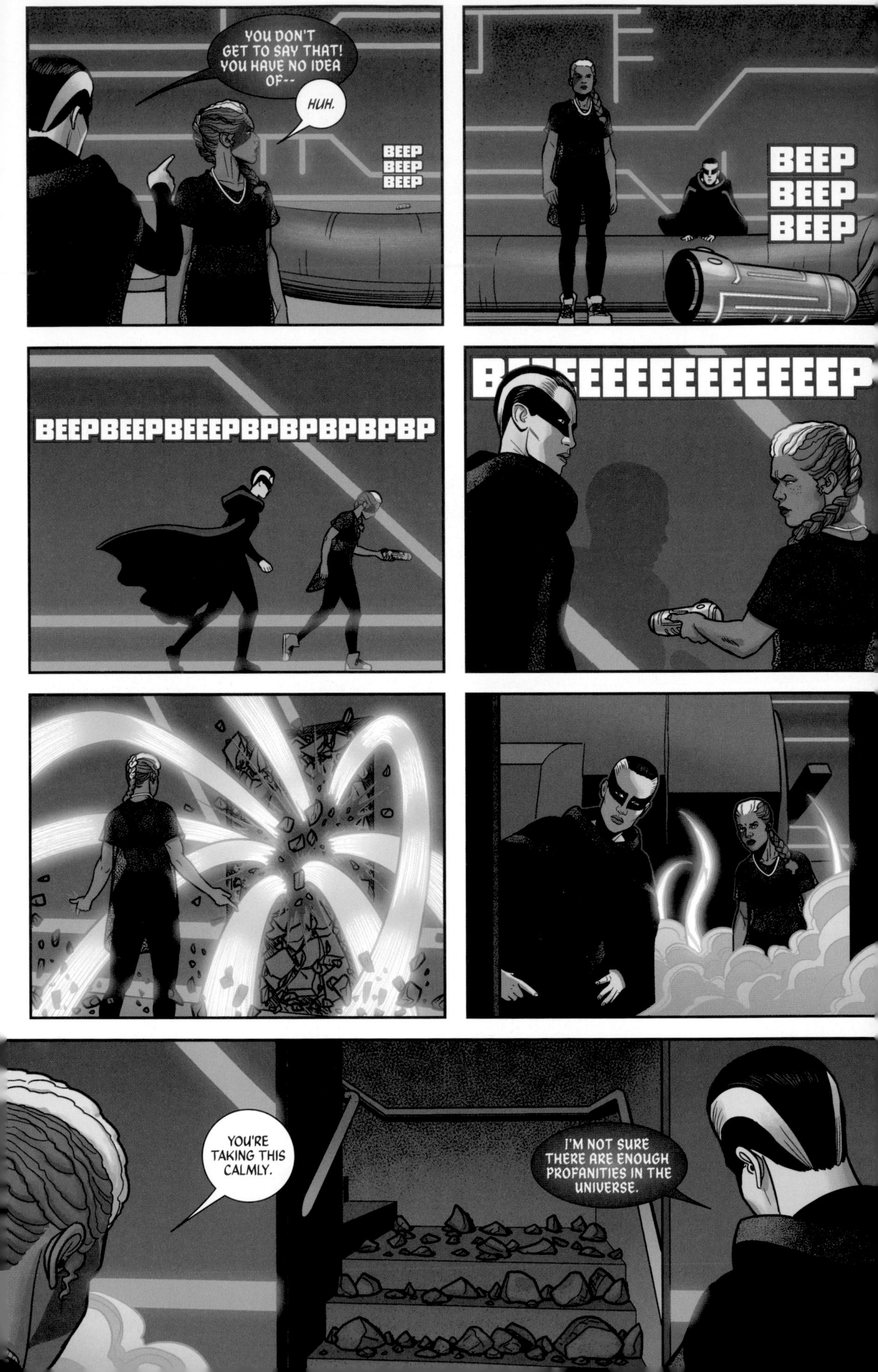
YOU DON'T GET TO SAY THAT! YOU HAVE NO IDEA OF--
HUH.
BEEP BEEP BEEP
BEEP BEEP BEEP
BEEPBEEPBEEEPBPBPBPBPBP
BEEEEEEEEEEEEEP
YOU'RE TAKING THIS CALMLY.
I'M NOT SURE THERE ARE ENOUGH PROFANITIES IN THE UNIVERSE.

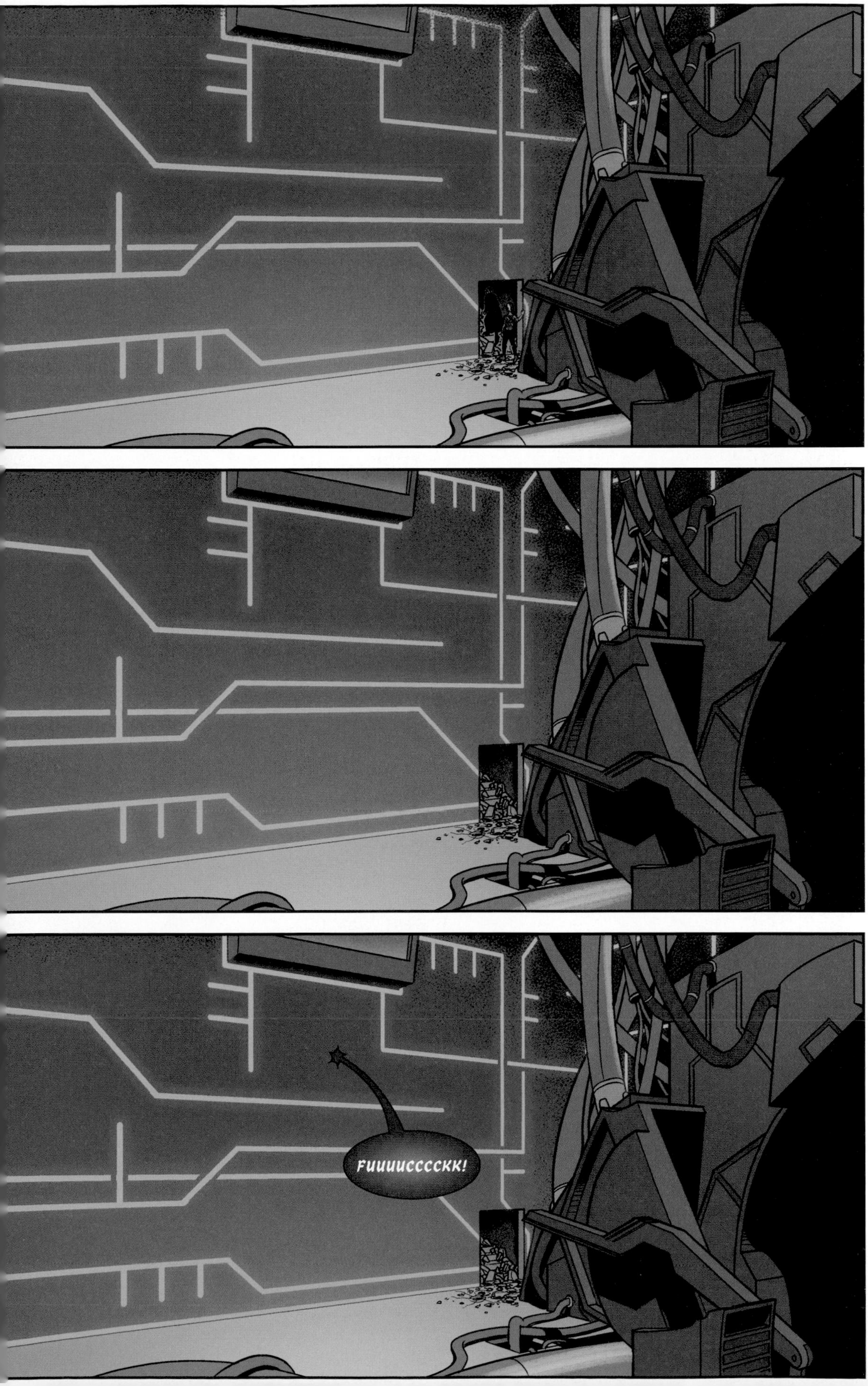
FUUUUCCCCCKK!

THE BEEP TEST

9 MARCH 2015

THE
WICKED
+
THE DIVINE

33

THE
WICKED
+
THE DIVINE

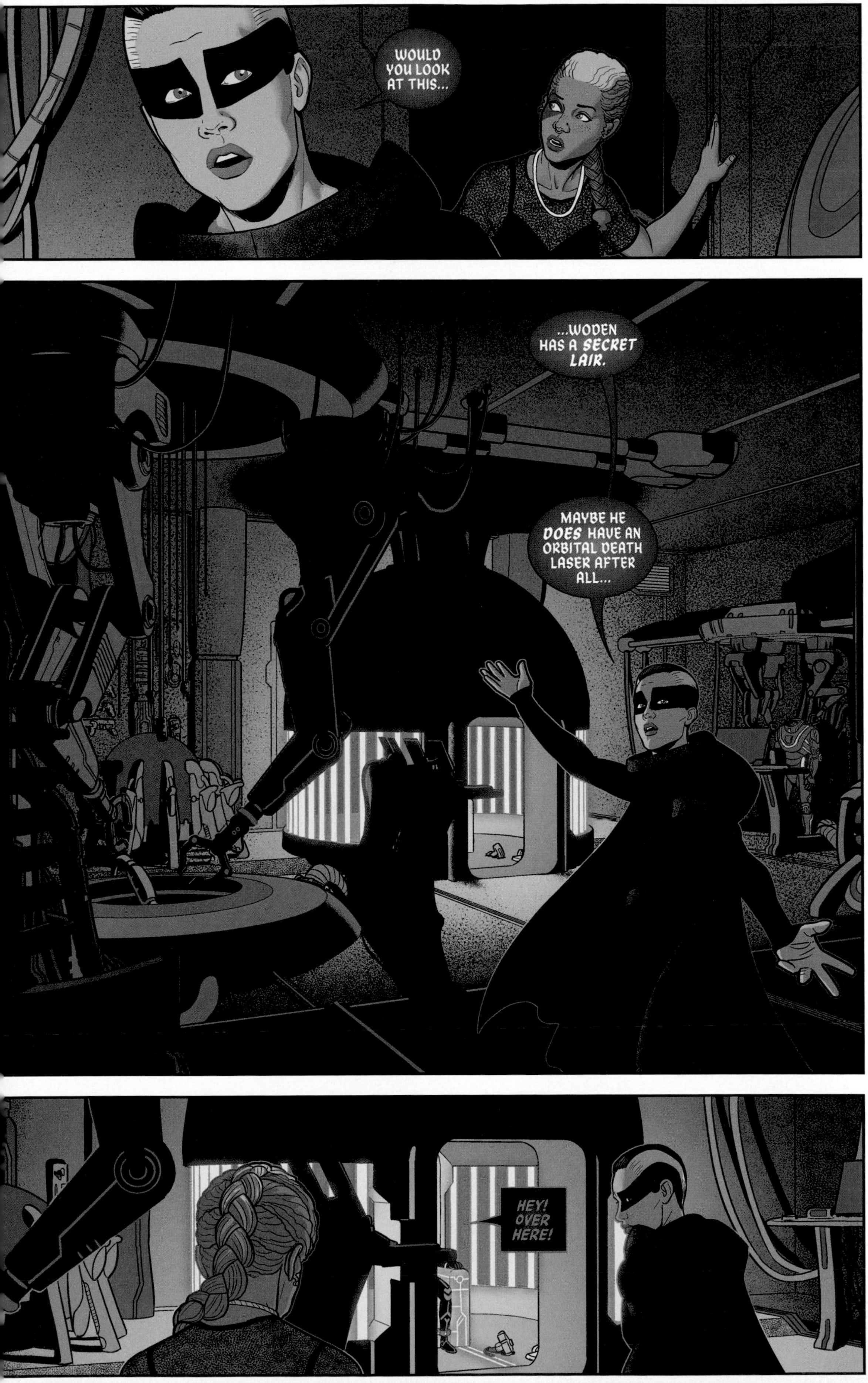
WOULD YOU LOOK AT THIS...
...WODEN HAS A SECRET LAIR.
MAYBE HE DOES HAVE AN ORBITAL DEATH LASER AFTER ALL...
HEY! OVER HERE!

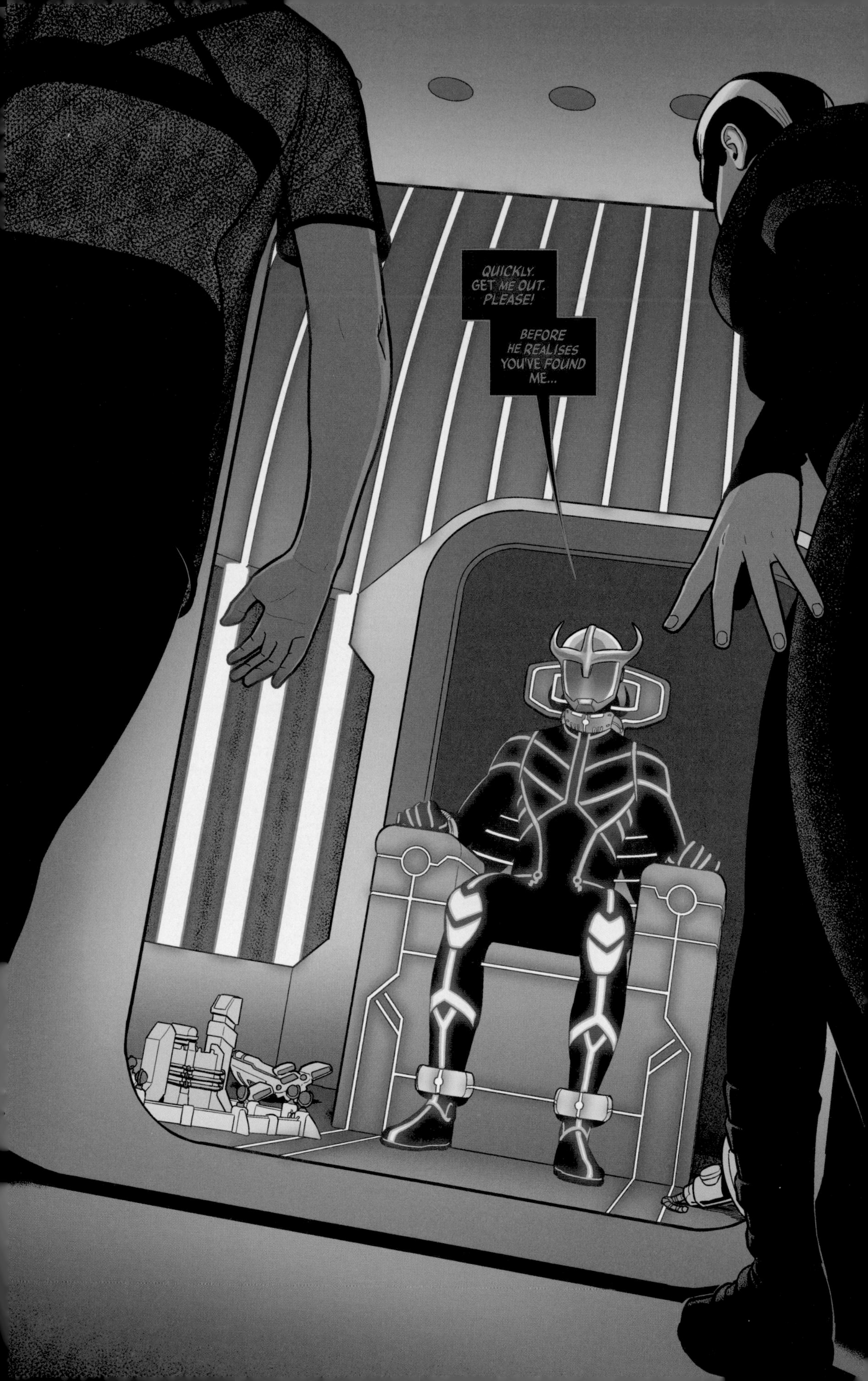
QUICKLY. GET ME OUT. PLEASE!
BEFORE HE REALISES YOU'VE FOUND ME...

FUCK! YOU KNOW, THE ONLY REAL SURPRISE IS THAT THE PRISONER WODEN HAS IN HIS DUNGEON IS A *BOY*.

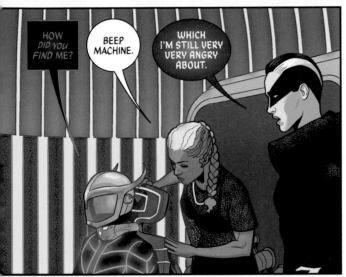

HOW DID YOU FIND ME?

BEEP MACHINE.

WHICH I'M STILL VERY VERY ANGRY ABOUT.

I WAS WORKING TO THEIR PLANS. GETTING SOMETHING OF MY OWN IN THERE WHICH THEY'D MISS WAS NEARLY IMPOSSIBLE.

IT WAS THE BEST I COULD DO. IT...WAS A SMALL HOPE.

HOPE WAS ALL I HAD.

BACK OFF. I'LL TEAR HIM FREE...

WHO THE HELL ARE YOU, ANYWAY?

SURELY YOU'VE WORKED THIS OUT, MISS IGARASHI?

I THOUGHT YOU WERE CLEVER.

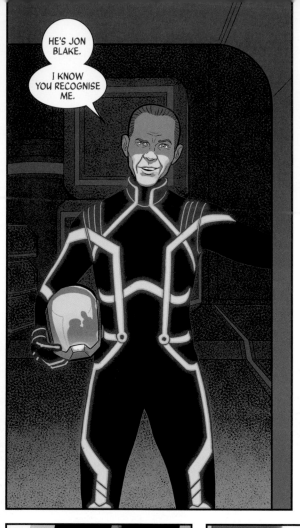

HE'S JON BLAKE.

I KNOW YOU RECOGNISE ME.

NOT AFTER I'VE TORN YOUR FACE OFF.

CLK

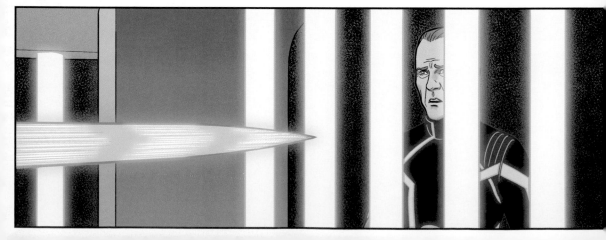

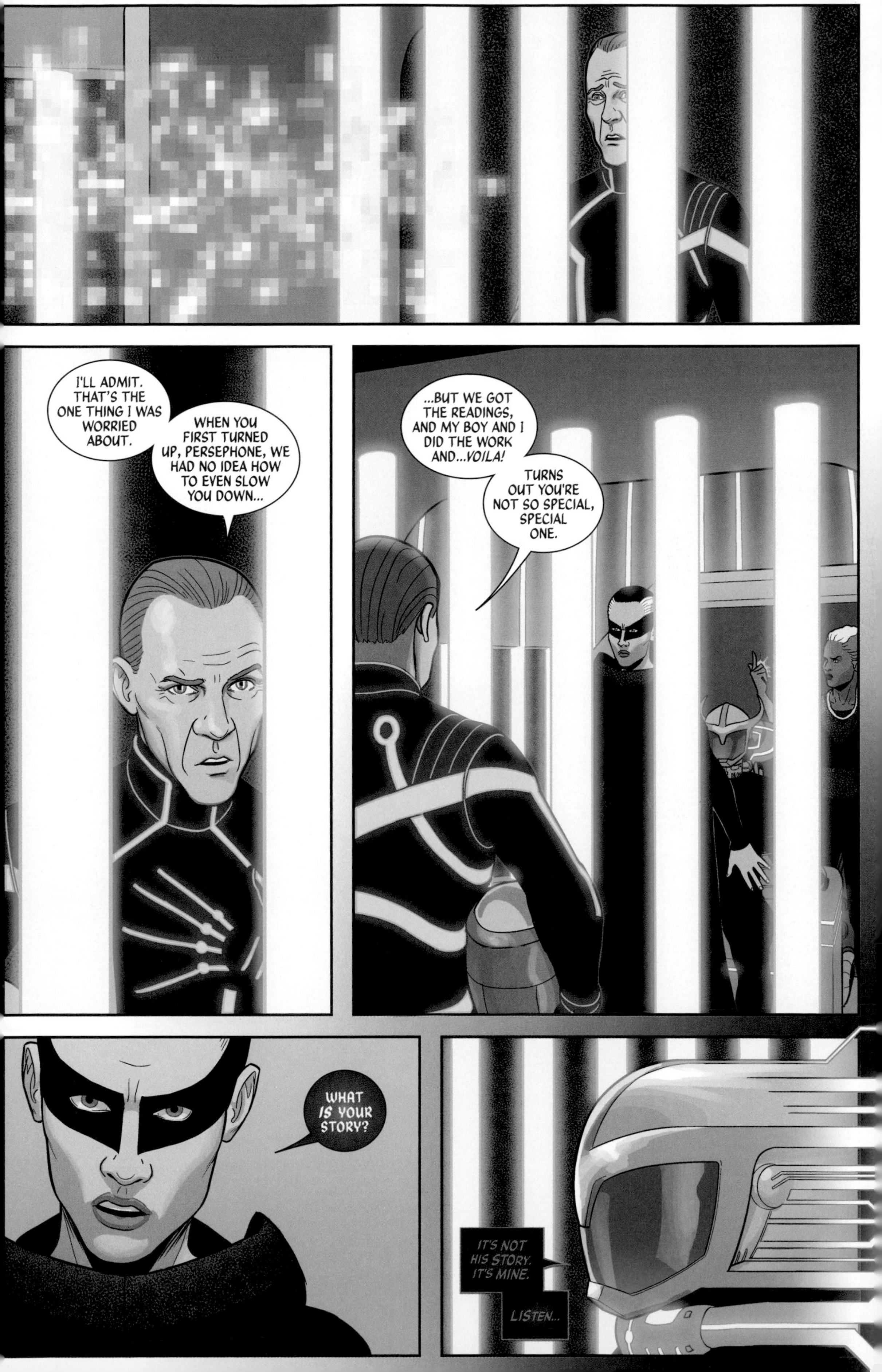
I'LL ADMIT. THAT'S THE ONE THING I WAS WORRIED ABOUT.
WHEN YOU FIRST TURNED UP, PERSEPHONE, WE HAD NO IDEA HOW TO EVEN SLOW YOU DOWN...
...BUT WE GOT THE READINGS, AND MY BOY AND I DID THE WORK AND...VOILA!
TURNS OUT YOU'RE NOT SO SPECIAL, SPECIAL ONE.
WHAT IS YOUR STORY?
IT'S NOT HIS STORY. IT'S MINE.
LISTEN...

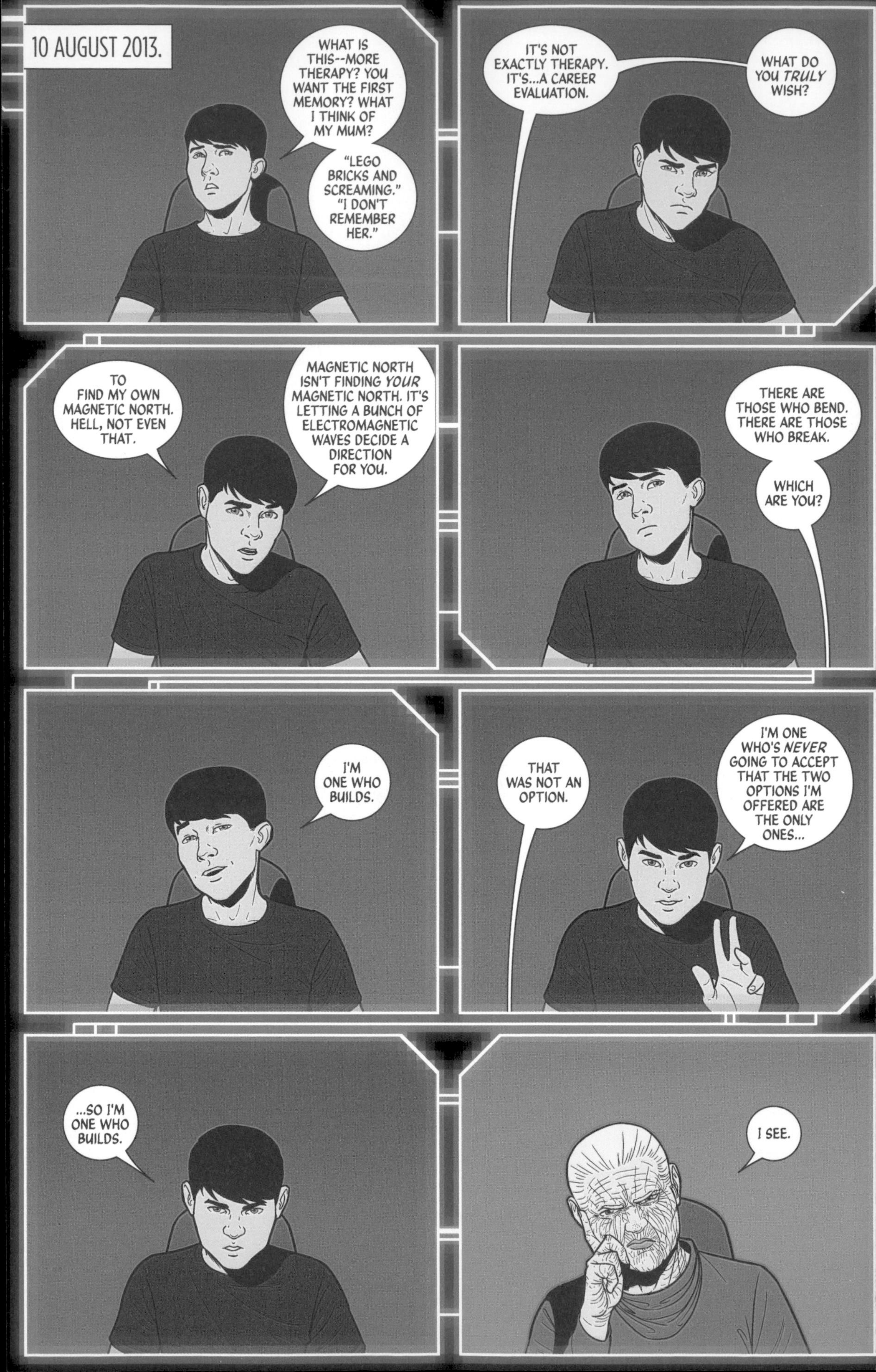
10 AUGUST 2013.
WHAT IS THIS--MORE THERAPY? YOU WANT THE FIRST MEMORY? WHAT I THINK OF MY MUM?
"LEGO BRICKS AND SCREAMING." "I DON'T REMEMBER HER."
IT'S NOT EXACTLY THERAPY. IT'S...A CAREER EVALUATION.
WHAT DO YOU *TRULY* WISH?
TO FIND MY OWN MAGNETIC NORTH. HELL, NOT EVEN THAT.
MAGNETIC NORTH ISN'T FINDING *YOUR* MAGNETIC NORTH. IT'S LETTING A BUNCH OF ELECTROMAGNETIC WAVES DECIDE A DIRECTION FOR YOU.
THERE ARE THOSE WHO BEND. THERE ARE THOSE WHO BREAK.
WHICH ARE YOU?
I'M ONE WHO BUILDS.
THAT WAS NOT AN OPTION.
I'M ONE WHO'S *NEVER* GOING TO ACCEPT THAT THE TWO OPTIONS I'M OFFERED ARE THE ONLY ONES...
...SO I'M ONE WHO BUILDS.
I SEE.

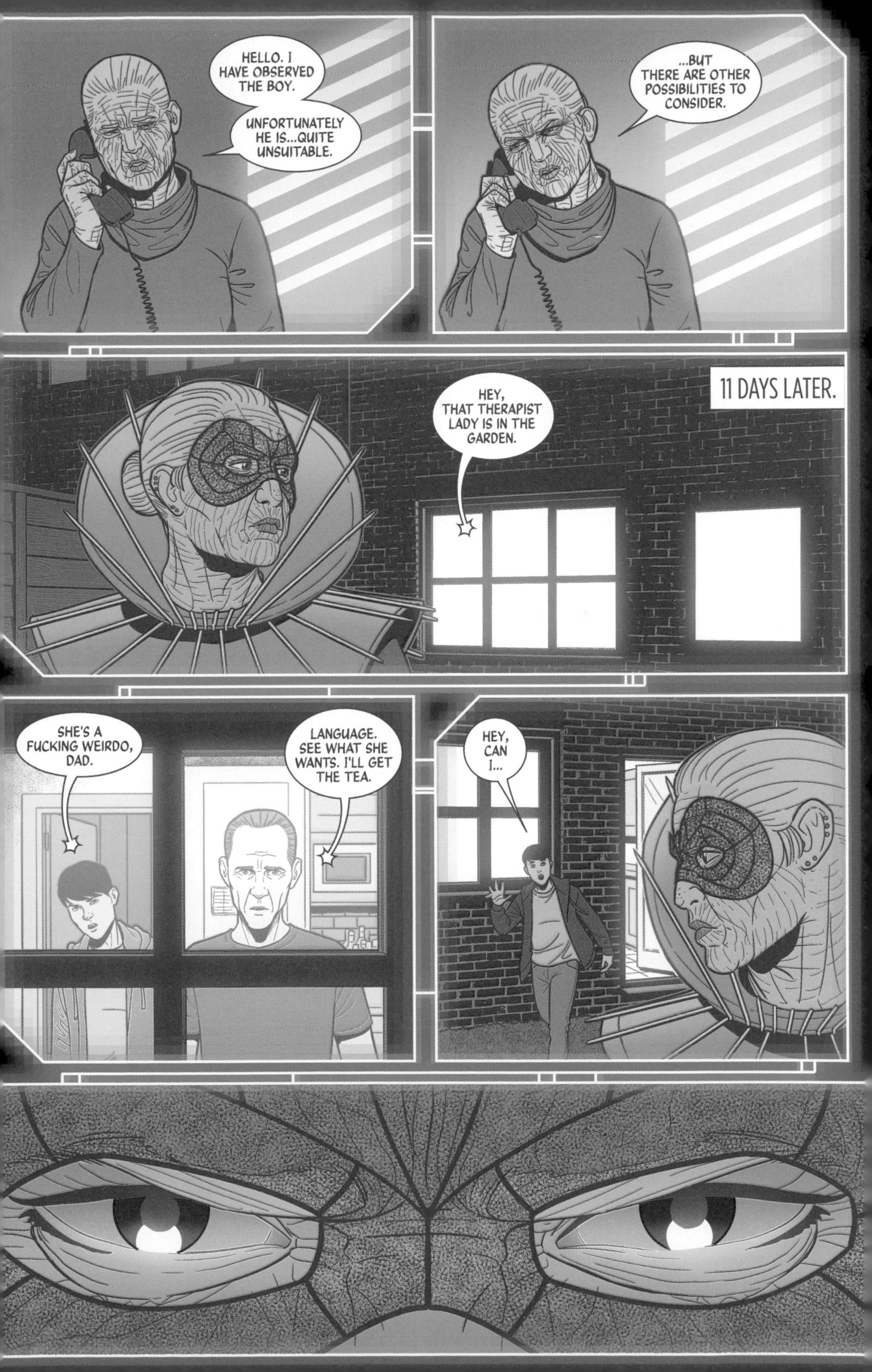
HELLO. I HAVE OBSERVED THE BOY.
UNFORTUNATELY HE IS...QUITE UNSUITABLE.
...BUT THERE ARE OTHER POSSIBILITIES TO CONSIDER.
11 DAYS LATER.
HEY, THAT THERAPIST LADY IS IN THE GARDEN.
SHE'S A FUCKING WEIRDO, DAD.
LANGUAGE. SEE WHAT SHE WANTS. I'LL GET THE TEA.
HEY, CAN I...

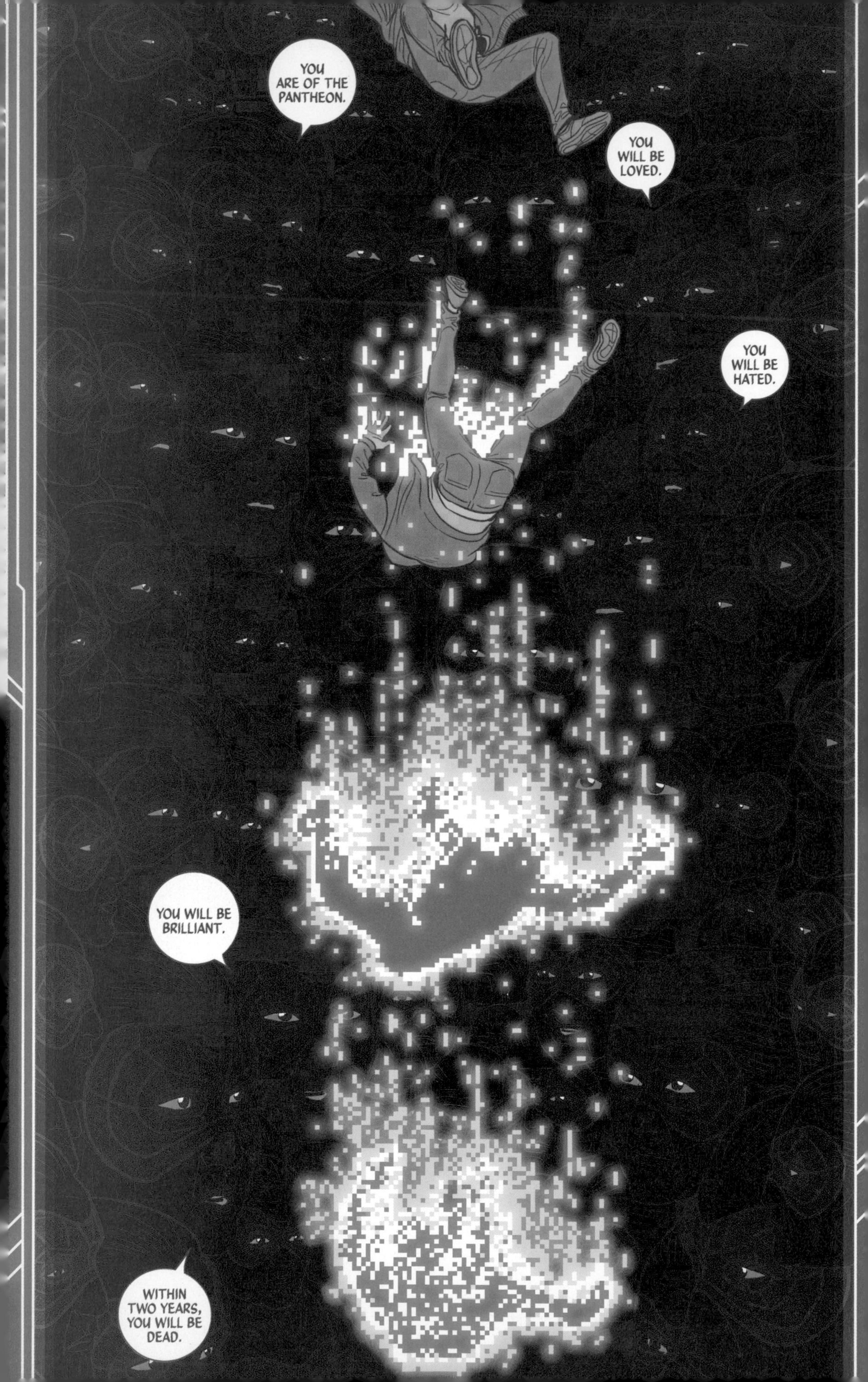
YOU ARE OF THE PANTHEON.
YOU WILL BE LOVED.
YOU WILL BE HATED.
YOU WILL BE BRILLIANT.
WITHIN TWO YEARS, YOU WILL BE DEAD.

YOU WALKED AMONG YOUR FOES FOR THE SAKE OF LOVE.
STRUCK DOWN YOU ARE RAISED UP, THE SKY KING'S GRANDEST TREASURE.
THE WELL OF YOUR SOUL.
YOUR MIND.
YOUR HEAD.

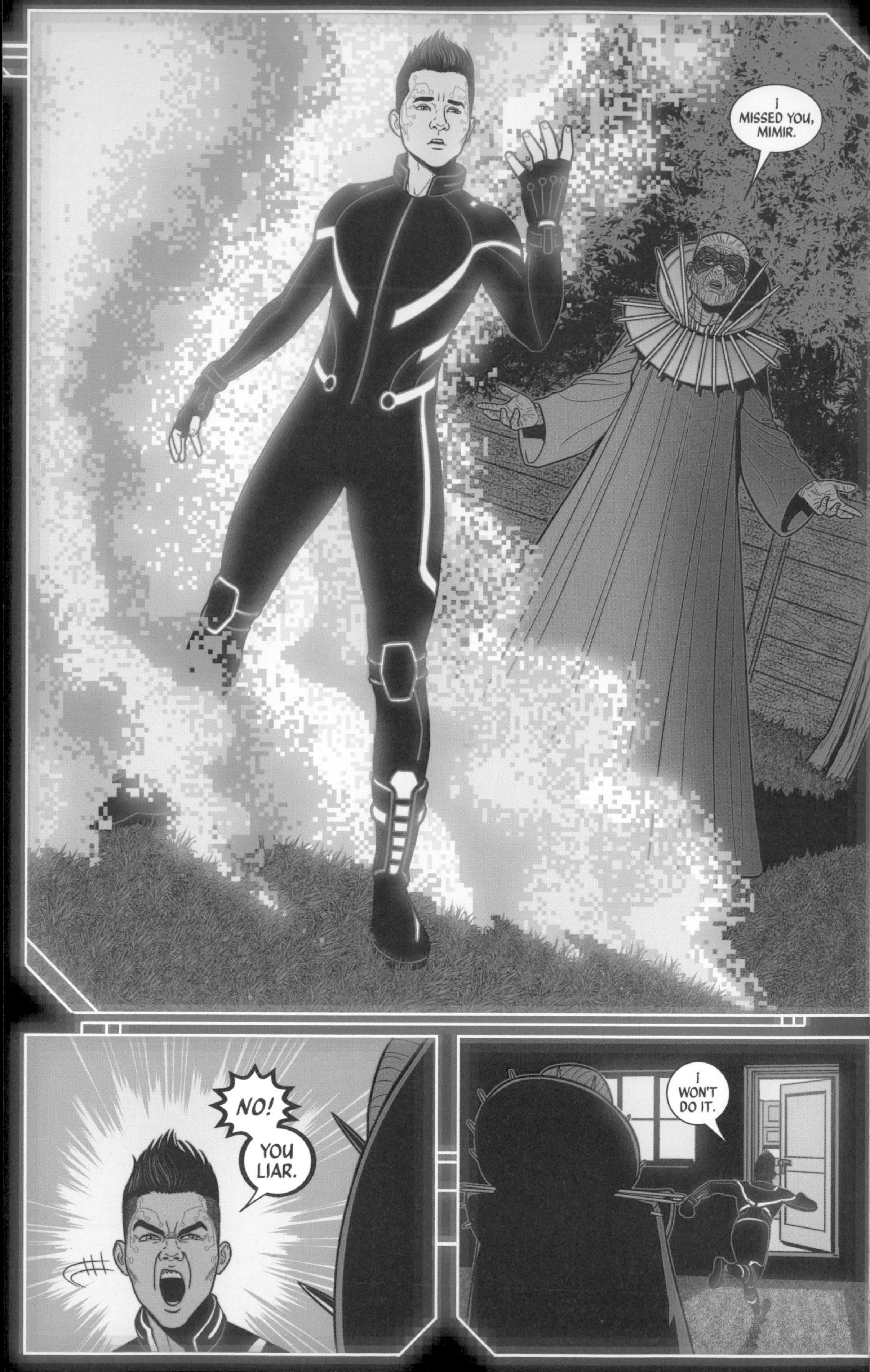
I MISSED YOU, MIMIR.
NO!
YOU LIAR.
I WON'T DO IT.

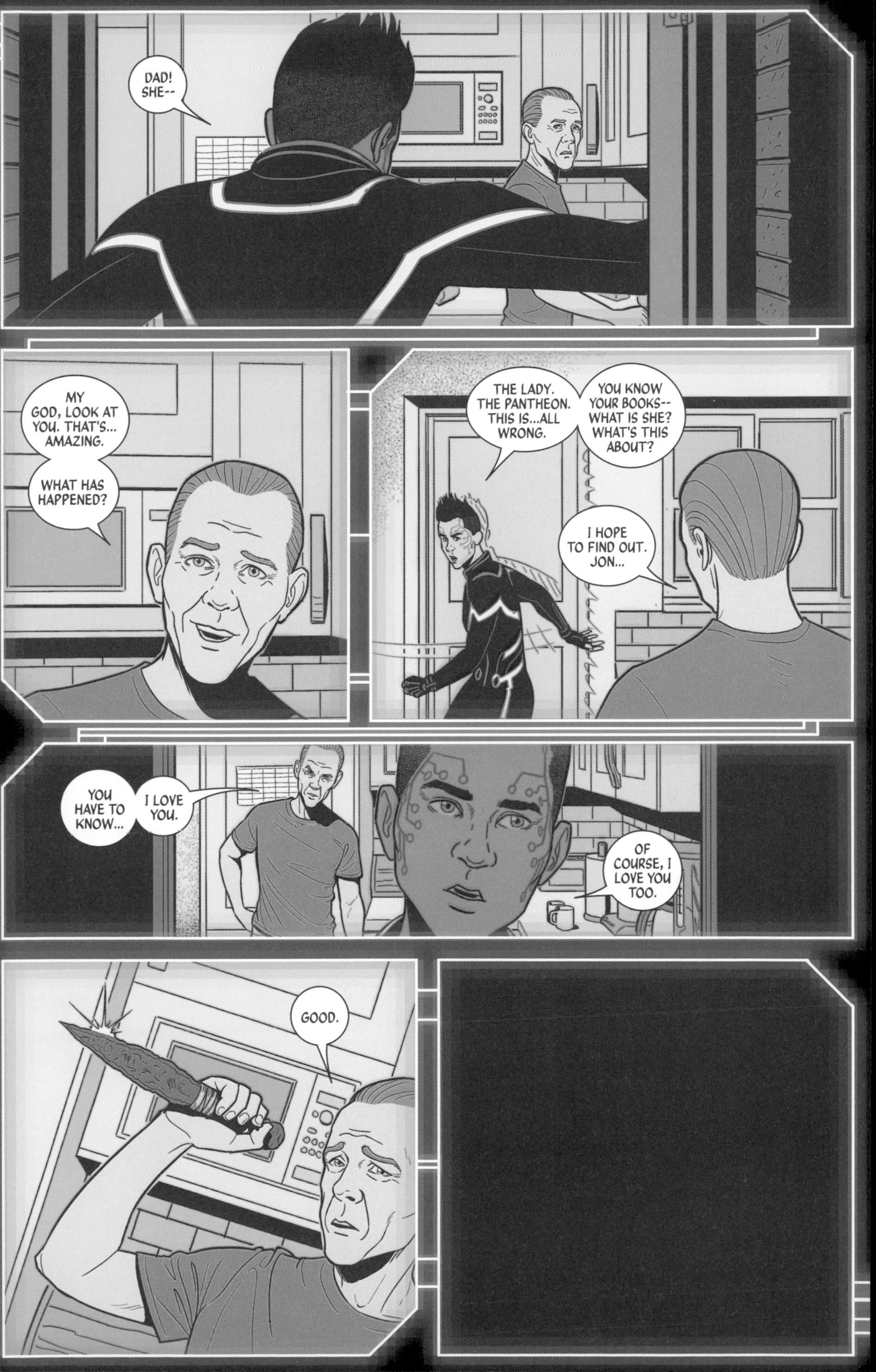
DAD! SHE--
MY GOD, LOOK AT YOU. THAT'S... AMAZING.
WHAT HAS HAPPENED?
THE LADY. THE PANTHEON. THIS IS...ALL WRONG.
YOU KNOW YOUR BOOKS-- WHAT IS SHE? WHAT'S THIS ABOUT?
I HOPE TO FIND OUT. JON...
YOU HAVE TO KNOW...
I LOVE YOU.
OF COURSE, I LOVE YOU TOO.
GOOD.

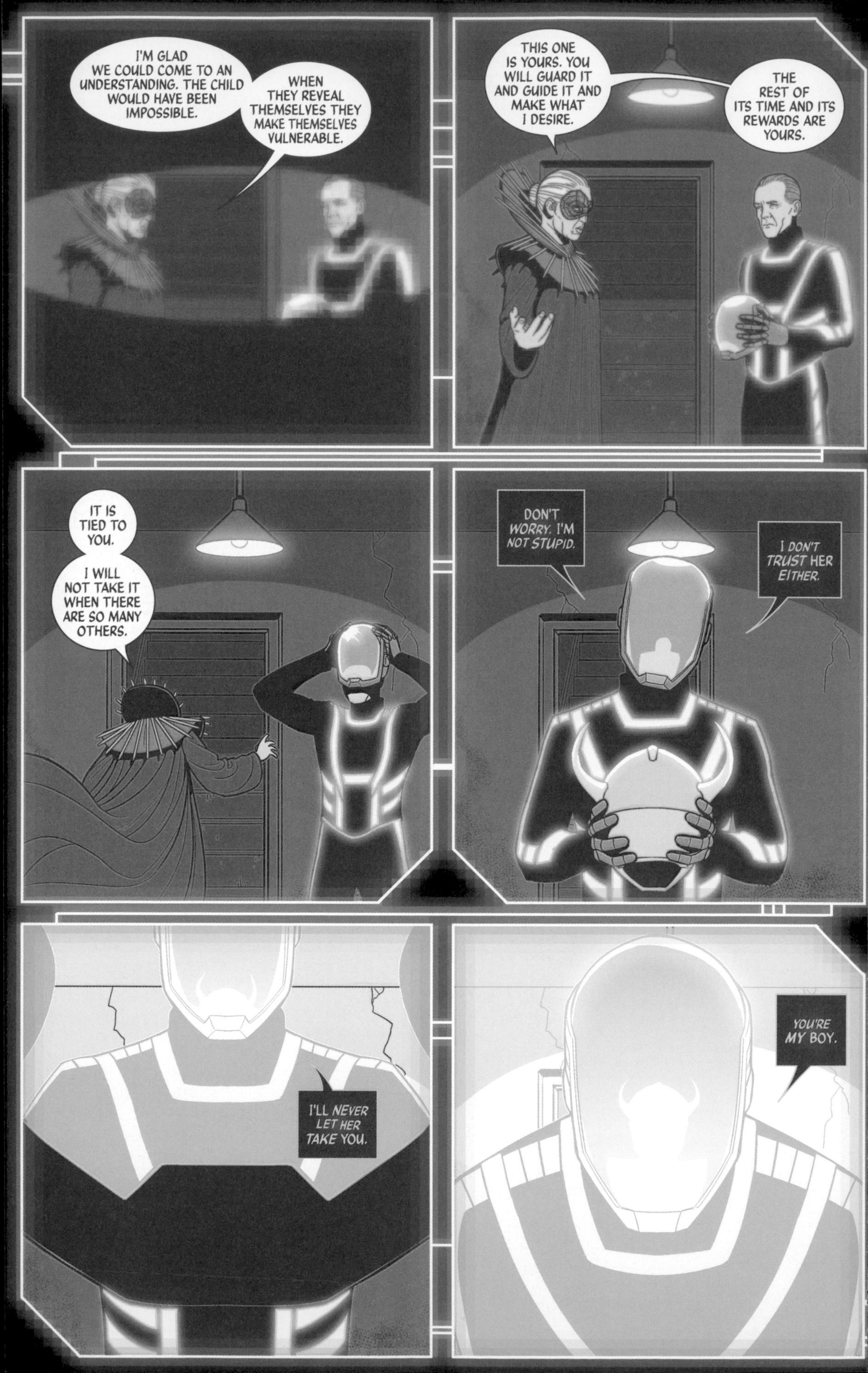
I'M GLAD WE COULD COME TO AN UNDERSTANDING. THE CHILD WOULD HAVE BEEN IMPOSSIBLE.
WHEN THEY REVEAL THEMSELVES THEY MAKE THEMSELVES VULNERABLE.
THIS ONE IS YOURS. YOU WILL GUARD IT AND GUIDE IT AND MAKE WHAT I DESIRE.
THE REST OF ITS TIME AND ITS REWARDS ARE YOURS.
IT IS TIED TO YOU.
I WILL NOT TAKE IT WHEN THERE ARE SO MANY OTHERS.
DON'T WORRY. I'M NOT STUPID.
I DON'T TRUST HER EITHER.
I'LL NEVER LET HER TAKE YOU.
YOU'RE MY BOY.

A LITTLE
WODEN BOY

21 AUGUST 2013

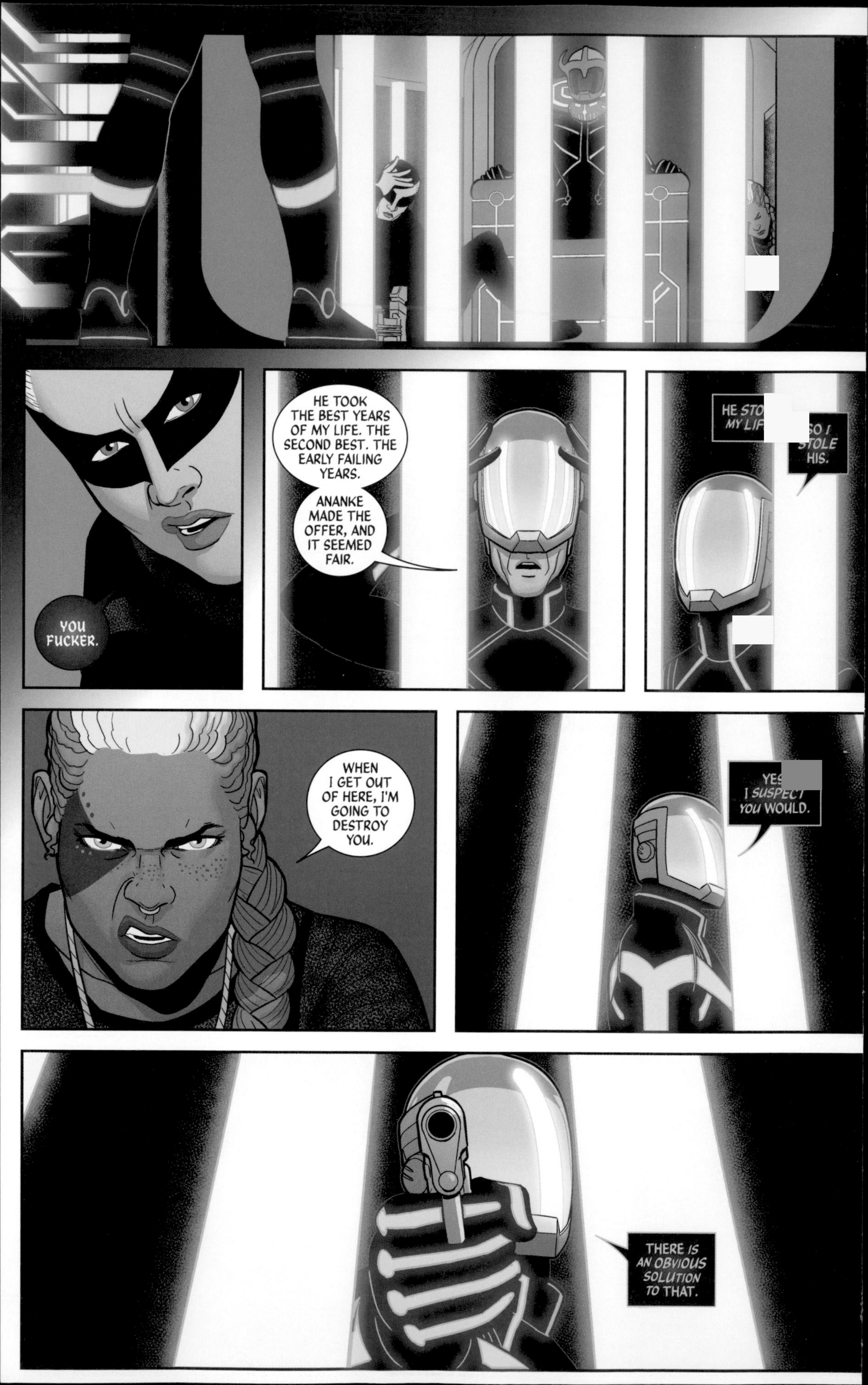
YOU FUCKER.
HE TOOK THE BEST YEARS OF MY LIFE. THE SECOND BEST. THE EARLY FAILING YEARS.
ANANKE MADE THE OFFER, AND IT SEEMED FAIR.
HE STO MY LIF
SO I STOLE HIS.
WHEN I GET OUT OF HERE, I'M GOING TO DESTROY YOU.
YES I SUSPECT YOU WOULD.
THERE IS AN OBVIOUS SOLUTION TO THAT.

I KNOW I NEED CASSANDRA.

I'M PRETTY SURE YOU'RE SURPLUS TO REQUIREMENTS.

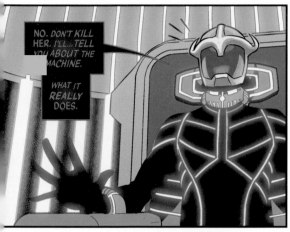

NO. DON'T KILL HER. I'LL...TELL YOU ABOUT THE MACHINE.

WHAT IT REALLY DOES.

ANANKE GAVE YOU EXACT SPECIFICATIONS. YOU WERE JUST FOLLOWING ORDERS.

YOU HAD NO IDEA.

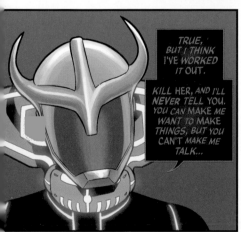

TRUE, BUT I THINK I'VE WORKED IT OUT.

KILL HER, AND I'LL NEVER TELL YOU. YOU CAN MAKE ME WANT TO MAKE THINGS, BUT YOU CAN'T MAKE ME TALK...

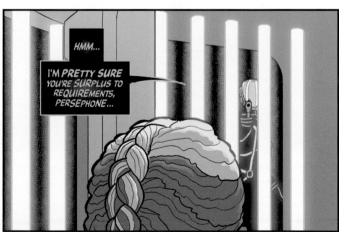

HMM...

I'M PRETTY SURE YOU'RE SURPLUS TO REQUIREMENTS, PERSEPHONE...

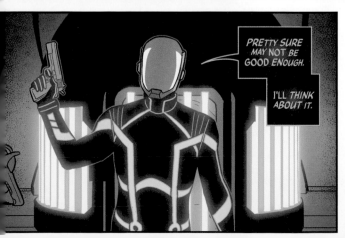

PRETTY SURE MAY NOT BE GOOD ENOUGH.

I'LL THINK ABOUT IT.

YOU SHOULD HAVE LET HIM SHOOT.

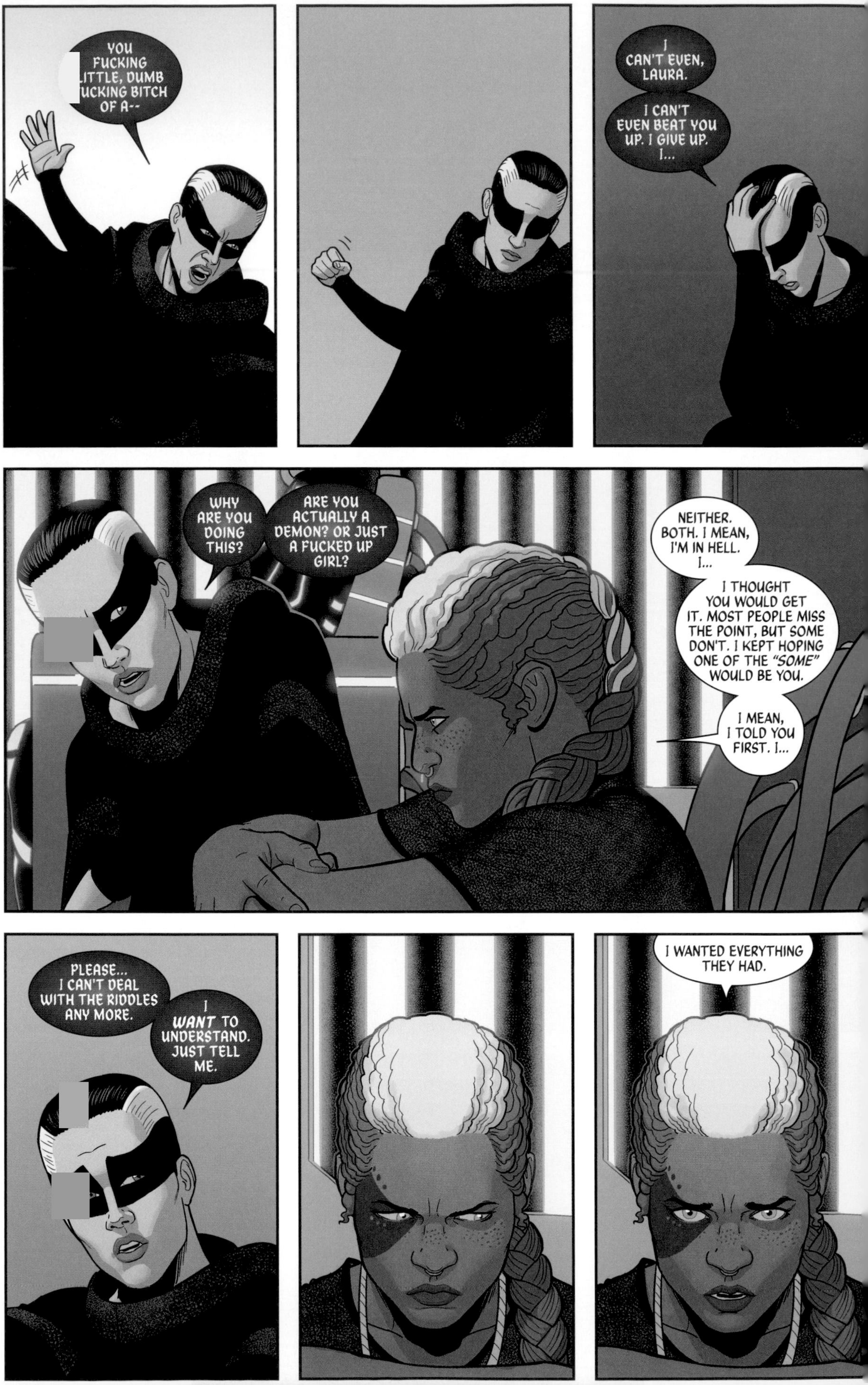
YOU FUCKING ITTLE, DUMB UCKING BITCH OF A--
I CAN'T EVEN, LAURA.
I CAN'T EVEN BEAT YOU UP. I GIVE UP. I...
WHY ARE YOU DOING THIS?
ARE YOU ACTUALLY A DEMON? OR JUST A FUCKED UP GIRL?
NEITHER. BOTH. I MEAN, I'M IN HELL. I...
I THOUGHT YOU WOULD GET IT. MOST PEOPLE MISS THE POINT, BUT SOME DON'T. I KEPT HOPING ONE OF THE *"SOME"* WOULD BE YOU.
I MEAN, I TOLD YOU FIRST. I...
PLEASE... I CAN'T DEAL WITH THE RIDDLES ANY MORE.
I *WANT* TO UNDERSTAND. JUST TELL ME.
I WANTED EVERYTHING THEY HAD.

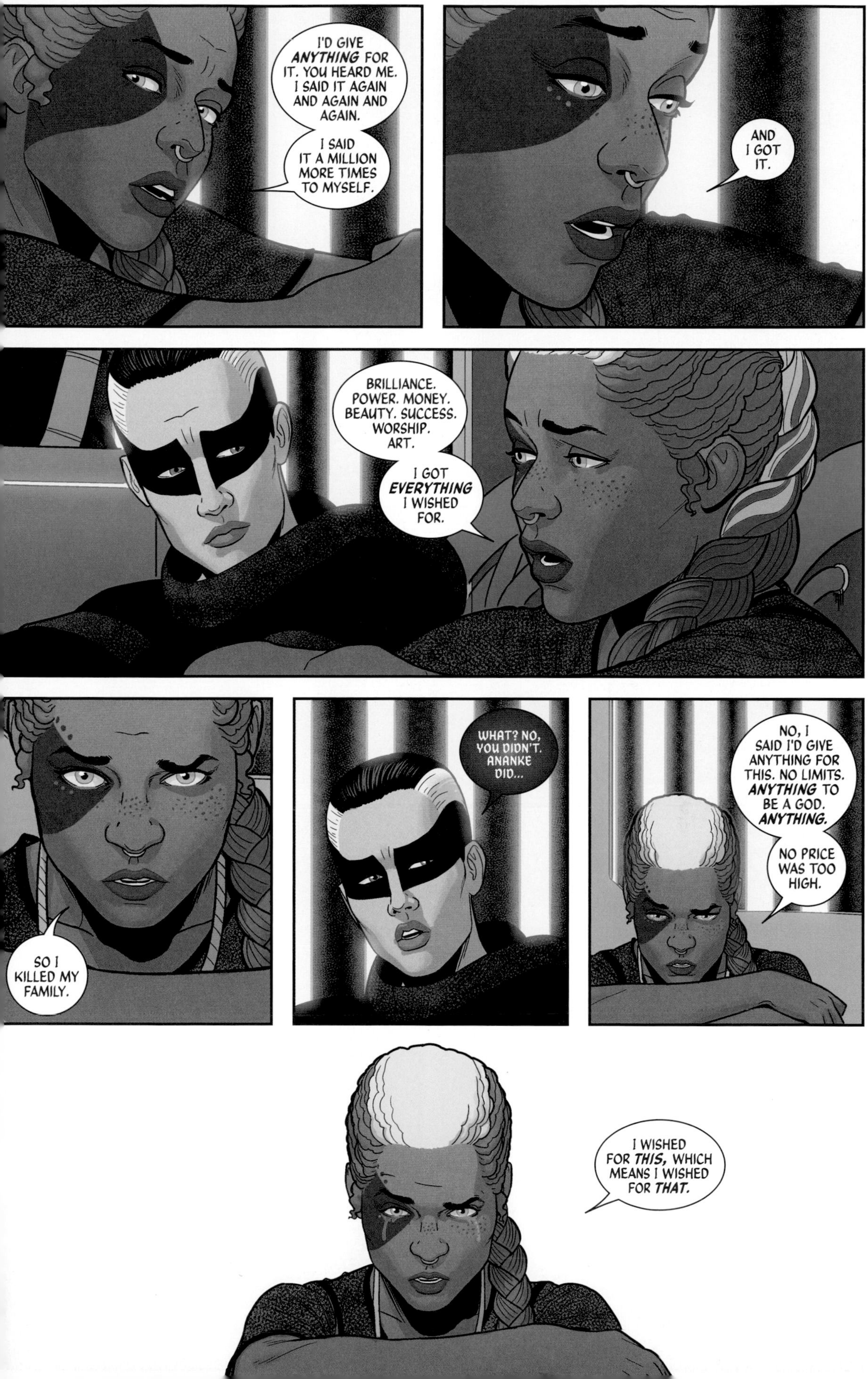
I'D GIVE ANYTHING FOR IT. YOU HEARD ME. I SAID IT AGAIN AND AGAIN AND AGAIN.
I SAID IT A MILLION MORE TIMES TO MYSELF.
AND I GOT IT.
BRILLIANCE. POWER. MONEY. BEAUTY. SUCCESS. WORSHIP. ART.
I GOT EVERYTHING I WISHED FOR.
SO I KILLED MY FAMILY.
WHAT? NO, YOU DIDN'T. ANANKE DID...
NO, I SAID I'D GIVE ANYTHING FOR THIS. NO LIMITS. ANYTHING TO BE A GOD. ANYTHING.
NO PRICE WAS TOO HIGH.
I WISHED FOR THIS, WHICH MEANS I WISHED FOR THAT.

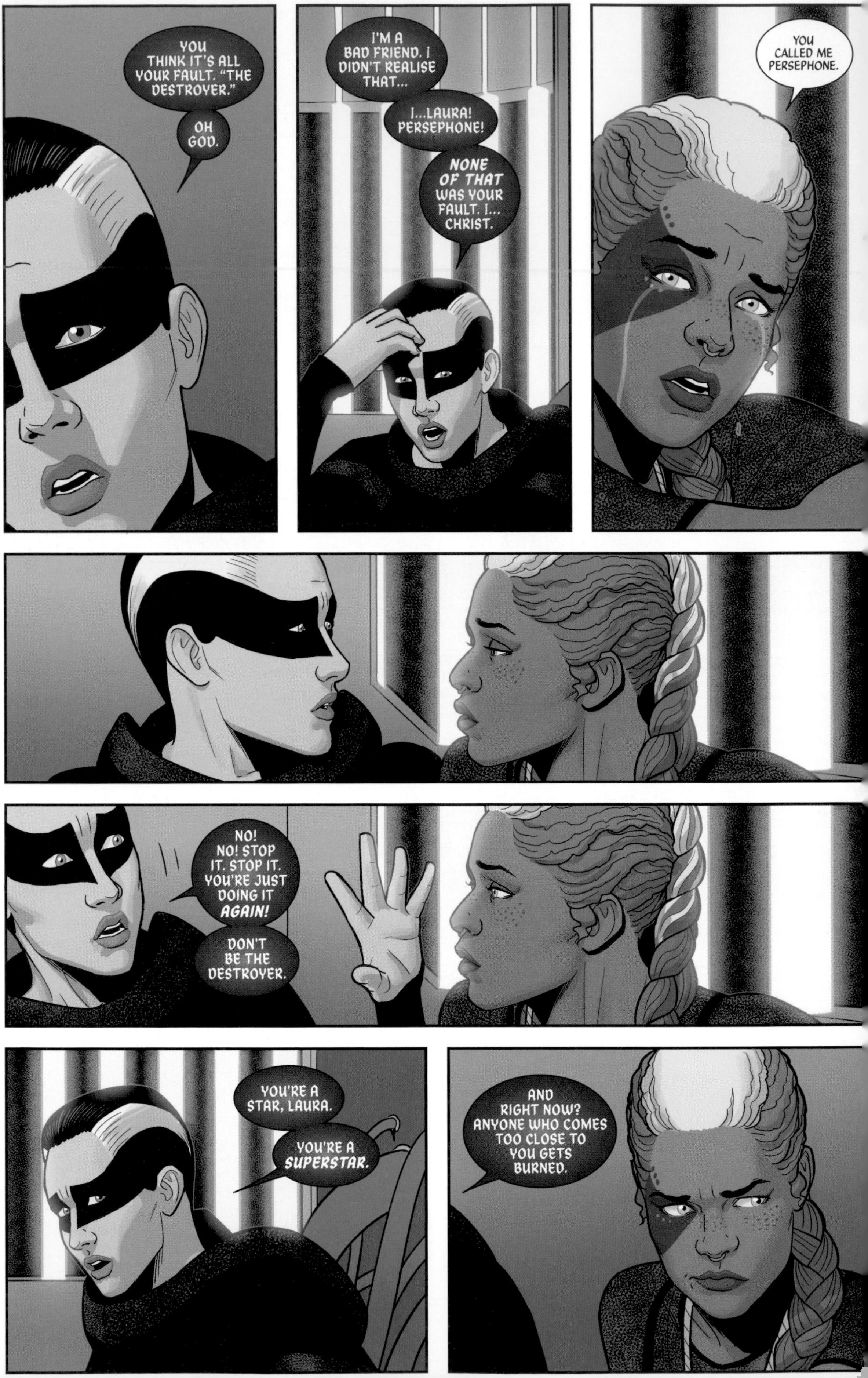
YOU THINK IT'S ALL YOUR FAULT. "THE DESTROYER."
OH GOD.
I'M A BAD FRIEND. I DIDN'T REALISE THAT...
I...LAURA! PERSEPHONE!
NONE OF THAT WAS YOUR FAULT. I... CHRIST.
YOU CALLED ME PERSEPHONE.
NO! NO! STOP IT. STOP IT. YOU'RE JUST DOING IT AGAIN!
DON'T BE THE DESTROYER.
YOU'RE A STAR, LAURA.
YOU'RE A SUPERSTAR.
AND RIGHT NOW? ANYONE WHO COMES TOO CLOSE TO YOU GETS BURNED.

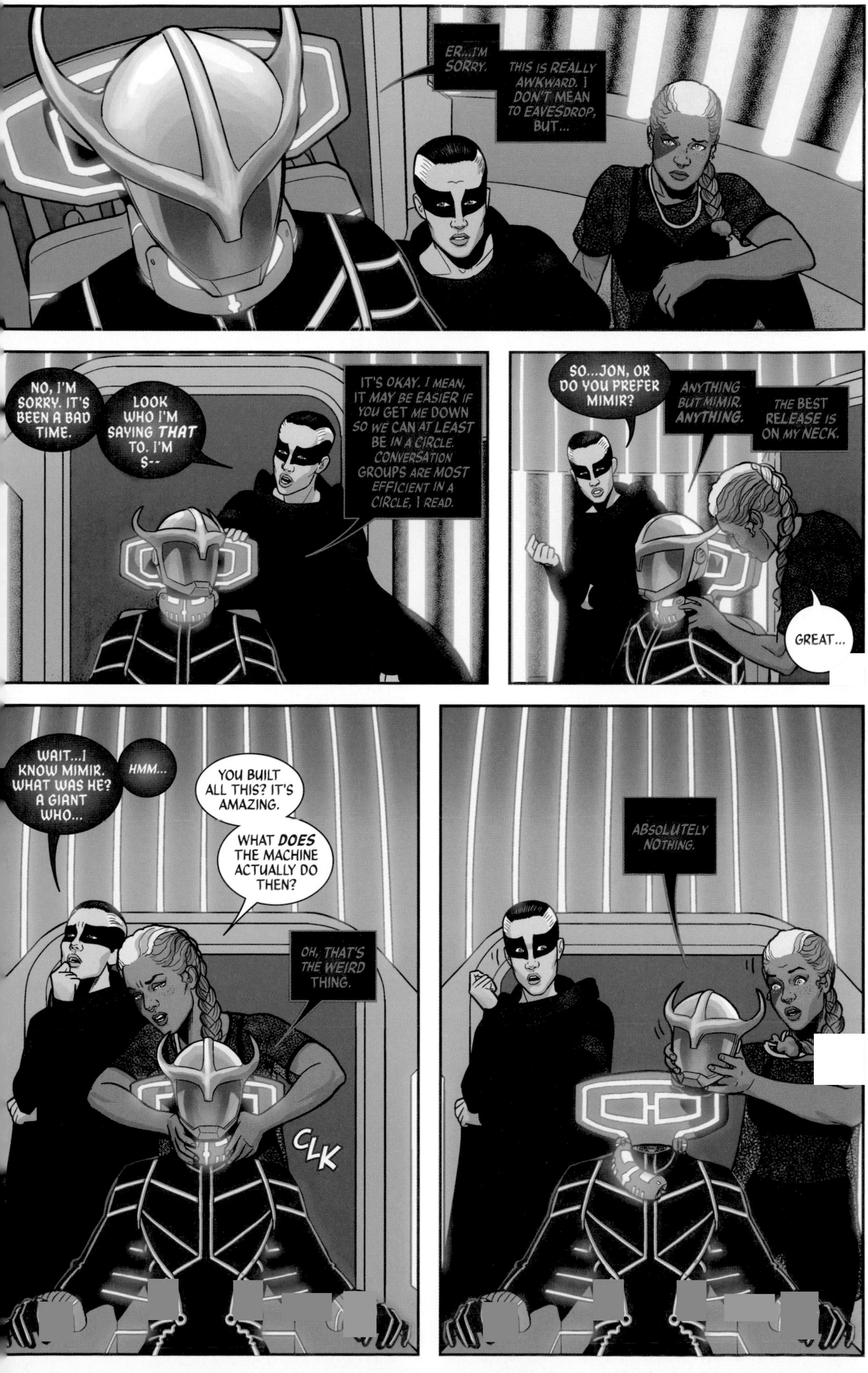
ER...I'M SORRY.
THIS IS REALLY AWKWARD. I DON'T MEAN TO EAVESDROP, BUT...
NO, I'M SORRY. IT'S BEEN A BAD TIME.
LOOK WHO I'M SAYING THAT TO. I'M S--
IT'S OKAY. I MEAN, IT MAY BE EASIER IF YOU GET ME DOWN SO WE CAN AT LEAST BE IN A CIRCLE. CONVERSATION GROUPS ARE MOST EFFICIENT IN A CIRCLE, I READ.
SO...JON, OR DO YOU PREFER MIMIR?
ANYTHING BUT MIMIR. ANYTHING.
THE BEST RELEASE IS ON MY NECK.
GREAT...
WAIT...I KNOW MIMIR. WHAT WAS HE? A GIANT WHO...
HMM...
YOU BUILT ALL THIS? IT'S AMAZING.
WHAT DOES THE MACHINE ACTUALLY DO THEN?
OH, THAT'S THE WEIRD THING.
CLK
ABSOLUTELY NOTHING.

NO.
NO.

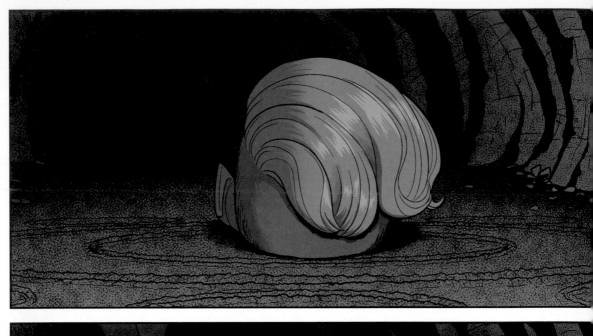

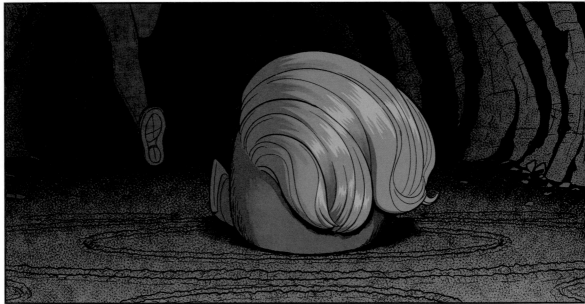

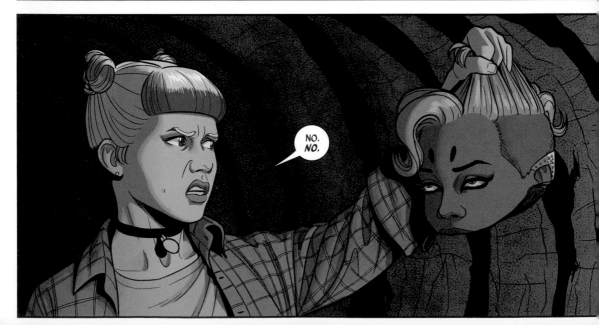

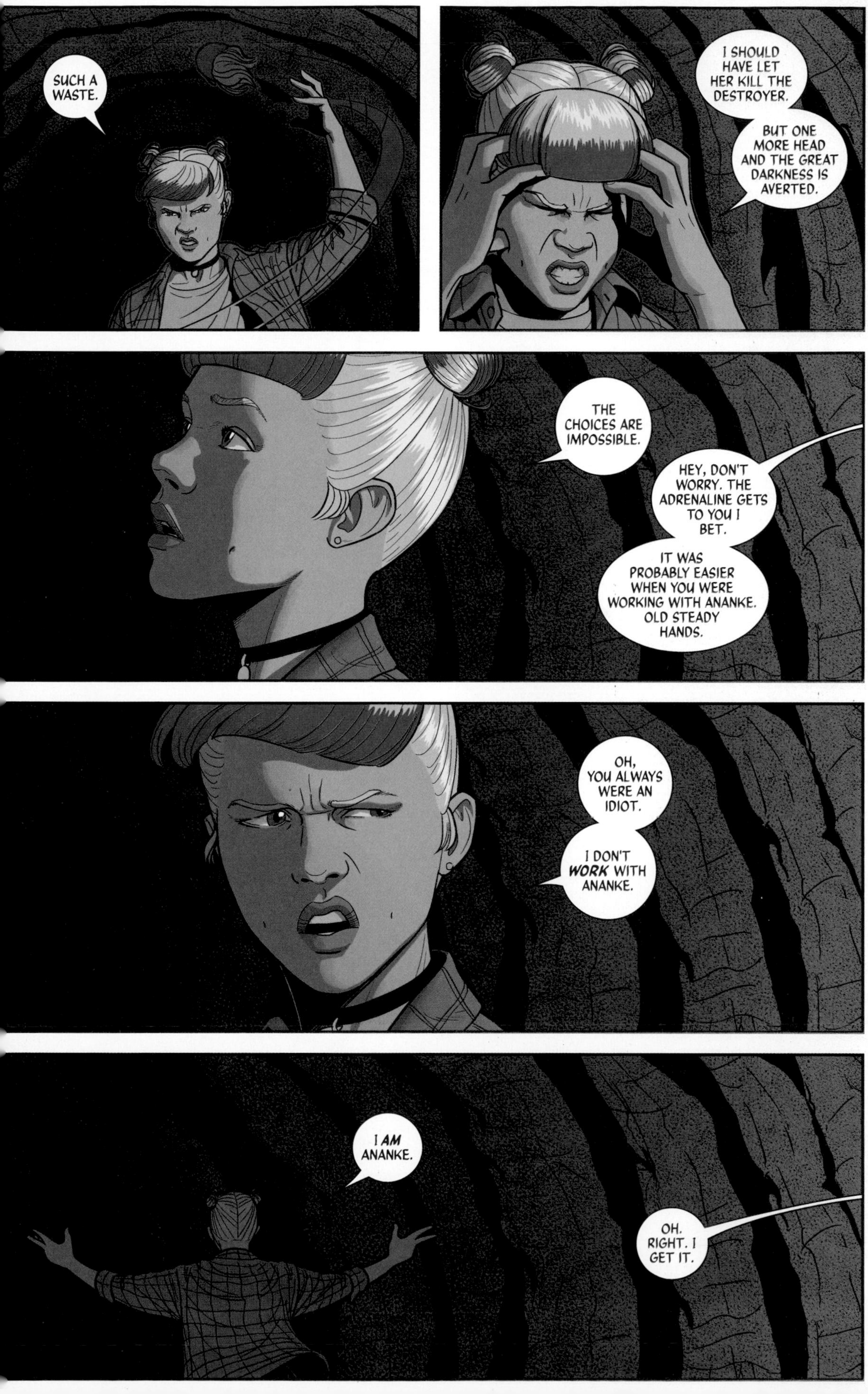
SUCH A WASTE.
I SHOULD HAVE LET HER KILL THE DESTROYER.
BUT ONE MORE HEAD AND THE GREAT DARKNESS IS AVERTED.
THE CHOICES ARE IMPOSSIBLE.
HEY, DON'T WORRY. THE ADRENALINE GETS TO YOU I BET.
IT WAS PROBABLY EASIER WHEN YOU WERE WORKING WITH ANANKE. OLD STEADY HANDS.
OH, YOU ALWAYS WERE AN IDIOT.
I DON'T *WORK* WITH ANANKE.
I *AM* ANANKE.
OH. RIGHT. I GET IT.

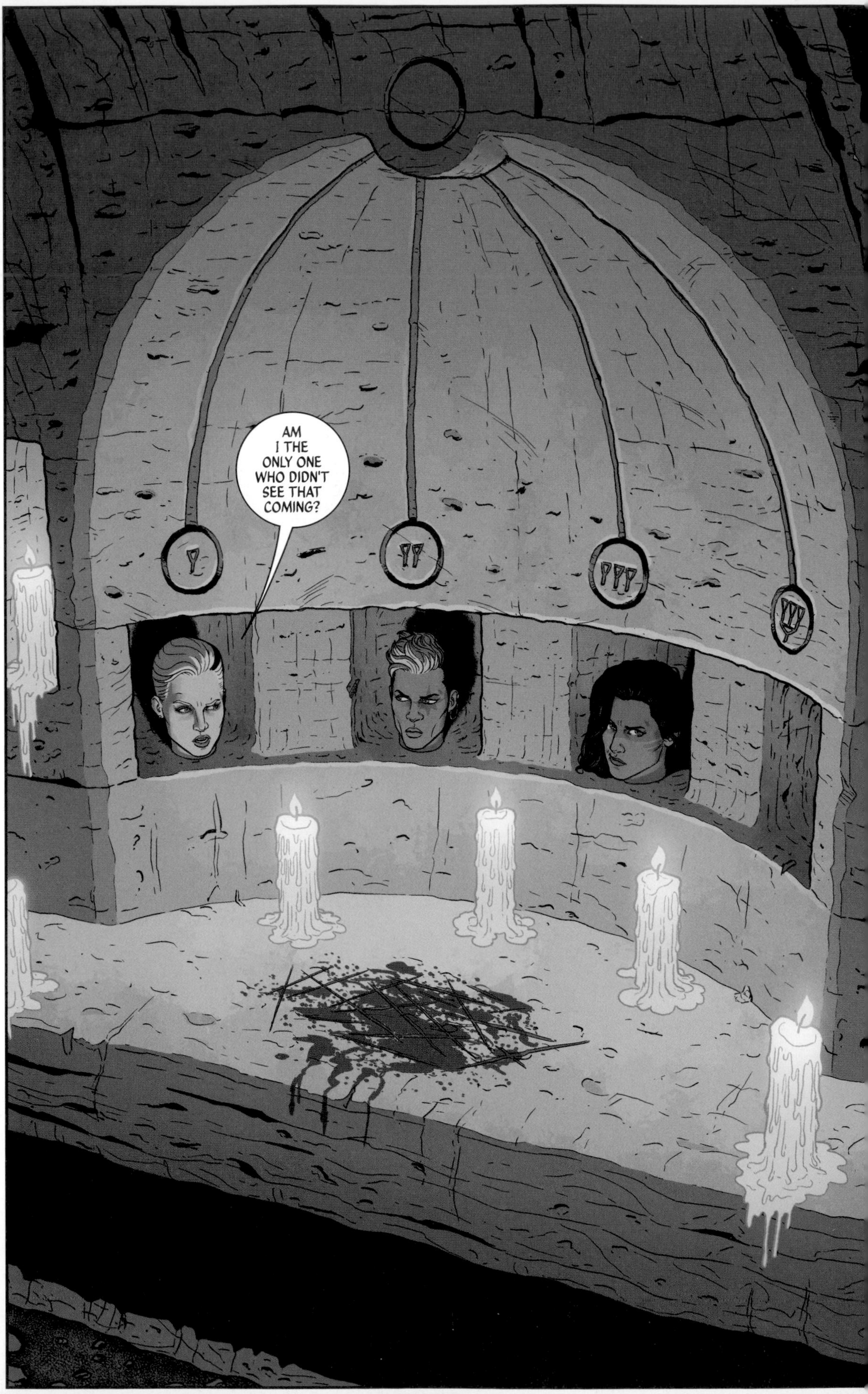
AM I THE ONLY ONE WHO DIDN'T SEE THAT COMING?

TALKING HEADS

9 MARCH 2015

VARIANT ART

How talented are your friends? Our friends are THIS talented. You can't see how far apart our hands are, as these are just words we're writing, but they are extremely far apart. In fact, Kieron's hands are in London and Jamie's hands are in Edinburgh. Our friends are over 400 miles talented, and for proof of this claim, look at the gallery of alternate covers they did for the comic in the pages that follow. Look at them, and don't wonder what kind of keyboard Kieron and Jamie are using to write this when they're so far apart. Actually, it's googledocs. We're sharing a googledoc. Phew. Literary conceit saved.

Jock
Issue 29 cover

Jamie McKelvie and Matthew Wilson
Issue 29 cover for Image Comics "Images of Tomorrow"

Meredith McClaren
Issue 30 cover

Jonathan Hickman
Issue 30 cover

Sophie Campbell
Issue 31 cover

Noelle Stevenson
Issue 32 cover

Jamie McKelvie
Issue 32 cover for Image Comics *Walking Dead* Tribute

Russell Dauterman and Matthew Wilson
Issue 33 cover

Jamie McKelvie and Matthew Wilson
Forbidden Planet Bookplate

Jamie McKelvie and Matthew Wilson
French Edition cover for Vol. 1

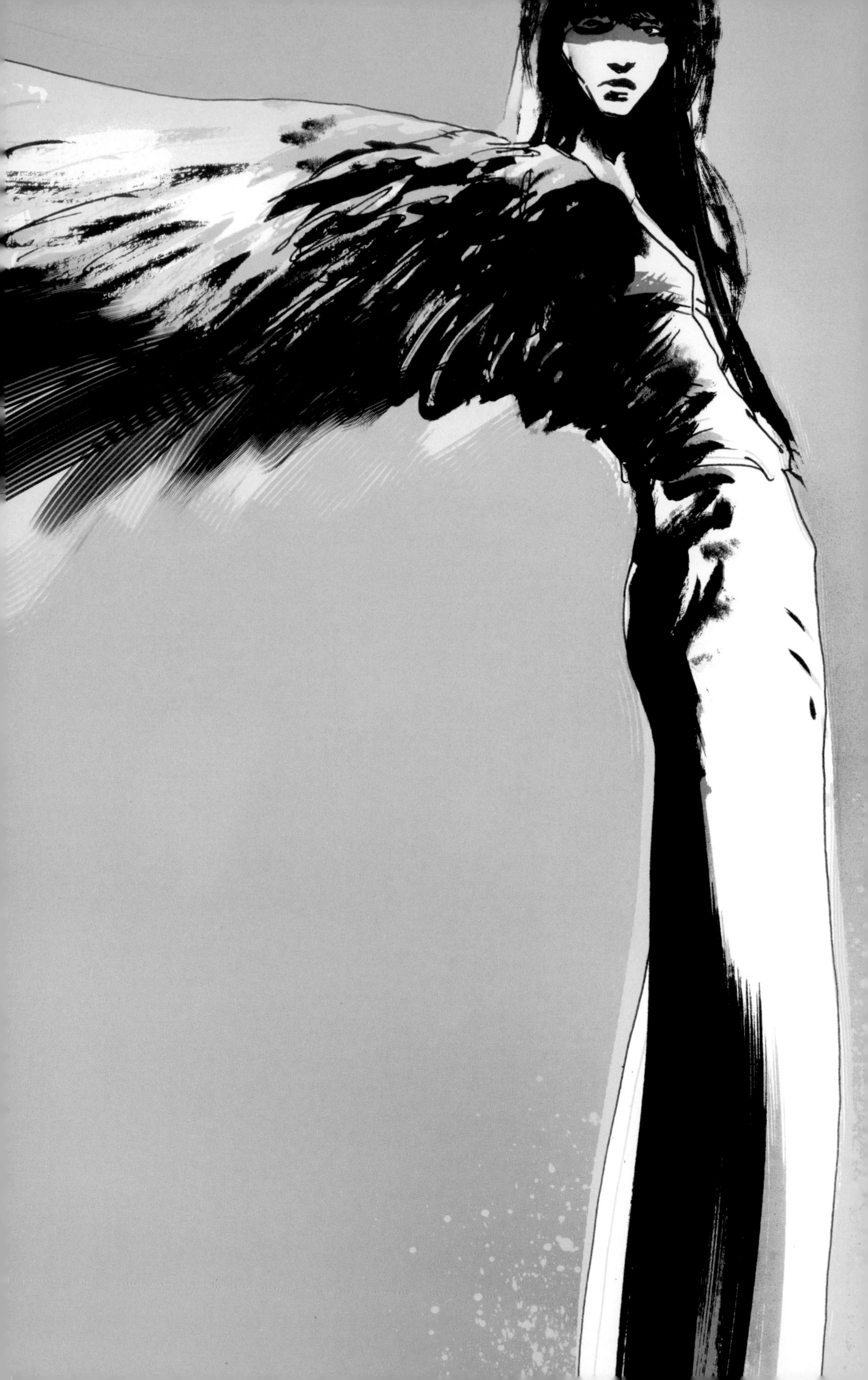

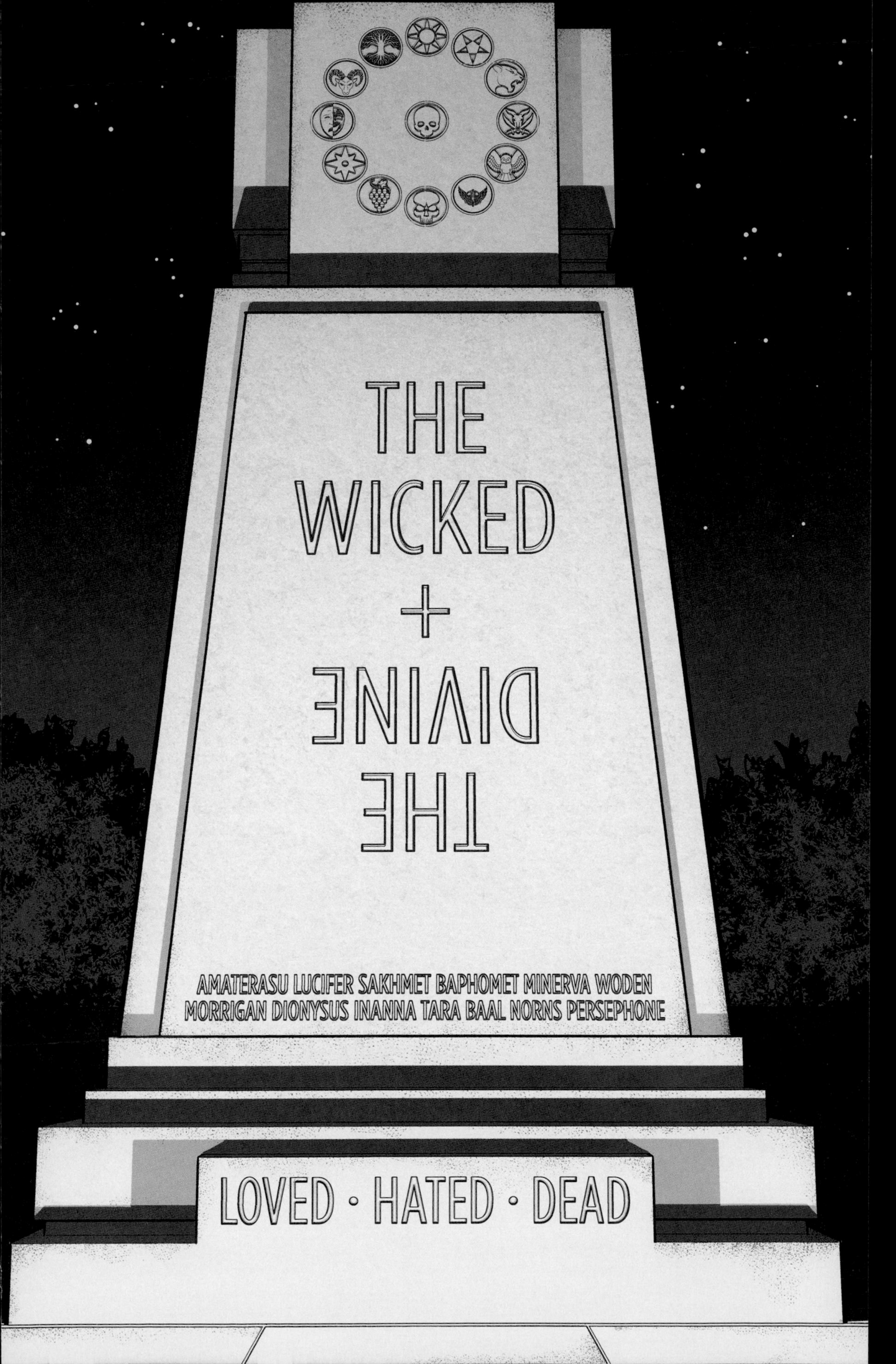
THE WICKED + THE DIVINE
AMATERASU LUCIFER SAKHMET BAPHOMET MINERVA WODEN
MORRIGAN DIONYSUS INANNA TARA BAAL NORNS PERSEPHONE
LOVED · HATED · DEAD

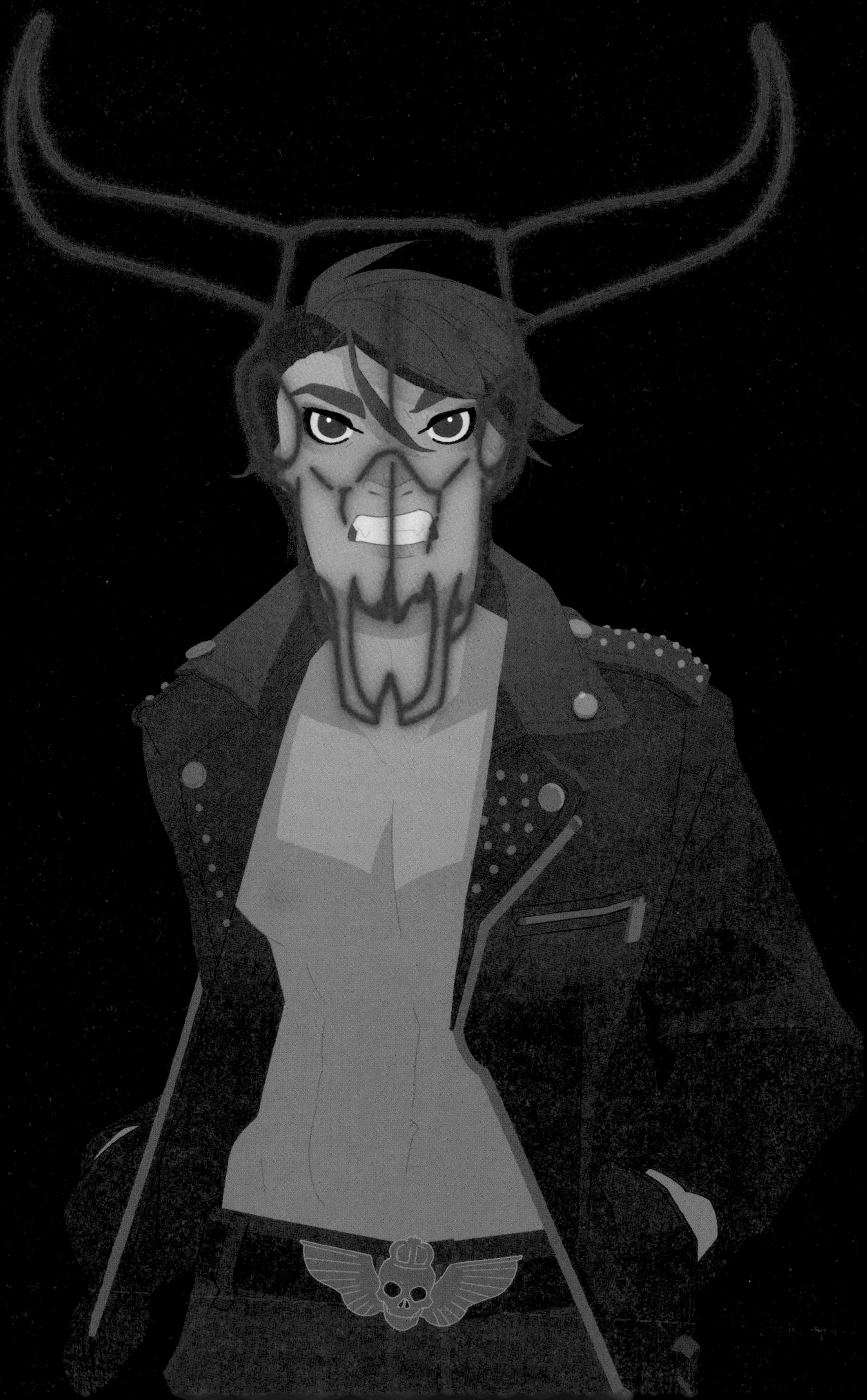

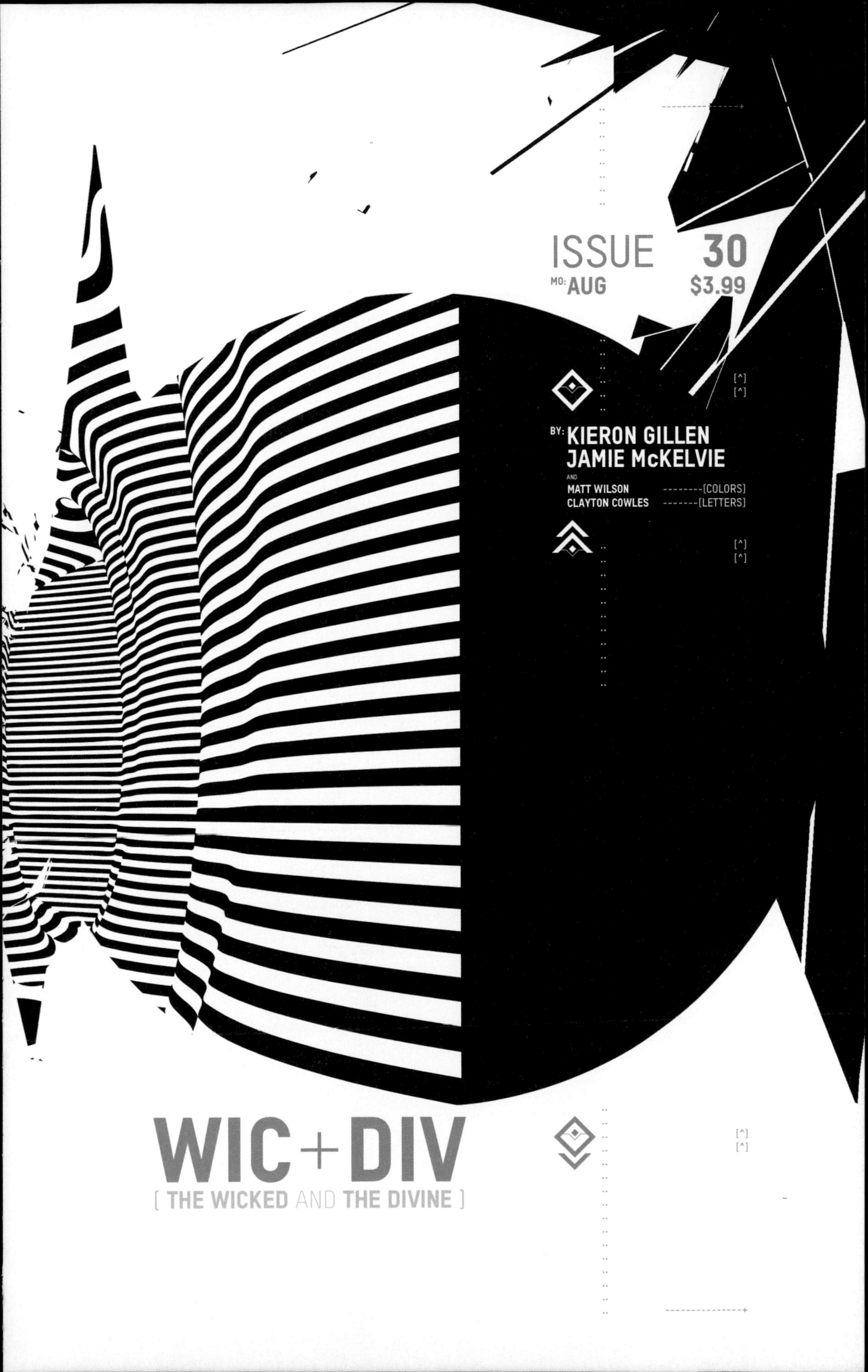

ISSUE 30
MO: AUG
$3.99
BY: KIERON GILLEN
JAMIE McKELVIE
AND
MATT WILSON --------[COLORS]
CLAYTON COWLES -------[LETTERS]
WIC+DIV
[THE WICKED AND THE DIVINE]

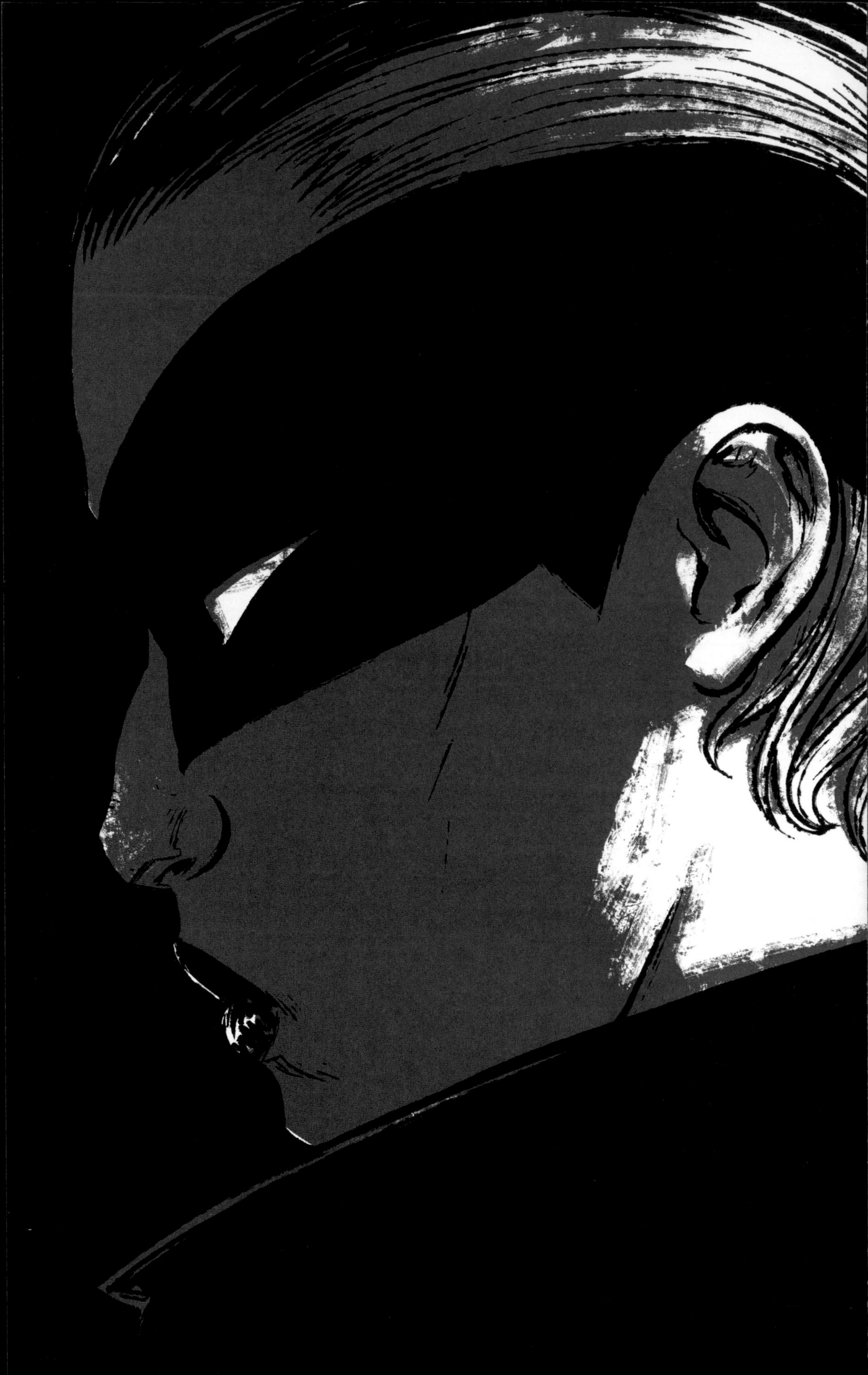

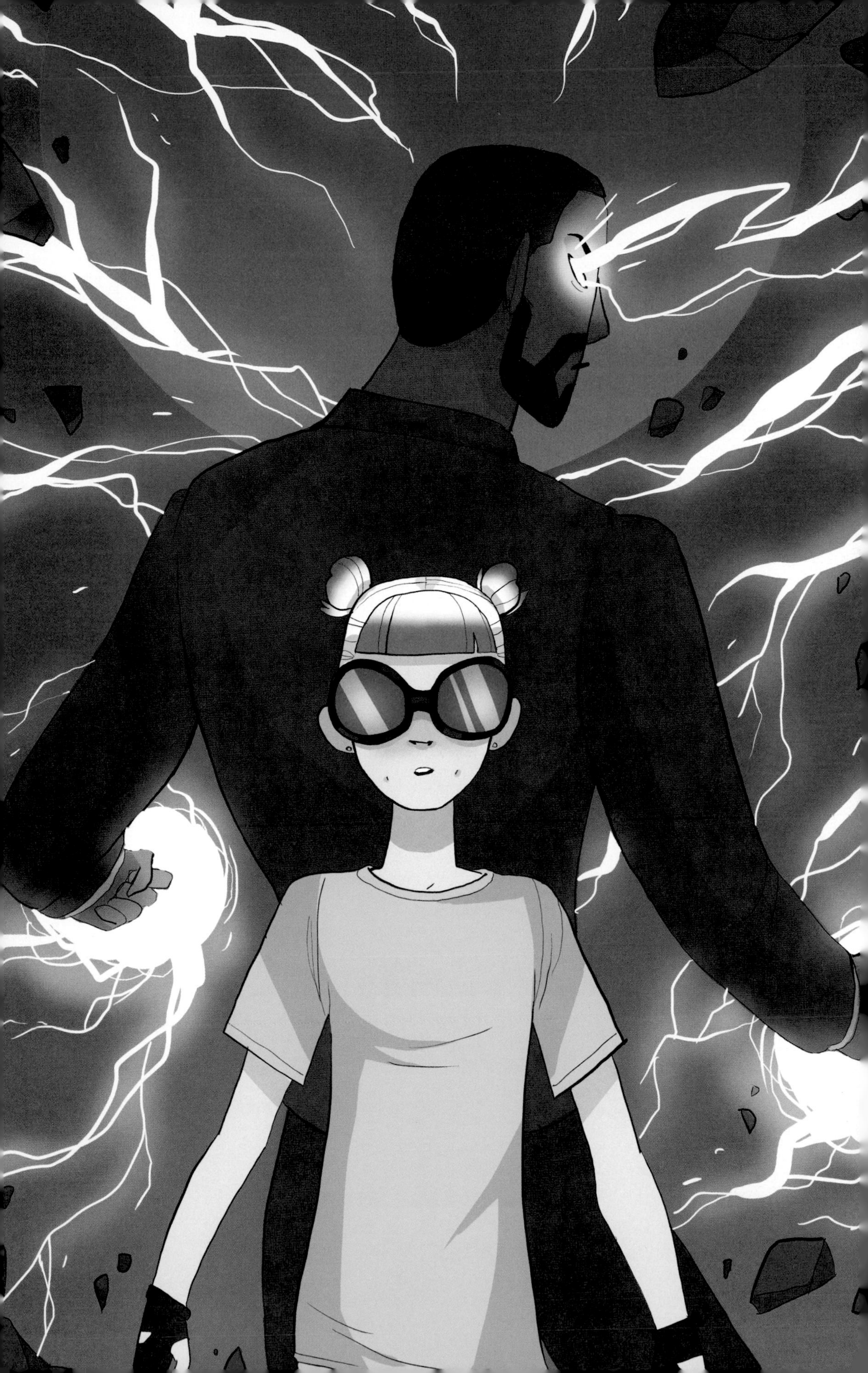

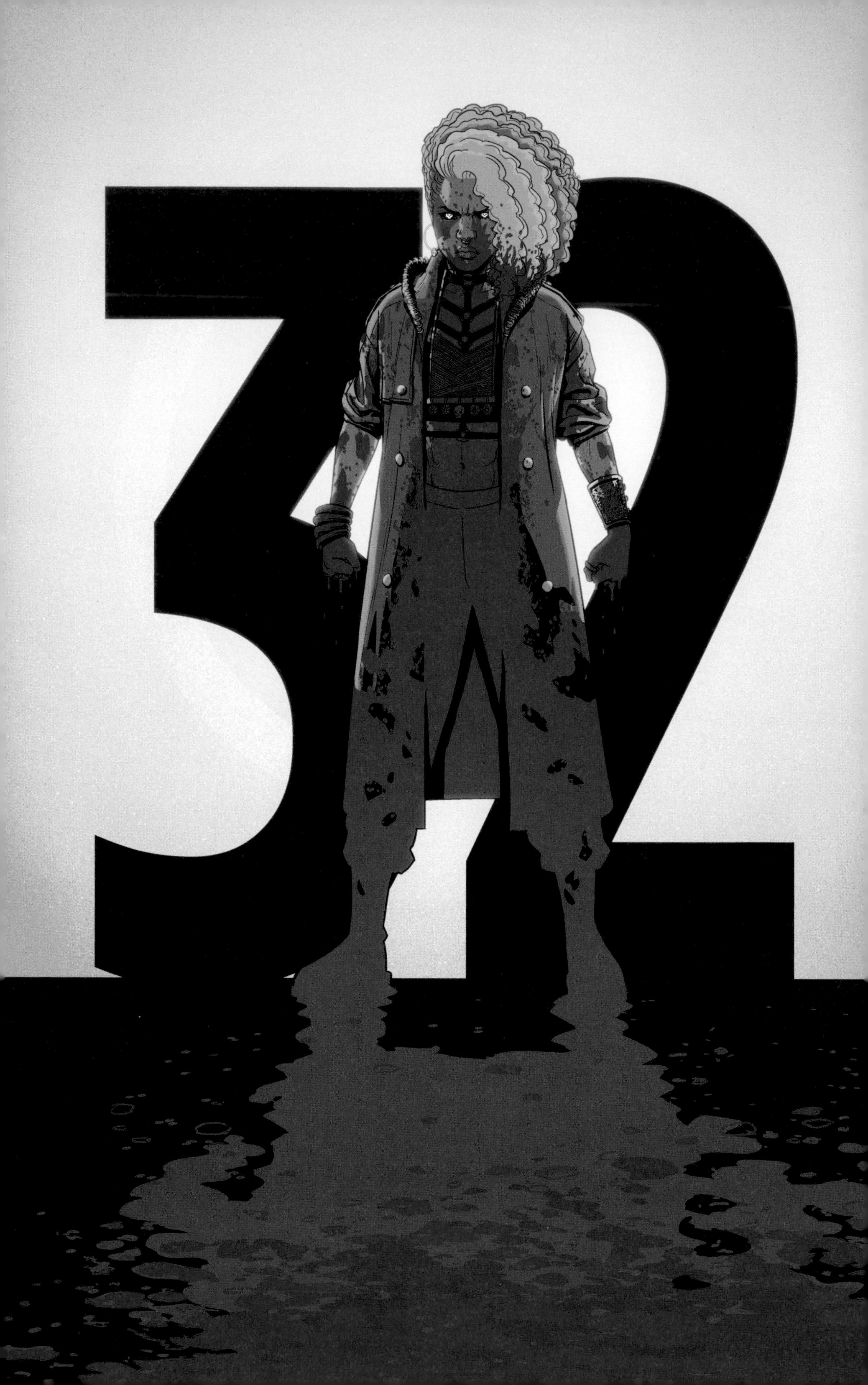
32

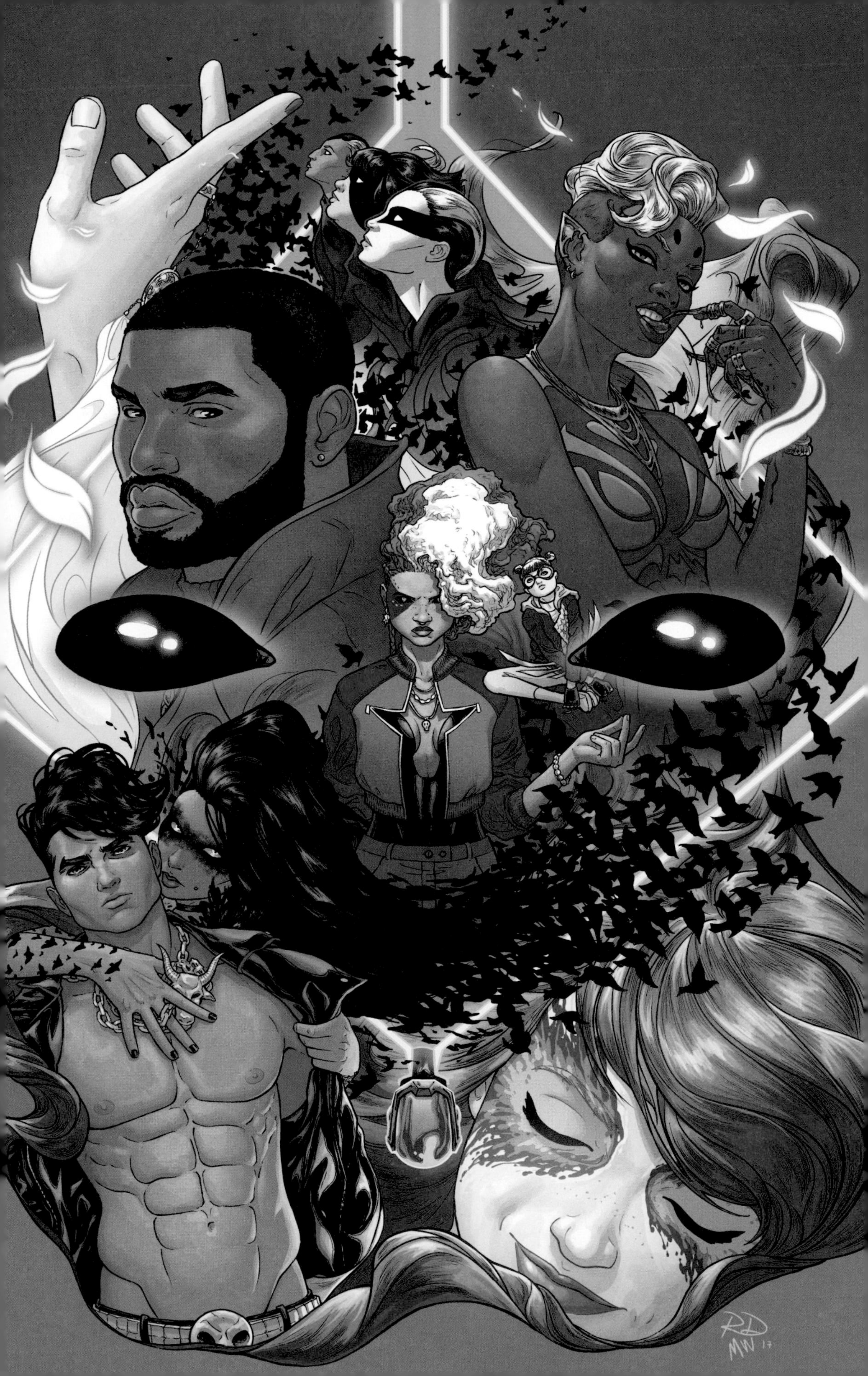

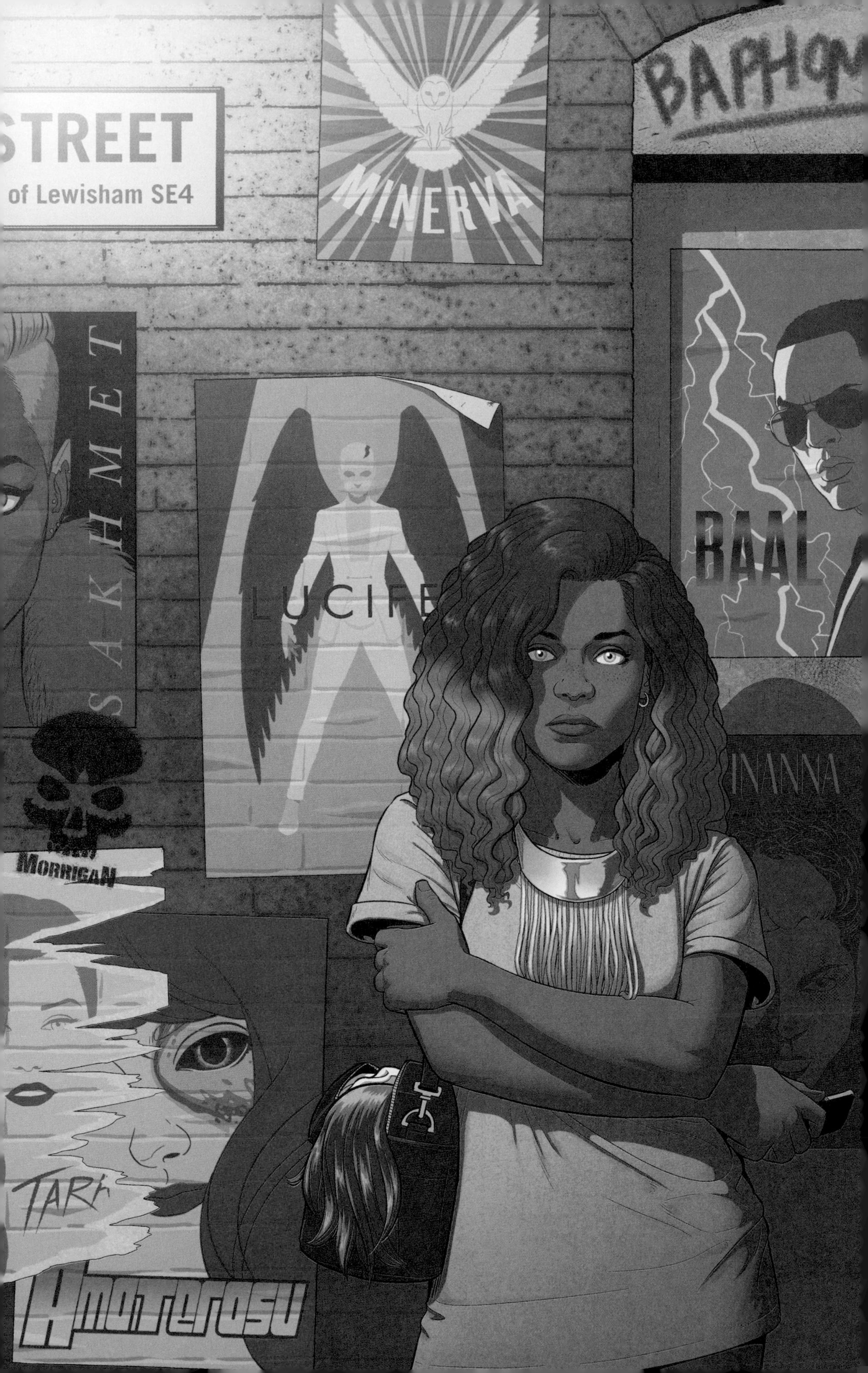

STREET
of Lewisham SE4
MINERVA
BAPHO
SAKHMET
LUCIFE
BAAL
INANNA
MORRIGAN
AMATERASU

Script to page is a standard in our 'Making Of' sections, but we often also say that the script is the start of a conversation rather than the end of it. We figured we should include some of the conversation for once, in this case based around page 5 from issue 29. The Marvel Method pages like below are inevitably the ones where there's the most change between script and page, as is only right.

PAGE 5

Marvel Method!

And Baal slides past Sakhmet with a grin, tagging her like it's a wrestling match. Sakhmet, entering, challenging, like the cat who has got all the cream in the entire world. Clothes are magnificent, but also less opulent — this is the very beginning. I want there to be a gap here as well, in terms of the distance from the gods in *Imperial Phase* to where they started. Don't push it too far, because the gods get to do the god stuff... but there's definitely less of it.

BAAL: Baal took your virginity...

BAAL: ...Sakhmet's taking everything else.

And we explode into an awesome gig effect. Sakhmet style. Sex, release, a hedonistic bliss, sweat. Perhaps claw rips as the panel effects? As in, if the murder scene from last issue was on ecstasy.

Cutting between the two of them — Laura, fan, Sakhmet, god. The "I want everything you have" of Amaterasu's performance, merging into "I want you."

We could talk about this scene. It's a performance scene. I would have a couple of slivers of black in here, where I can put Laura's performance captions — the "Back then, I didn't even think of wanting what you had. I just wanted you. I wanted you like oxygen. Instantly."

Basically, this is our chance to do a TASTE of a Baal and Sakhmet performance.

Anyway — either way, page ends with a CAP from the real world, as we're going to hard cut...

POLICE CAP: "Laura Wilson?"

KIERON'S SCRIPT TO JAMIE

Sakhmet

Jamie McKelvie
to Kieron Gillen

Morning,

Here it all is. I am really struggling with the panel of Sakhmet singing, so it's left blank at the moment. Could you maybe explain more what you were after? Trying to communicate what's in the script, I'm finding it tough.

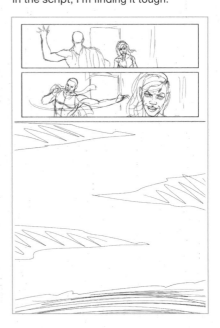

1 Attachment

 sakhmet.jpg

JAMIE'S PENCILS BACK WITH
EMAIL QUESTION TO KIERON

KIERON’S REPLY TO JAMIE

Re: Sakhmet

Kieron Gillen

to Jamie McKelvie

Re: Sakhmet. Good question. Leaving it as open as I did does perhaps leave it too open. It does kind of suggest “can you draw the most awesome fight scene ever!” in a Millar-esque fashion.

I mean, I was throwing “Sakhmet” aspects we could turn into a performance. The rips but done “good” could be fun. A colour tweak on the scene to make it feel primal and urgent? Pinks, reds, blacks. Just moments of her performance, and Laura’s response, etc. Implicit sensuality of it.

I suggest Laura text in the background, or integrated, but I suspect that may be too much—or one element too much.

Is this better? Basically “a Sakhmet gig performance” is all I need. Cool, but about that instant connection between the two of them... or rather, Laura’s connection with Sakhmet.

•••

1 Attachment

sakhmet.jpg

JAMIE’S INKS

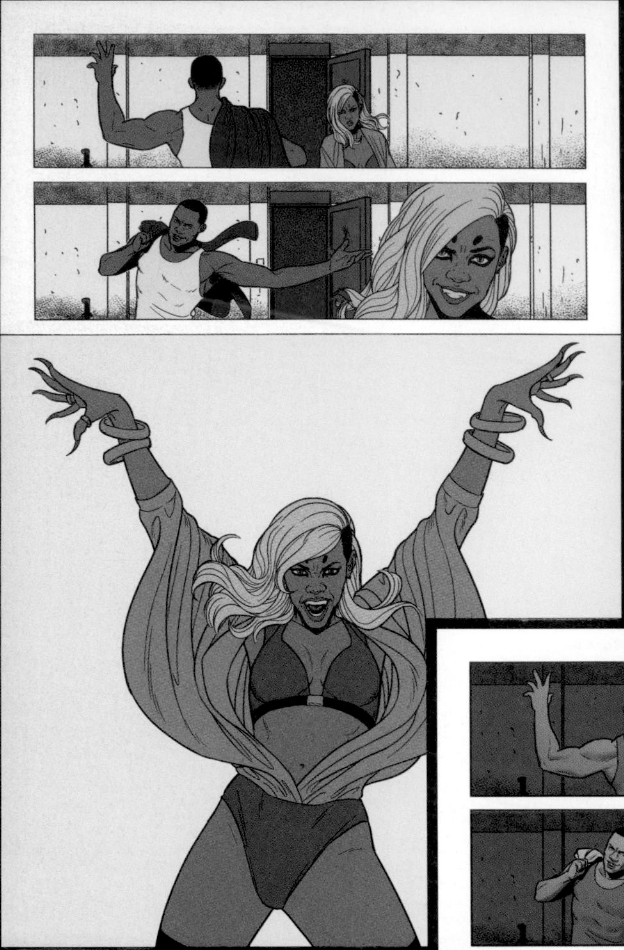

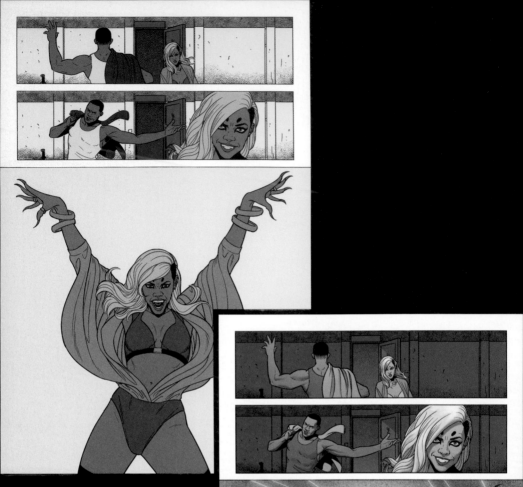

FLATS

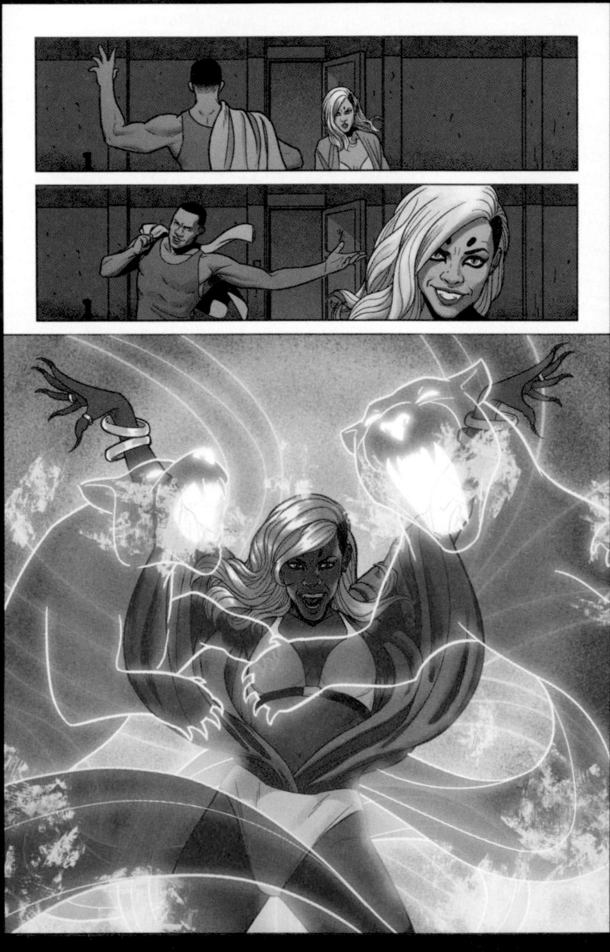

COLOURS

VALHALLA

As well as being a startling image, this is an interesting page that shows the other side of the equation. As well as the spectacle, this is an example of how many guidelines for plot elements and world building can get worked into a splash. It's a checklist of things to think about. It's also telling that Kieron didn't ask for an actual stage, but Jamie added one anyway, because Jamie is clever.

PAGE 2 (1 panel)

2.1
And reveal on Valhalla.

Valhalla is... complicated. It's still running down, but has been patched together with bits of new technology. It's not "Awake" yet but hints that interesting things will be going on when this machinery gets switched on.

Basically, Valhalla? It looks a lot like the machine, doesn't it? If you squint. Woden has plugged the machine into the whole structure, and is using it as a resonating device — think Russian Dolls, the machine being a tiny version of Valhalla in the base of it.

The garden outside has a spiral of cables stretching out to the walls, with Tesla-esque things on the walls.

When it activates, they're going to create a dome above the whole park, sealing them in. If you want, I can tell you more about how this goes, and show the later scripts that exist in a draft state, but I suspect you can get what you need from here. "The walls will generate a dome" is basically all you need. Do talk. As if you weren't going to.

Now — we could have the IT'D BETTER coming from Woden who is tiny, as we've pulled out entirely to show this sprawl, or we could have the reveal on the first panel and a panel at the bottom of a tight shot on Woden/Cass as they walk away from it. The 2/3rd panel and a 1/3rd panel is very us, of course, but I wrote it as a splash as a thought to maybe change it up. Either is great for our purpose.

Woden's dialogue always being recognisable helps us with the storytelling, of course.

As well as all the tech stuff, we maybe see other, more usual gig stuff — toilet cubicles, bars, whatever. This beat is a WicDiv version of a festival setting up. There's normal workers, as well as the Valkyries. Trucks coming in would also be strong.

(The Valkyries who teleported may be visible at the top of Valhalla, attaching the machinery they teleported with to the tip of the whole thing.)

WODEN: It'd better.

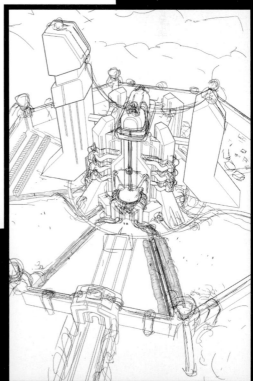

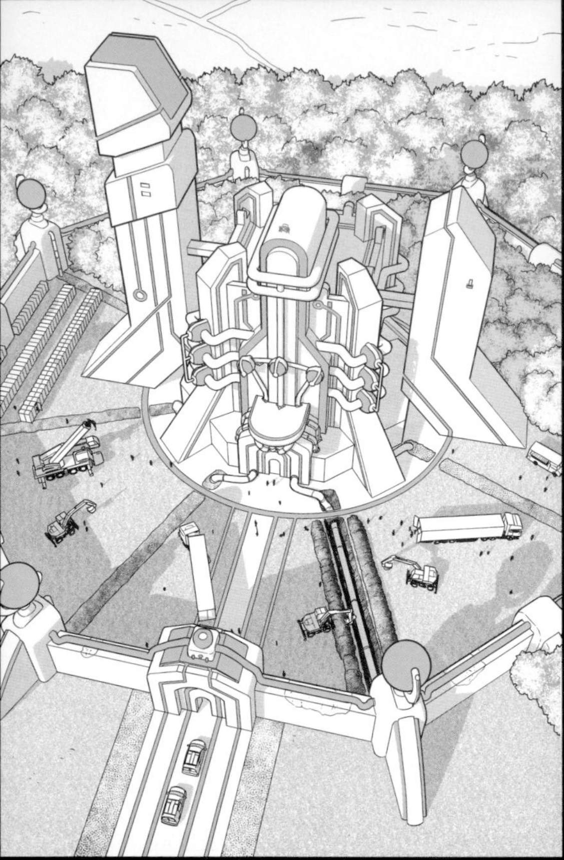

INKS

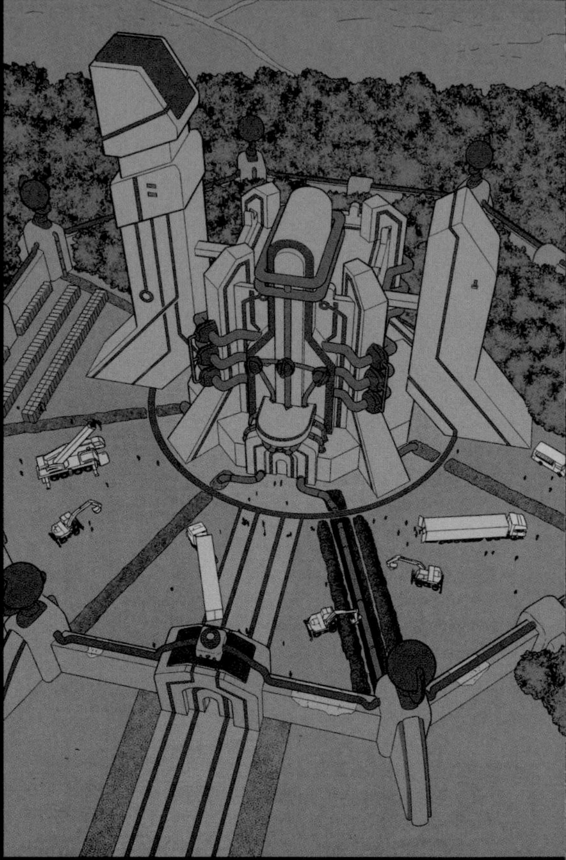

FLATS

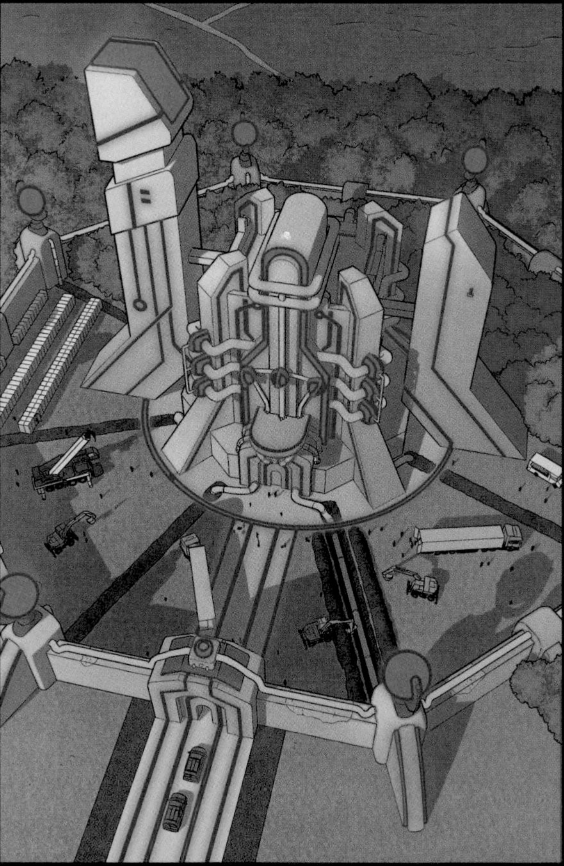

COLOURS

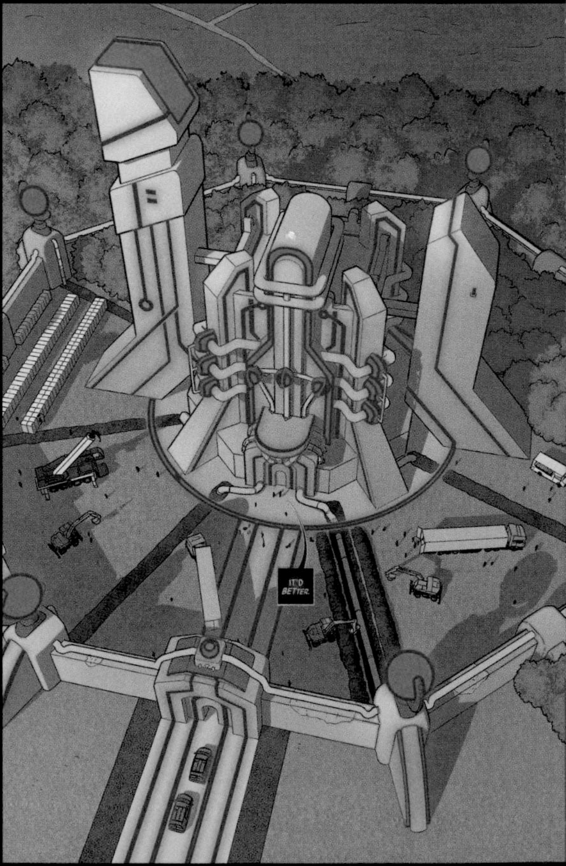
IT'D BETTER.

LETTERING

THE WODEN EFFECT

This page shows some of the more visual experimentation. You'll see rather than a simple panel of the distortion as the Norns are falling apart, the left of the panel is normal with the countdown and the right of the panel is the swirl as Cass' perceptions are taken apart. This bit is all about inter-team interplay.

SCRIPT

```
PAGE 14 — 5 panels


14.1
And we're on Woden shooting the Norns from behind
with concentric waves of energy. It passes through
the Norns. It's like a stun-blaster in Star Wars,
that wave of energy — that "that doesn't look
fatal, but does look weird."


NO DIALOGUE


14.2
And the Norns turn around, confused.
Something is kicking in...

NORN: What are you--
WODEN: 4, 3, 2, and...

14.3
And Cass's perspective on Woden...
and Woden has fractured like a kaleidoscope.


NO DIALOGUE


14.4
And the Norns are collapsing to the floor,
eyes staring wildly, hallucinating awfully...

WODEN: Seer. One who sees.

WODEN: The volume's been turned up on
your powers and...well, have a rest.


14.5
The Norns on the floor, knocked out.
Woden on the DJ booth, pressing the
buttons, setting up his move...

WODEN: Oh, Cass. You and your machine.
WODEN: As if that was the only mystery.
```

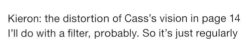

Re: Cass's vision

Jamie McKelvie   📎 ★ ↩
to Kieron Gillen ➕

Kieron: the distortion of Cass's vision in page 14 I'll do with a filter, probably. So it's just regularly pencilled for now.

....

1 Attachment   ⬇ ☁

📄 WicDiv31_014.jpg

EMAIL FROM JAMIE WITH PENCILS

INKS

FLATS

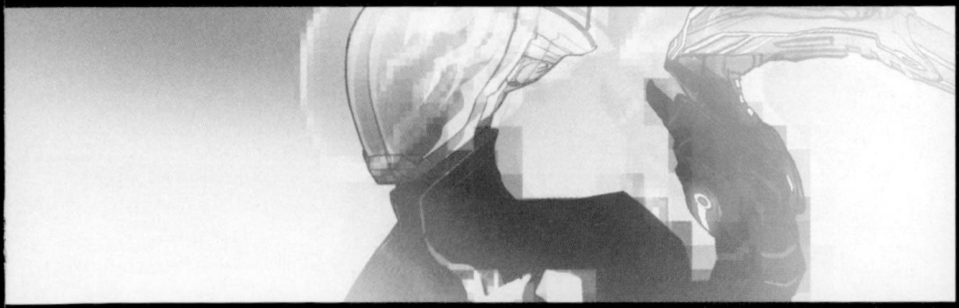

COLOURS

AMATERASU'S RED LETTER DAY

We've talked about Amaterasu's performances throughout the book, but when we're reaching the climax of her arc, we want to try and show something in her lettering choice. We automatically know she's 'performing' to Sakhmet. To match the red of her design, a red choice was made, and great... but when the colours came in, it merged with the actual page. Clayton went back and had a play, ultimately adding an outline to the balloon to ensure the elements are kept separate.

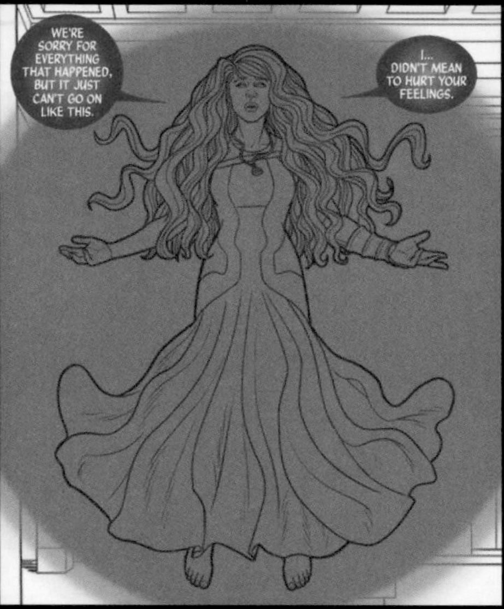
WE'RE SORRY FOR EVERYTHING THAT HAPPENED, BUT IT JUST CAN'T GO ON LIKE THIS.
I... DIDN'T MEAN TO HURT YOUR FEELINGS.

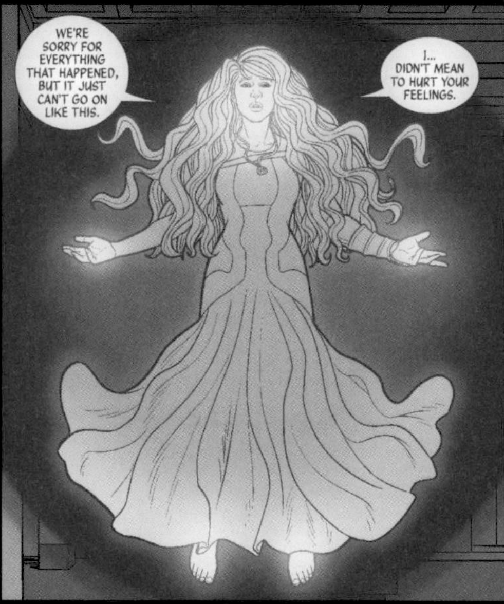
WE'RE SORRY FOR EVERYTHING THAT HAPPENED, BUT IT JUST CAN'T GO ON LIKE THIS.
I... DIDN'T MEAN TO HURT YOUR FEELINGS.

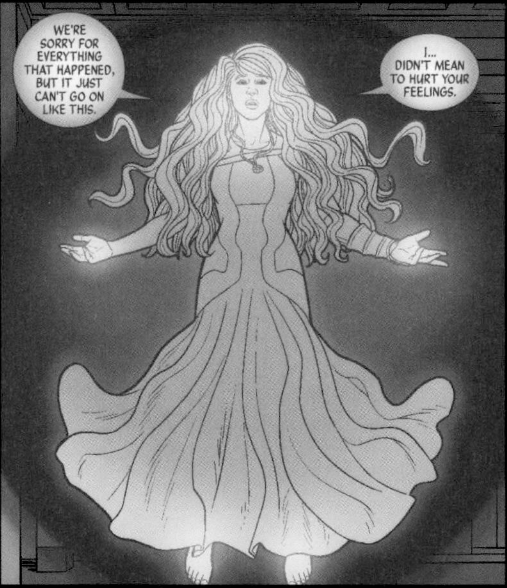
WE'RE SORRY FOR EVERYTHING THAT HAPPENED, BUT IT JUST CAN'T GO ON LIKE THIS.
I... DIDN'T MEAN TO HURT YOUR FEELINGS.

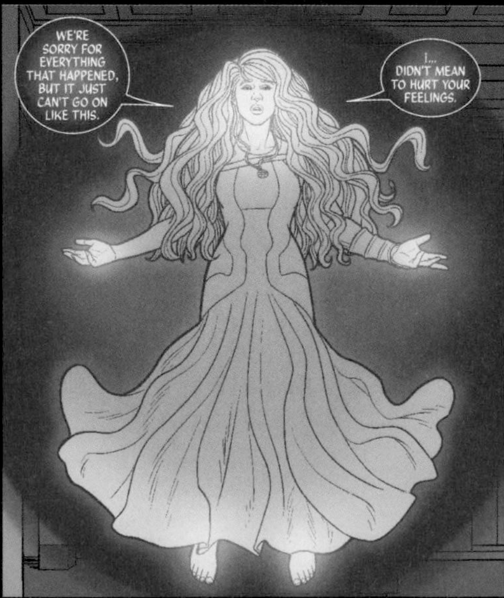
WE'RE SORRY FOR EVERYTHING THAT HAPPENED, BUT IT JUST CAN'T GO ON LIKE THIS.
I... DIDN'T MEAN TO HURT YOUR FEELINGS.

DIONYSUS' FIGHT

Dio's *Red Shoes* dance/fight sequence was, appropriately, carefully choreographed. The rhythm of the panels and captions is key, and as you see we lose some of the 'beats' when we realise that a caption is distracting or just not needed. Letting us drop that verbal beat when Dio pops his nunchaku, before it kicks in with the splash, is key. Sniff.

PAGE 3 – 5 panels

3.1
Same angle, and his eyes are opening weakly. Like, only a sliver. But he's alive, and we know he's not done yet.
And for the first time, we have a Dionysus caption. As you can imagine, this isn't exactly a good sign for Dionysus.

DIO CAP: No.

3.2
And Dio, lurching to his feet, somehow managing it. It's clearly done in pain.

DIO CAP: Not like this.

3.3
People are perhaps turning to him, with obvious hostility. There is an intruder in their midst. Perhaps to the point of literally doing an INVASION OF THE BODYSNATCHERS finger point at him.

DIO CAP: He's stolen my crowd.

3.4
And Dio reaches out to one side, materialising his staff out of nowhere, glowing perfectly...

DIO CAP: Cass.

DIO CAP: Norns.

3.5
He snaps it before his face, into the two separate bits. We have his look of calm, tired determination. His nose is bleeding. If we have his non-black eyes, we see they're bloodshot. Perhaps the blackness of his eyes is cracking into red? That could be creepy.

DIO CAP: I can save them.

PAGE 4 - splash

4.1
Splash.
From behind Dio, leaping forward, those nunchuks spinning in the glo-stick way. He's in the air, hanging magnificently, as the crowd is converging, like a rave dance floor turned zombie movie. In the middle distance there's Valhalla, and the stage, and specifically the concentration of light where Woden is.
This is both a heroic and pyrrhic image. We don't think he can do it. The scale and horror and humanity. But he's going to try and...
Surely he can't do it?
Woden colouring on everything else. Dionysus colouring on Dionysus.
Oh man. You have no idea how upsetting I find this image.

CAP: I can save everyone.

SCRIPT

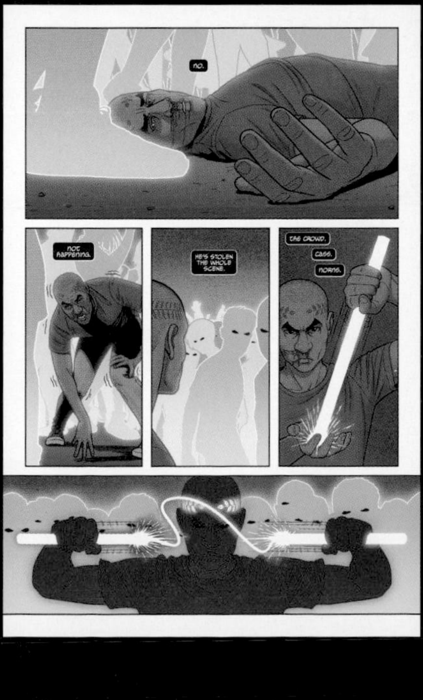
no.
not happening.
He's stolen the whole scene.
the crowd.
cass.
norns.

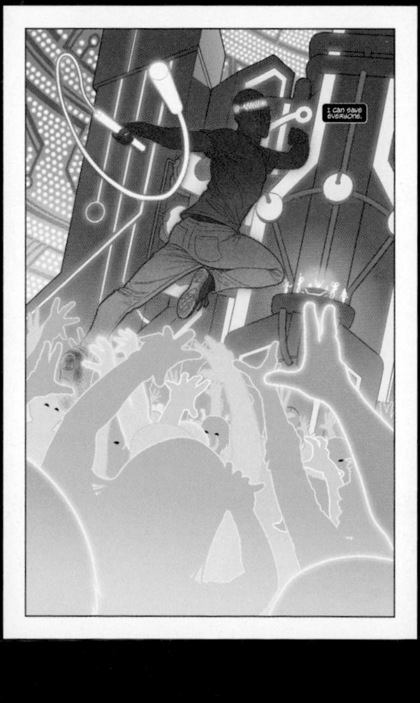
I can save everyone.

MORE MARVEL METHOD

Marvel Method is basically where rather than the script being broken into individual captions, it's left to the artist to decide the choices. In *WicDiv* we primarily use it for action sequences or performance sequences... but even when Kieron writes full script, there's always room for interpretation. It's not holy writ.

PAGE 14 – marvel method
And let's go to Marvel Method...

The Eleusinia phone, ringing, on the bed, or by it...

Pull out. We catch Baal, in a half second after we've seen him, moving in, Sakhmet in her lying position. Baal moving with speed and desperation, the fist raised, crackling... Maybe he can hit her before she does her thing?

And Baal hits the bed, smashing it. Persephone is sent rolling backwards. Baal is at the end of attack position... but there's multiple images of Sakhmet moving around him, coloured simply, perhaps just in outline, with tiny claw marks showing tiny hits.

And Baal is just in the process of finishing dropping, as Sakhmet is on top of him, blood flying... and we angle past her to the Owly, watching. It would be great to get the broken phone in the image if we could, but it's really not important.

And tight on Owly's eye, coldly watching, the reflection in its eyes.

(We could lose all of the Owly to give more room for the combat, and then include a bit of the fight scene in the monitor in the first panel on the next page.)

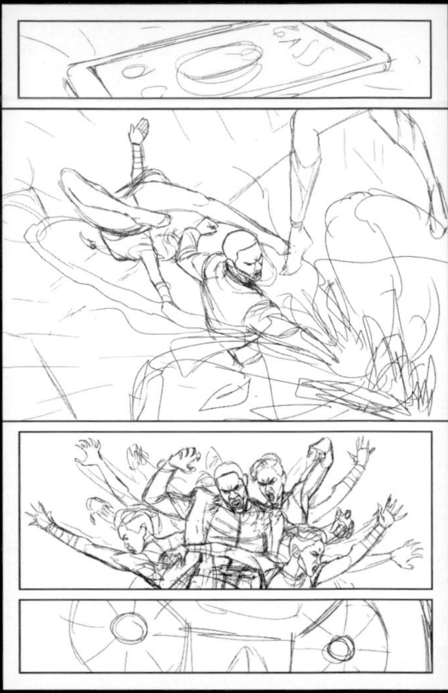

PENCILS

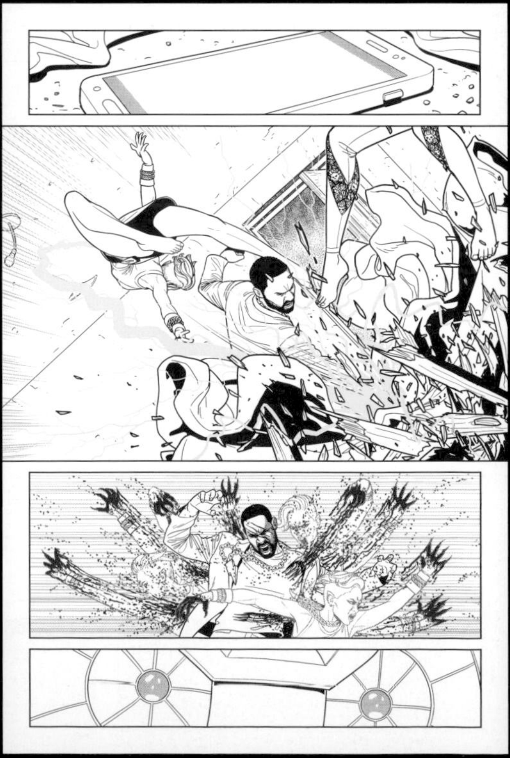

INKS

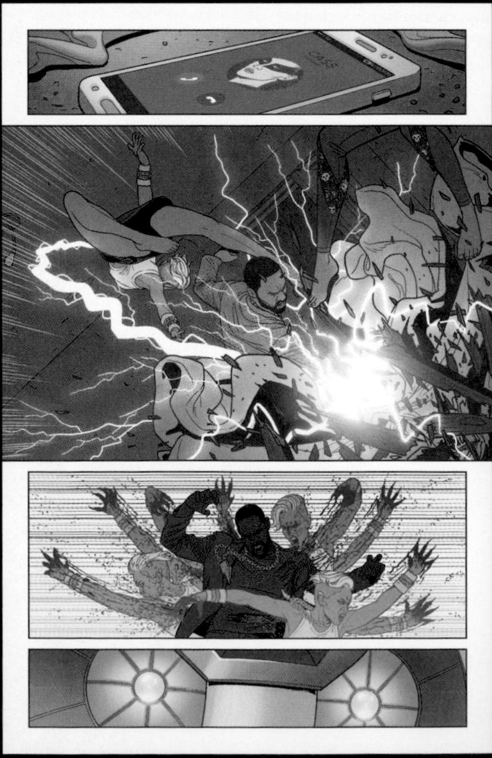

COLOURS

THE CAGE

Yeah, scripts are the start of a conversation, but sometimes conversation just fails. Then it's time for Kieron to bust open his pens and doodle what he actual means. Then Jamie stares at it and goes "You are terrible at art" and then Kieron hangs his head. Woden's cage is an example of that process.

1.2
And we reveal... and it's Woden's secret lair.
The secret lair has all manner of stuff in it. Half-developed teleporters, armours, designs. This is really a BATMAN BASE. Hell, we could give it a giant penny, or a half-built robot skeleton.

It's worth noting that one person has actually been here – namely, Laurie Penny.

Relevantly, towards the middle/back right is a cage. A Woden Cage, which is like a circle. There's a force-field encasing it, of soft energy, ala Morrigan's Cage. The whole thing turns is glowing pink. This is because it's suppressing MIMIR's powers. There's a door into it, and controls by the door, ala controls by a door in Star Wars.

The cage is about 10ft in a semi-circle. It is the only thing glowing Pink in the room.

It should be against the wall, because there's a window on one wall – as in, the majority of the wall can see into the Machine room.

SCRIPT p1

WAY IN!
CAGE
WINDOW
WINDOW
ENERGY WHEN DOOR SHUT
STAIRS
CAGE

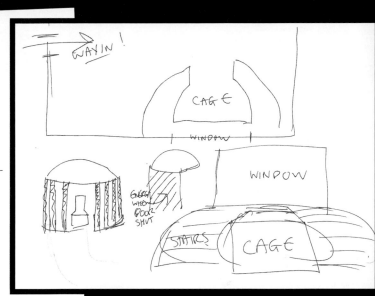

KIERON'S PLAN

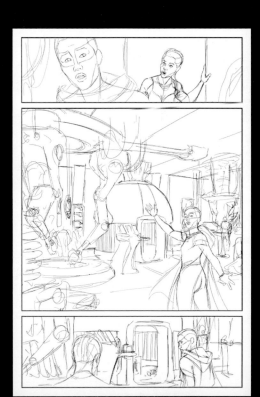

INKS p1

FLATS p1

COLOURS p1

PAGE 2 (splash)

2.1
And reveal on the contents of the cage.

The cage is a large cage. As in, it is its got room inside it to walk around — hell, there's a small workshop in there. The door is open to it, which is what we're looking through.

Think of our take on a Hannibal-lecter-esque cell, with the door open.

Sitting in the middle is MIMIR, aka Pink Woden.

He's in a chair. It's got heavy duty clasps over it — Woden tech. There's cables running out into the floor, into the chair. This is like something out of the Matrix. His helmet is pressed against the back of it. There would be perhaps some clasps visible around the neck of the armour, which is going to come into play soon enough.

It's worth noting that a whole page for this reveal is pretty hefty commitment of space — we could move panels from the next page on here, but when we want Page 4 to be ANOTHER reveal we can't exactly claw back extra space. Unless we decide that the Woden reveal isn't worth a page turn.

There would be various bits of tech in the room, half-constructed. The purpose wouldn't be clear, to say the least. Models of the gig machinery may be a good idea — the idea it was all building towards this.

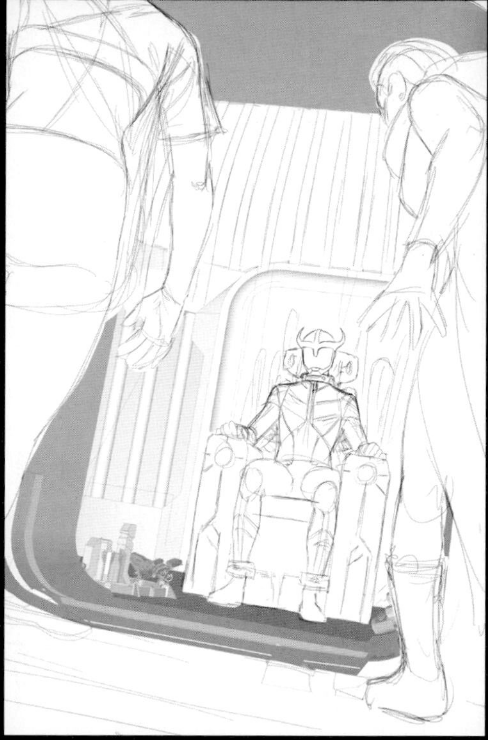

PENCILS p2

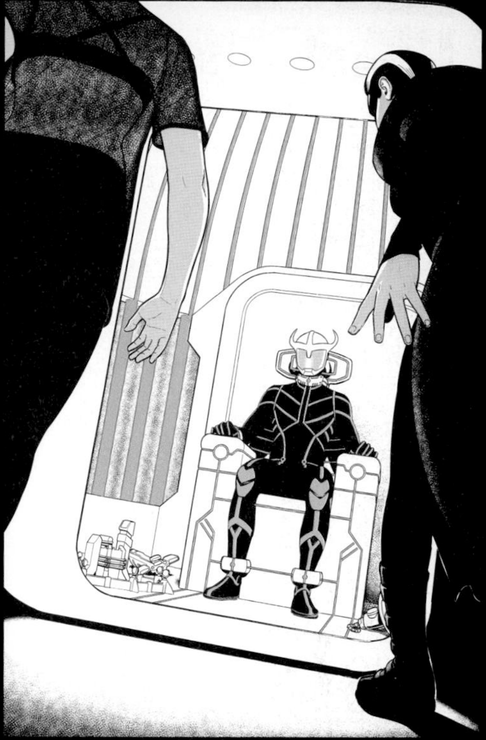

INKS p2

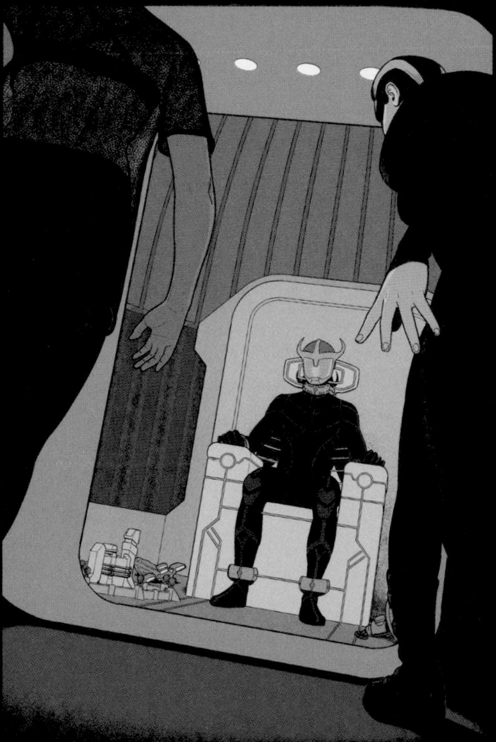

FLATS p2

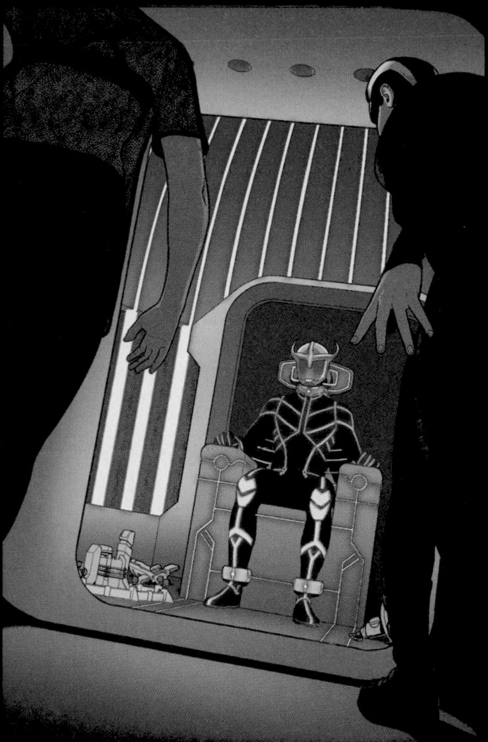

COLOURS p2

THE WICKED + THE DIVINE

VOL. 1:
THE FAUST ACT
#1—5 COLLECTED

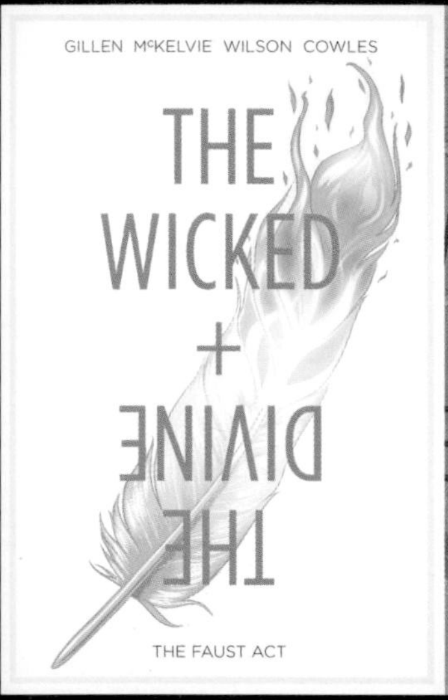
GILLEN McKELVIE WILSON COWLES
THE WICKED + DIVINE THE
THE FAUST ACT

VOL. 2:
FANDEMONIUM
#6—11 COLLECTED

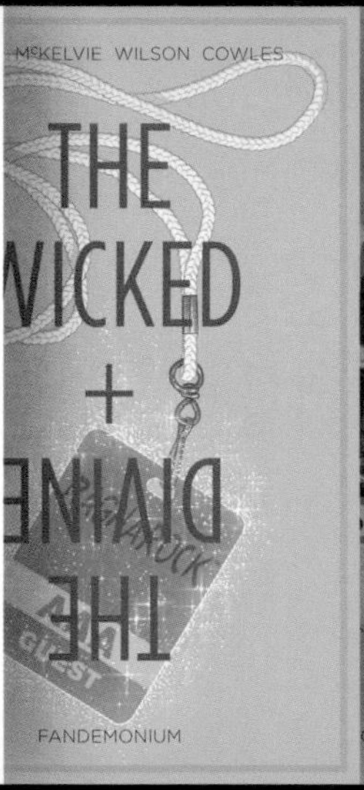
McKELVIE WILSON COWLES
THE WICKED + DIVINE THE
FANDEMONIUM

VOL. 3:
COMMERCIAL
SUICIDE
#12—17 COLLECTED

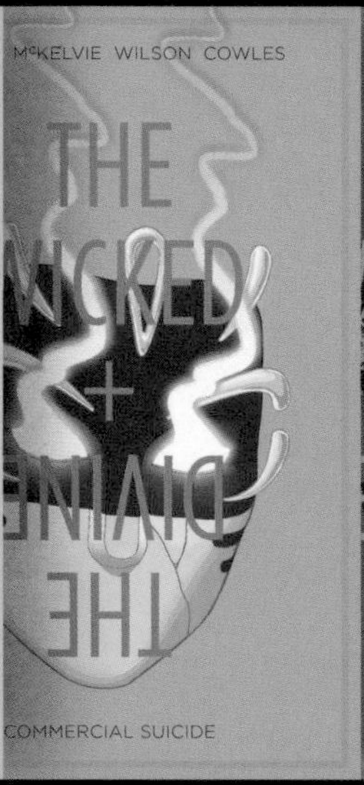
McKELVIE WILSON COWLES
THE WICKED + DIVINE THE
COMMERCIAL SUICIDE

VOL. 4:
RISING ACTION
#18—22 COLLECTED

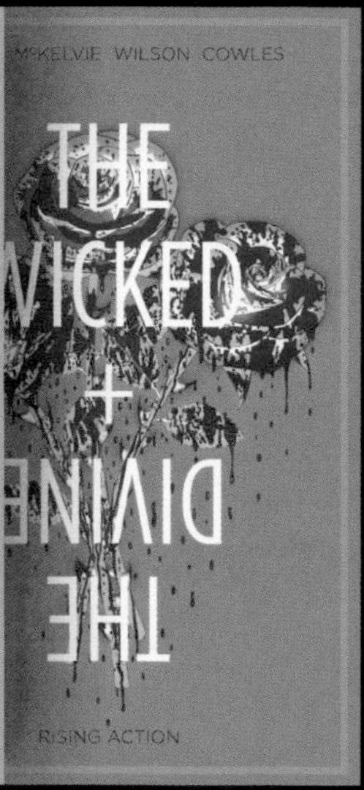
McKELVIE WILSON COWLES
THE WICKED + DIVINE THE
RISING ACTION

VOL. 5:
IMPERIAL PHASE I
#23—28 COLLECTED

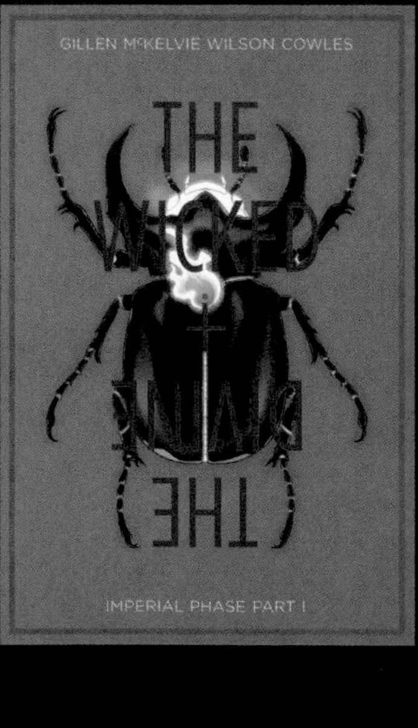
GILLEN McKELVIE WILSON COWLES
IMPERIAL PHASE PART I

BOOK ONE:
#1—11 COLLECTED

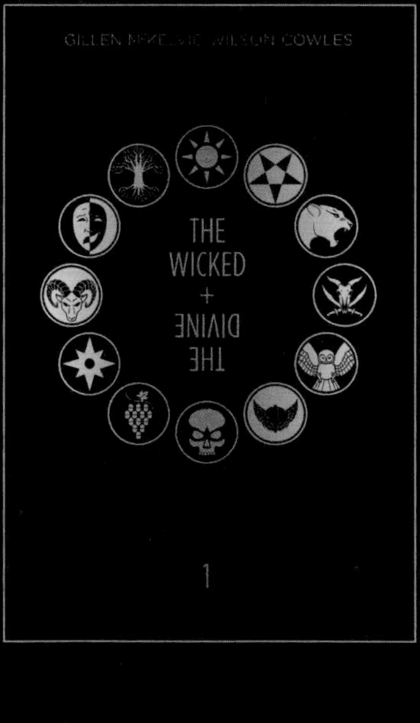
THE WICKED + DIVINE THE
1

BOOK TWO:
#12—22 COLLECTED

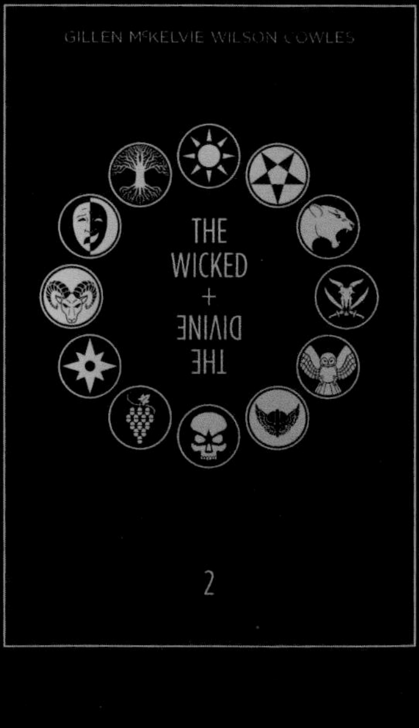
GILLEN McKELVIE WILSON COWLES
THE WICKED + DIVINE THE
2

ALSO BY THE CREATORS

PHONOGRAM

VOL. 1:
RUE BRITANNIA

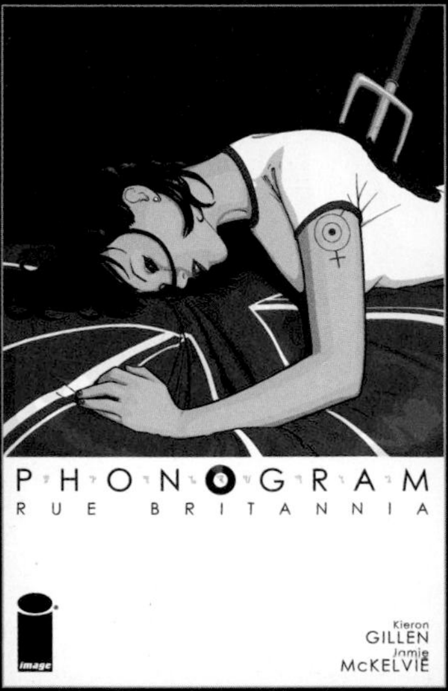
P·H·O·N·O·G·R·A·M
R U E B R I T A N N I A
image
Kieron
GILLEN
Jamie
McKELVIE

VOL. 2:
THE SINGLES CLUB

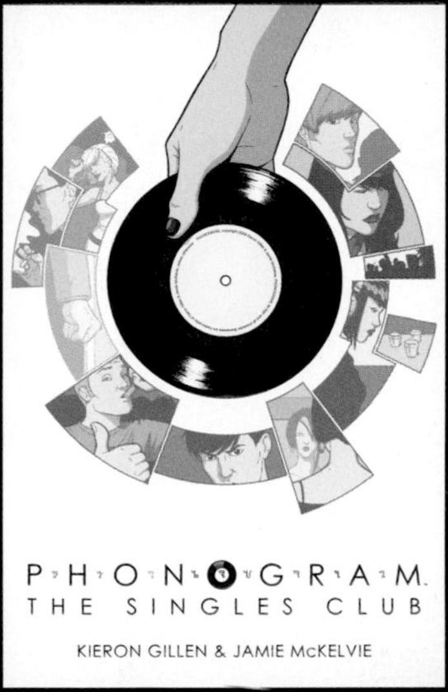
P·H·O·N·O·G·R·A·M.
THE SINGLES CLUB
KIERON GILLEN & JAMIE McKELVIE

VOL. 3:
THE IMMATERIAL GIRL

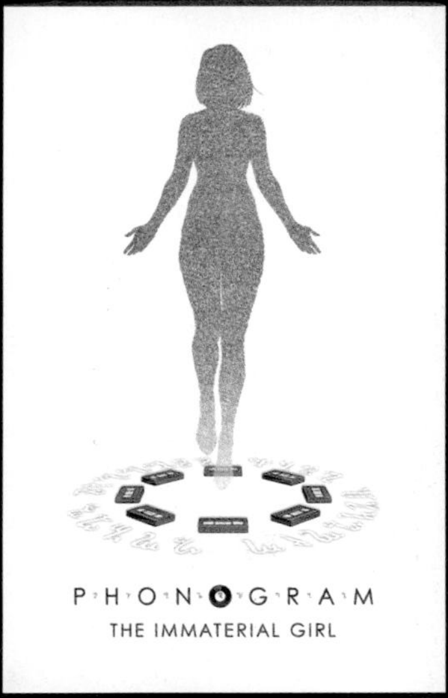
P·H·O·N·O·G·R·A·M
THE IMMATERIAL GIRL

THE COMPLETE
PHONOGRAM

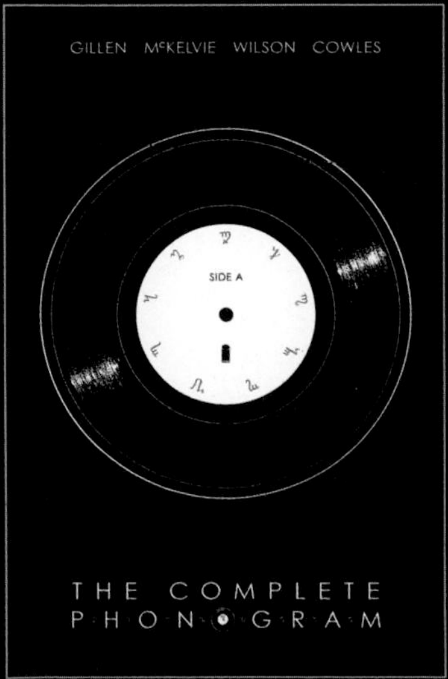
GILLEN McKELVIE WILSON COWLES
SIDE A
THE COMPLETE
P·H·O·N·O·G·R·A·M

THE COMPLETE PHONOGRAM COLLECTS

Vol. 1: Rue Britannia

Vol. 2: The Singles Club

Vol. 3: The Immaterial Girl

And the previously uncollected B-side stories.

FOR FURTHER INFORMATION ON

THE WICKED + THE DIVINE:

www.wicdiv.com

major news, new issues, merchandise.

#WicDiv

the hashtag on twitter for WicDiv Discussion

WicDiv

the general tag on tumblr for the community.

bit.ly/WicDivPlaylist

the ever-updated Spotify Playlist for the series.

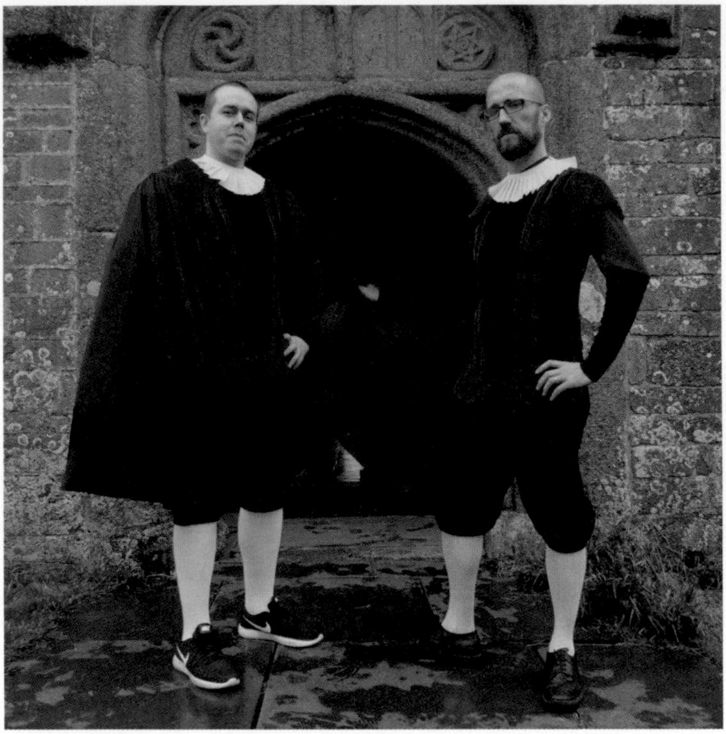

Kieron Gillen is verily a writer.

Jamie McKelvie is verily an artist.

Matt Wilson is an actual Eisner Award-winning professional colourist and can't believe he has to work with these people.

Photograph by Katie West